AVID
READER
PRESS

Also by Dan Senor and Saul Singer

Start-Up Nation: The Story of Israel's Economic Miracle

THE GENIUS OF ISRAEL

The Surprising Resilience of a
Divided Nation in a Turbulent World

DAN SENOR AND SAUL SINGER

AVID READER PRESS

New York   London   Toronto   Sydney   New Delhi

Avid Reader Press
An Imprint of Simon & Schuster, Inc.
1230 Avenue of the Americas
New York, NY 10020

First Avid Reader Press hardcover edition November 2023

AVID READER PRESS and colophon are trademarks of Simon & Schuster, Inc.

For information about special discounts for bulk purchases, please contact Simon & Schuster Special Sales at 1-866-506-1949 or business@simonandschuster.com.

The Simon & Schuster Speakers Bureau can bring authors to your live event. For more information or to book an event, contact the Simon & Schuster Speakers Bureau at 1-866-248-3049 or visit our website at www.simonspeakers.com.

Interior design by Wendy Blum

Manufactured in the United States of America

1   3   5   7   9   10   8   6   4   2

Library of Congress Cataloging-in-Publication Data

Names: Senor, Dan, author. | Singer, Saul, author.
Title: The genius of Israel : the surprising resilience of a divided nation in a turbulent world / Dan Senor and Saul Singer.
Other titles: Surprising resilience of a divided nation in a turbulent world
Identifiers: LCCN 2023026253 (print) | LCCN 2023026254 (ebook) |
ISBN 9781982115760 | ISBN 9781982115777 (trade paperback) |
ISBN 9781982115784 (ebook)
Subjects: LCSH: National characteristics, Israeli. | Entrepreneurship—Israel. |
Israel—History. | BISAC: BUSINESS & ECONOMICS / Economic Conditions
TECHNOLOGY & ENGINEERING / Inventions
Classification: LCC DS113.3 .S46 2023 (print) | LCC DS113.3 (ebook) |
DDC 956.94—dc23/eng/20230612
LC record available at https://lccn.loc.gov/2023026253
LC ebook record available at https://lccn.loc.gov/2023026254

ISBN 978-1-9821-1576-0
ISBN 978-1-9821-1578-4 (ebook)

To my mother, Helen Senor, who taught me about resilience
through every chapter of her story.
—*Dan Senor*

To my father, Max Singer, who taught me the craft of
thinking differently. To my mother, Suzanne Singer, who
taught me how to live joyously.
—*Saul Singer*

We are forever grateful that the life journeys of Helen, Max,
and Sue led them to Israel.

CONTENTS

THE
GENIUS
OF
ISRAEL

AUTHORS' NOTE

As this book goes to press in the summer of 2023, Israel is embroiled in a conflict—not against external foes but within itself. For six months and counting, Israelis have come out to the streets by the hundreds of thousands in a struggle over the fundamental structure of Israel's government.

As we discuss in chapter 10 ("The Wars of the Jews"), Israeli and Jewish history is ridden with internal conflicts. In that chapter we attempt to place the current conflict over Israel's judicial system into historical context. Here, in this note, we feel obliged to address a different question: Has a core theme of this book—that one of Israeli society's great strengths is its sense of solidarity, belonging, and caring for the country—been overtaken by events?

Political polarization is on the rise in many Western democracies. There are numerous studies chronicling this trend. According to the 2023 Edelman Trust Barometer, surveying over 32,000 people in 28 countries, majorities in 15 of those countries believed that their countries were more divided today than in the past. Three Western countries—U.S., Spain, and Sweden—were found to be "severely divided." The heated events of 2023 show that Israel is not immune to this global trend. So how is Israel different?

The difference is that Israel has a reservoir of social solidarity that it can draw upon. There is an ideal of solidarity that, even if sometimes honored in the breach, is a powerful aspiration across the political spectrum.

One stunning finding of the Edelman survey was that less than one-third of respondents said they would help someone in need with whom they strongly disagree politically. Only one-fifth said they would be willing to live in the same neighborhood with a political opponent or have them as a coworker.

In Israel, to even ask these questions would be strange. Disagreeing—with gusto—is not only normal, but central. Nor can Israelis avoid engaging across "tribal" lines. The country is too small and families are too large. Extended families often include religious and secular members. Marriages between Ashkenazi and Mizrahi Jews are common, so families also blend across this divide. People with starkly opposing views live not just in the same neighborhood but also in the same apartment buildings, and often sit around the same Shabbat dinner table. And then there is, of course, military service, which for a majority of Israelis is the most powerful melting pot of all.

Often in this book, when we refer to "Israelis" or "Israeli society," we have in mind the approximate two-thirds of Israelis who may be ethnically, economically, religiously, and ideologically diverse but this majority still does not include Haredi ("ultra-Orthodox") Jews or Israeli Arabs. While Israel's two largest minorities are slowly becoming more intertwined with broader society, by and large they live in separate worlds (see chapter 11: "The Other Israel"). But these three worlds are more interconnected than it seems, and there is a complex interplay between the forces that are bringing them together and prying them apart.

The gaps between Israelis are real. The two-thirds majority, the ultra-Orthodox minority, and the Israeli Arab minority generally, though not always, live separately and study in separate school systems. But it wouldn't occur to an Israeli not to help someone in need because they disagreed politically. Jews and Arabs are literally saving one another's lives daily in hospitals and through emergency services, as we also discuss in chapter 11.

• • •

But solidarity cannot be built just on daily interactions or a high tolerance for arguing. Solidarity must stand on something profound that is shared. And Jewish Israelis share a common story and fate. For Israelis, "united we stand, divided we fall" is not just a cliche, it's reality. Israelis know that if their common bond is shattered their country will cease to exist.

In other polarized countries, the yearning for unity that cuts across deep political divides might not be as strong. You can't yearn for what you can't imagine. In Israel, the solidarity is just beneath the surface, like a frame holding a mosaic together.

One evening at the height of the protests over judicial reform, the long escalators going down into the Jerusalem station for the train to Tel Aviv were packed with protesters, many of them carrying Israeli flags. On that day, the main pro-government rally was in Tel Aviv while the main anti-government protest was in Jerusalem, opposite the Knesset (Israel's parliament).

After the rallies, the up escalators were filled with government supporters returning to Jerusalem while the down escalators were packed with government opponents returning to Tel Aviv. Spontaneously, people started stretching across the wide divider between the escalators to shake hands with their opponents. A video of the scene went viral and became an instant icon. In the video, a young bandana-wearing protester reached across, his sign turned toward the other escalator. The sign read "equality, justice, democracy." As he was shaking hand after hand he shouted, "I love you, you don't know how much I love you."

In Israel, such a scene is not surprising. It is reflective of a culture that celebrates disagreement and lionizes unity. In other politically divided countries, the shaking-hands scene would be unimaginable, partly because the two sides don't rub shoulders and partly because there is no sense of an underlying bond.

When Israelis look back at this time, they will remember the bitterness and the passions, but we hope they will also remember the hands reaching across the escalators. Much of this book is about what brings Israelis together as well as what pushes them apart. The unifying forces should not be taken for granted. That these forces have withstood so many tests is a miracle, and miracles take a lot of work to maintain.

"Israel isn't a paragon of democracy because it cannot be," writes Yossi Klein Halevi. "But Israel is a paragon of the struggle for democratic norms under near-impossible circumstances," as many episodes in Israeli history demonstrate. "Israel is a laboratory for democracy under extremity, and that is its value for the world."

—Dan Senor (New York City) & Saul Singer (Jerusalem)
August 1, 2023

THE ISRAELI PARADOX

*Humans don't mind hardship, in fact they thrive on it; what
they mind is not feeling necessary. Modern society has perfected the
art of making people not feel necessary.*

—Sebastian Junger

Tiffanie Wen lay on the massage mat. It was that brief moment when you
are there alone, waiting for the masseur you had met a moment ago to
return. Wen thought, *Should I tell him, or would that be out of place? Or
would he mention it on his own?*

He didn't. She didn't like to point things out to people. But if she
didn't, she knew that the niggling thought would be there. Better to get
it out and over with.

"I'm sure you remember, but the siren is going to go off in the middle
of our massage," she said, speaking to the wall, the side of her face nestling
into the towel covering the mat. "Oh, yeah, today is Yom HaZikaron," he
said, conscious of the role reversal. As the Israeli in the room, he should
have been doing the reminding. It was Memorial Day, when Israel re-
members its fallen soldiers.

"When the siren goes off," he said, recovering his authority, "you just
lie on the mat. Don't worry about getting up in the middle of your massage. But I'll stop and stand during the siren."

Wen, an Asian American journalist from San Francisco who had followed her Israeli boyfriend back to Tel Aviv, was studying for a master's

1

degree in Middle Eastern Studies at Tel Aviv University. She savored being the knowing local for a moment, but no matter how many times she experienced it, this uniquely Israeli communal ritual continued to astound her. At exactly 11:00 a.m., Israel's national air-raid siren system would fill the air with a loud, plaintive note—a blaring high-pitched sound that could be heard everywhere, as if it were coming out of the air itself.

For two minutes the world would stop, as in a sci-fi movie. Cars would stop on the highways, their drivers standing like sentries next to them. In restaurants and hotels, schools and offices, stadiums and homes, everyone would stand in silence. Diners, waiters, and kitchen staff would all stand. Students and teachers in school would stand. Foreign news outlets would post videos of street scenes frozen in time while the jarring, inescapable wail filled the air.

The sirens actually sound on two days each year, one week apart: Yom HaShoah (Holocaust Memorial Day) and Yom HaZikaron (Memorial Day, for soldiers and victims of terror).

Two minutes was a long time to be still and silent. *What, or who, were they all thinking about as they looked down, stared out, or closed their eyes?* Wen wondered. If she hadn't been flat on a mat, she would have stood, too. Participating made her, in a small way, feel part of the collective. But it wasn't just that Israelis were *doing* the same thing—they were tuned to the same channel, a channel she couldn't access. The channel was at once collective and personal, as Israelis focused on someone they lost: a brother, a son, a girlfriend, a parent, a childhood friend, a teacher, a student, a nearby shopkeeper, a soldier from their unit.

Wen remembered another Memorial Day siren, when she was Skyping from San Francisco with her boyfriend, who was in Israel. "We'll have to stop talking for a couple minutes or so, but it's okay, just stay on." Wen marveled. "He wasn't in public, he was in his apartment by himself," she told us. "Nobody would notice what he did. Yet he stood up and had that moment."

Joe McCormack felt a similar sense of awe. "The siren always sends chills down my back. Even now," he said. The name, the fair skin, the open face, the accent—these were all giveaways that McCormack was not a typical Israeli. Even for a place to which people had come from over seventy different countries, McCormack stood out. "I remember the first time I heard the siren," he said. "It was on Holocaust Remembrance Day, on a train to Haifa. And all of a sudden, the train stops, in the middle of nowhere. Fields all around. No buildings. And everyone in the train stood up. It was very intense. You could see on everyone's faces, their minds racing with emotions.

"I grew up in rural Scotland," McCormack explained. "I had never met a Jew. I was nine years old when we learned about the Second World War, and Hitler, and what happened to the Jewish people. I remember the school and the teacher. And I remember being in that classroom and hearing the stories about how murderous people have been towards the Jews, and then fast-forwarding to this moment—I'm in Israel standing in silence on a train with all these people whose country came into existence out of the ashes of the Holocaust."

McCormack was one of the first people on Facebook when it opened to people outside of college campuses in 2006. That's where he met Adi, an Israeli who also was there to check out this buzzy social media start-up. They got to know each other virtually for six months, and then McCormack decided to come for a two-week visit.

"I had no idea about the Middle East, less about Israel. I thought it was a place with camels and that Yasser Arafat was president," McCormack admitted. "I was so nervous. I was shocked at this big modern airport. It was nighttime and I went to this cool and hopping city . . . Tel Aviv. I was like, 'Wow. This is a lot different from Scotland.'"

McCormack stayed with Adi's family. "It was a real Israeli household," he recalled. "A big family that would gather each week for Friday night dinner. Three—sometimes four—generations getting together for dinner . . . *every week*. I had never experienced anything like it. And I just really loved the place." He quit his job and stayed for three months, until his tourist visa ran out. McCormack went back to the UK for a while to get a new visa, and returned to work in Israel's thriving high-tech sector.

Parts of life in Israel mystified McCormack. On the one hand, there was the moving experience of seeing Israelis stand as one during the siren. But at Tel Aviv's main open-air fruit and vegetable market, he would see a more typical side of Israelis. "People would be shouting and arguing, and it just felt to me like a very aggressive place. No one would queue up and people would push in line, and that used to drive me crazy," he said.

If Israelis were constantly tussling, how could they be capable of switching over to performing such a tremendous act of unity? McCormack couldn't figure it out. One incident brought this paradox right before his eyes.

"I was on my bike, and I saw a bus cutting off a motorcyclist," McCormack recalled. "And then I saw the cyclist take off his helmet and start banging on the side of the bus. And the bus driver opened the door, and they're shouting at each other. And I'm thinking, 'Oh my God, this is not going to end well.' And then suddenly, the guy with his helmet off starts asking the bus driver for directions, and he says, 'Okay, thanks.' And then he speeds off. And I just stood there with my mouth open. What just happened?"

Soon enough, Tiffanie Wen got to experience another kind of siren. This time she found herself crumpled into a ball in the hallway of her Tel Aviv apartment building, sobbing into her dog's fur. Out of nowhere, the rising howl of air-raid sirens had pierced the night. She went with her neighbors to the most rocket-proof part of the building. One neighbor, an eighty-six-year-old ex-paratrooper named Fishkay, gave her a look that said, *Nothing scares me*. But even the younger people didn't seem fazed. The neighbors knew the drill. You wait for the all-clear siren and then go about your business.

"Why aren't they scared?" she and her American friends asked one another the next day. She also had a practical problem: What would she do if the sirens went off while she was at the university?

Wen asked one of the supervisors of her program. The first thing she said was not to panic, because more people get hurt running for shelter than from rockets. Then she smiled and told her, "Look out your window. If you see Israelis panicking, that's the time to panic. Just copy the Israelis. You'll be fine."

The ability to take all this in stride was incredible to her. Israelis, including her boyfriend, seemed so much more resilient than Wen and her friends. An argument on the street or a disagreement on the job could easily ruin Wen's day or week. But for Israelis, "my thinking about these things one minute after they happen seems like overhyped drama."

We have been observers of Israel for decades. In our previous book, *Start-Up Nation: The Story of Israel's Economic Miracle*, we sought to understand and explain one prominent aspect of Israel—its booming high-tech sector. But at some level, we were just as mystified as Tiffanie Wen and Joe McCormack about what made Israeli society tick.

In many respects, Israel looks like the modern and prosperous democracies of North America, Europe, and Asia. As of 2021, its GDP per capita has surpassed those of Germany, the UK, France, and Japan, and its economy has been growing faster than the U.S. and EU. Tel Aviv, Jerusalem, and other cities are festooned with construction cranes building new office towers, hotels, and apartment buildings. Israel's economic and military strengths are visible and known. What no one seemed to have noticed, including us and most Israelis, was the evidence that Israel was an outlier in *societal* health.

We had been so dazzled by Israel's high-tech scene that we hadn't paid attention to how Israel stacked up on the societal level. And the more we looked into it, the more the results surprised us.

Why Are Israelis So Damn Happy?

Wen told us that "every time I thought I understood the place, something happened that didn't make sense." One paradox stood out because it encompassed all the rest. A United Nations report had recently ranked countries on happiness, and Israel came out near the top.

It didn't take long for Wen to become aware of the stresses of daily life in Israel. Income inequality and the cost of living were rising. In 2021, the *Economist* ranked Tel Aviv as the most expensive city in the world. An average apartment costs about 150 times the average annual salary, more than double the figure in the United States. And all that's before you get to the part about living under perpetual threat. During certain periods over the past twenty-five years, more than half of Israeli adults surveyed said they had been victims of terror attacks or had family or friends who had experienced one.

Israel's happiness score piqued Wen's curiosity. Partly to explain it to herself, she wrote an article for the *Daily Beast* titled "Why Are the Israelis So Damn Happy?" It became one of the most popular she had ever written. In Israel, it seemed as if everyone knew about their country's unlikely standing in the happiness sweepstakes.

"The piece sparked a lot of discussion among my Israeli friends," Wen said. One of her professors read the piece, but didn't know who she was. "He called out in my class, 'Who is Tiffanie Wen?' He very much agreed with the piece and gave me some nice feedback." But some people disagreed with her. A psychologist she spoke with said that Israelis weren't happy; all her patients were miserable.

We knew that Israelis had plenty to complain about and that they certainly do just that. Talking to Wen added to our questions. What did it mean to say that Israelis are happy? Where did the happiness ranking come from, anyway?

The source was the annual *World Happiness Report*, a well-regarded and research-based compilation issued by an organization affiliated with the United Nations. When Wen first came across the report, Israel ranked among the top fifteen out of over 150 countries. By the 2022 report, Israel had jumped to ninth place. Then, in the 2023 report, Israel jumped another five spots, to fourth in the world. While most countries' ranking stayed steady year after year, Israel—from a starting point that was already at a high level—rose ten places in three years.

It was hard to dismiss the results of the report. In its tenth year and based on a massive global poll by the Gallup organization, the results over time were remarkably consistent. Every year, Israel appeared in the top decile.

Promoting happiness has become part of the global policy agenda. Some countries, like the United Arab Emirates and Ecuador, even appointed ministers for happiness. (The UK has a minister for loneliness, but the mandate is the same.) The tiny country of Bhutan has attracted attention for declaring that it will no longer measure its progress according to the gross national product (GNP) but will focus instead on raising the country's "gross national happiness."

But how do you measure the happiness of a country? The whole idea of "happiness studies," at least on the country level, sounded slippery. The concept of a happy country brought to mind a place where everyone was walking around with a smile on their face. That certainly wasn't the Israel we knew.

The smiley version of happiness was not what Gallup was trying to measure. The report aimed at a deeper construct: life satisfaction. The pollsters employed a widely-used tool for measuring life satisfaction, called the "Cantril ladder." "Please imagine a ladder, with steps numbered from 0 at the bottom to 10 at the top," the question reads. "The top of the ladder represents the best possible life for you and the bottom of the ladder represents the worst possible life for you. On which step of the ladder would you say you personally feel you stand at this time?" Israelis placed themselves higher up the ladder of "the best possible life" than almost any country in the world.

This result is even more striking because the Jewish people have been complaining from the moment they became a people. In what must have been one of the earliest examples of chutzpah, the Jews had barely escaped Egypt when they started complaining to Moses about the food. "In Egypt we could eat all the fish we wanted, and there were cucumbers, melons, all kinds of onions, and garlic," the Israelites said. "But we're starving out here, and the only food we have is this manna." Modern Israelis complain no less. And Israelis, notoriously, have no problem telling you how they really feel, without sugarcoating. Yet, when asked to reflect on their lives, they express high levels of personal satisfaction. Why?

Israel is clearly the "odd man out" among the happiest nations. Geographically, the countries that ranked one through nine almost all fit in a tight circle centered around Copenhagen. Five were Nordic countries: Finland, Sweden, Denmark, Norway, and Iceland. The other three were close by: the Netherlands, Luxembourg, and Switzerland. These countries are peaceful, quiet, politically stable, and provide generous social welfare benefits.

Then there was Israel, far away in the Middle East, a region not known for tranquility. Noisy, argumentative Israelis rated their own lives more satisfying than did Swedes, Swiss, Americans, Australians, Canadians, and Singaporeans. Long before the COVID-19 pandemic, the affluent democracies of the world were struck by a panoply of societal sicknesses: loneliness, distrust, and even despair. Was Israel an exception?

Another sign of Israeli societal health is related to, but not the same as, happiness: optimism. The Pew Research Center, a blue-chip global polling organization, has periodically asked this question to measure optimism: "When children in your country grow up, will they be financially better or worse off than their parents?" Of all the wealthy countries polled, Israel and Singapore were the only countries where more people were optimistic about their children's financial future. Among the nineteen countries surveyed, the median of those answering "worse off" was 70 percent, while Israelis were the least pessimistic, at 27 percent. In almost all the other countries, the percentage answering "worse off" grew to record highs from 2019 to 2022. In Israel the number of pessimists *dropped* from an already low number to even lower. Why would Israelis, already among the most optimistic, become more so during a pandemic and when living amid a seemingly endless conflict?

And the conflicts confronting Israelis were not just based on external security threats, but sometimes toxic domestic political debates—over government decisions to accept Holocaust reparations from West Germany in 1952, to launch a controversial war in Lebanon in 1982, to uproot and forcibly relocate Jewish settlement communities in 2005, or to fast-track polarizing judicial reforms in 2023, to name a few. In the wake of the 1995 assassination of Yitzhak Rabin by a Jewish extremist, Israeli society appeared to be irreparably broken.

While there are thousands of academic studies—indeed a whole subfield of psychology—dissecting happiness among individuals, we were still unsure about relying on comparisons *at the country level* of something as culturally influenced as happiness. We wanted to look at incontrovertible data that measured aspects of societal health. So our next stop was a particularly comprehensive metric: longevity.

Living Longer

The most comprehensive measure of health in a country is life expectancy. We did not expect Israel to excel in this measure because Israelis have a lot of something unhealthy: stress. Young Israelis spend years in intense military service and security threats are constantly present throughout their lives. Economically, the growing gap between salaries and housing prices has added more stress. Traffic, another big stress inducer, is horrible. (According to Waze, which was invented in Israel, Tel Aviv is among the world's top five most congested cities.) Israelis joke that they go to Manhattan for relaxation.

In addition to these everyday stresses, there is the surround sound of ominous warnings that one or all of the tautly stretched seams of Israeli society will come undone: between hawks and doves, between the hedonists of Tel Aviv and the Haredim of Bnei Brak, between the high-tech bourgeois and the struggling towns on the periphery, between Jews from the East and Jews from the West, between Jews and Arabs—where they live together and where they live apart.

Bathing in stress would not seem to be a good recipe for a long life. Yet according to the World Health Organization, life expectancy in Israel was 82.6 years in 2019. This ranked Israel as the ninth highest in the world, slightly above France, Sweden, Canada, and New Zealand, and a full year above the UK, Germany, Finland, Belgium, and Denmark. On average, Israelis live more than four years longer than Americans and a decade longer than their wealthy neighbors in Persian Gulf countries like Saudi Arabia.

Another key metric is not how long people live (life span), but the average number of years they can expect to enjoy "full health" (health span). This measure is called "healthy life expectancy," or HALE. Here, too, Israel's ranking is extraordinary. Israeli men have the fourth highest healthy life expectancy globally, and Israeli women are in eighth place.

"Israel has been climbing the international rankings of life expectancy faster than any other country in the world," said Alex Weinreb, a demographer at the Taub Center for Social Policy Studies in Jerusalem. "But this is not happening during a time of peace and tranquility; the real growth happened for two decades when Israel was fighting multiple wars and absorbing a massive number of immigrants that required constantly building more schools, roads, and hospitals."

While Israel does have a world-class health care system—internationally recognized for its broad reach across socioeconomic divides—is that enough to explain why Israelis live so long and in better health? Probably not, because other affluent countries have health care systems that are just as good, or better, but with lower life expectancies.

Do Israelis just have healthier lifestyles or diets? Obesity levels in Israel are about average, and diabetes rates are relatively high. Israelis do have a Mediterranean diet, which is considered healthy, but so do many other countries.

So the question is, if Israelis' health takes a hit from stress, and health care, lifestyle, or diet don't explain the difference in life expectancy, what does? Why is Israel an outlier not only in happiness and optimism but also in longevity? The explanation is not obvious. But it would be hard to solve the puzzle if we only had part of it in front of us. We needed to see if Israel was an outlier in other respects. The next one wasn't hard to find.

Young and Growing

"The projections are reliable, and stark," the *New York Times* reported in July 2023. "By 2050, people age 65 and older will make up nearly 40 percent of the population in some parts of East Asia and Europe. That's almost twice the share of older adults in Florida, America's retirement capital." The article continued, "In all of recorded history, no country has ever been as old as these nations are expected to get."

It is difficult to imagine what such a world will look like. Except that there is a place where it already exists: Japan.

Japan has the world's highest life expectancy—a tremendous achievement. But with that success came a dire problem: not enough young people. In Japan, there are more people over seventy than under twenty. More adult diapers are sold in Japan than baby diapers. By 2060 there will be almost as many elderly people as those of working age. "Japan is standing on the verge of whether we can continue to function as a society," Japanese Prime Minister Fumio Kishida told his parliament in January 2023. And many wealthy countries, even some emerging nations, are on a similar path as their populations age.

Israel is on the other end of the scale—the youngest of the affluent democracies. In 2050 Israel is projected to be about twenty years younger than Italy, Spain, and Germany.

Look at these projected population pyramids for Israel and Japan in 2050. In Japan, there will be about twice as many seventy-five-to-eighty-year-olds as children five or younger. In Israel, the elderly-to-toddler ratio is reversed. There will be more than three times as many young children as those approaching eighty. And while Japan is leading the way toward a graying future, Europe is right behind.

In 2019, Israel's median age was 29, while Europe's was 41.3—

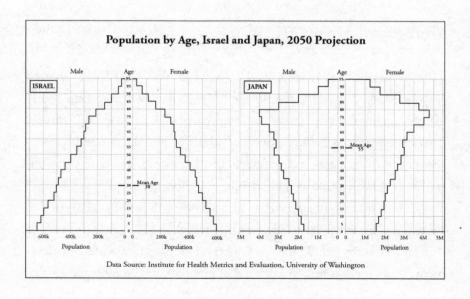

Data Source: Institute for Health Metrics and Evaluation, University of Washington

already a gap of over a decade. By 2050, Israel's median age is projected to rise moderately to 32.9, while Europe's jumps to 47.3—increasing the gap between Israel and Europe to over fourteen years. While the rest of the wealthy world will look increasingly like an old-age home, Israel will still be opening playgrounds and schools at a steady clip. Clearly, a country with more strollers than walkers has a different feel, energy, and excitement about the future.

In addition to rapid aging, the wealthy countries face a related demographic headwind: shrinking populations. Again, the rich countries are leading the way, but the rest of the world is following. In 2021, in a front-page feature titled "Long Slide Looms for World Population," the *New York Times* reported that the global population will go into "sustained decline" in the second half of this century. This trend would "upend how societies are organized," the paper warned. "Imagine entire regions where everyone is 70 or older. Imagine governments laying out huge bonuses for immigrants and mothers with lots of children. Imagine a gig economy filled with grandparents and Super Bowl ads promoting procreation."

Countries like Japan, Germany, South Korea, Denmark, and Italy are desperately trying to stave off this future. They are spending billions of dollars for day care programs and other inducements to encourage more births. Some governments have claimed that low birth rates are their nation's most pressing problem. There is only one wealthy country that has escaped this trend: Israel.

Israel and its wealthy peers part ways because they are on different sides of a sharp dividing line: the "replacement rate." If the fertility rate, or the average number of children a woman has in her lifetime, is above 2.1, the population will be young and growing. Below that rate the population will age and shrink. At 3.01 in 2019, Israel's fertility rate is well above replacement. The average among the Organisation for Economic Cooperation and Development (OECD) countries is 1.61. If these fertility rates stay stable, Israel and the rest of the rich world will move in opposite directions. By 2050, Japan's population is projected to shrink by almost one-fifth, while in Israel it is slated to increase by almost half.

There is also a social cost to population decline. "The arithmetic of below-replacement fertility eats away at the heart of the extended family structure," the demographer Nicholas Eberstadt told us. "It eats away at an extraordinarily important component of what we think of as social capital, right at the foundation of the resilience of the society."

Happiness, optimism, longevity, youth, and population growth are all positive measures where Israel stands out. We thought that one way to double-check these measures would be to look at the other end of the spectrum. To get a sense of the opposite of these indicators, we researched the toll from a truly tragic malady of modern societies: despair.

Don't Despair

In a 2015 study, the Princeton economists Anne Case and Angus Deaton examined a striking phenomenon. Since the year 2000, U.S. deaths from suicide, drugs, and other forms of substance abuse had turned upward, after having been flat from 1970 to 2000. By 2020 the number of these deaths in America had more than doubled.

Case and Deaton gave this devastating wave a name: "deaths of despair." The main component of these deaths was evident—the opioid epidemic. But this culprit was not solely to blame. Alcohol-related deaths had more than doubled from 1999 to 2017.

Case and Deaton argued that this phenomenon was uniquely American. In the UK and Europe, these kinds of deaths had dropped significantly over the same period. But this may be changing. In May 2019, the *Economist* reported that deaths of despair among middle-aged British men had been "moving in the wrong direction" over the previous eight years.

So here we see measurable signs of acute social decay in America and

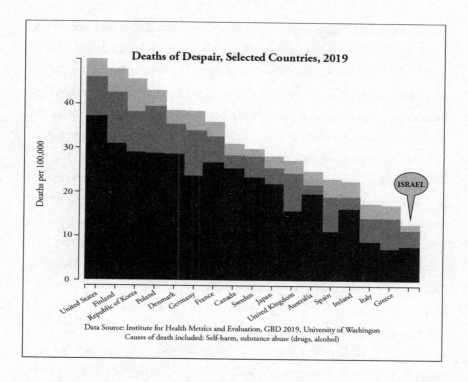

Deaths of Despair, Selected Countries, 2019

Data Source: Institute for Health Metrics and Evaluation, GBD 2019, University of Washingon
Causes of death included: Self-harm, substance abuse (drugs, alcohol)

the UK. What was happening in the other affluent democracies? The gold standard for international comparisons is the Global Burden of Disease (GBD) study, compiled at the University of Washington. The GBD measures all causes of death and disability—from road accidents to tuberculosis. We looked at the GBD to compare deaths of despair among wealthy nations.

Israel has been exposed to constant trauma. Yet countries often considered the most idyllic, like Sweden, Denmark, and Norway, suffer from two to three times higher rates of deaths of despair than Israel. Israel has the lowest rate of these deaths of all the wealthy nations in the OECD. Israel also has the world's third-lowest consumption level of alcohol on a per capita basis and even lower rates of deaths from opioid abuse. One way to get a better idea of what is behind these data is to look at what is happening with mental health.

In early 2023, new data were released on a trend that had been worsening long before the pandemic. "CDC Report on Teen Mental Health Is a Red Alert," wrote the *Washington Post*. The report found an "'overwhelming wave of violence and trauma' and never-before-seen levels of hopelessness and suicidal thoughts among high school students in the U.S.," according to NBC News. New "alarming levels of violence, sadness, suicide risk in teens," reported CBS News.

The CDC has been conducting the Youth Risk Behavior Surveillance Survey biennially for three decades. Over seventeen thousand high school students across the U.S. were polled. "High school should be a time for trailblazing, not trauma," declared the CDC's chief medical officer in a press release. The CDC's report echoed an earlier study by the American Academy of Pediatrics: "Across the country we have witnessed dramatic increases in Emergency Department visits for all mental health emergencies including suspected suicide attempts."

In New York, one Long Island hospital had 250 emergency room visits by suicidal adolescents in 1982; in 2010, the number had increased more than tenfold, to 3,000. In 2022, it was 8,000. After accidents, suicide has been overtaking homicide across the country as the second-leading cause of death in this age cohort.

And it wasn't just adolescents. In recent years there has been a near doubling of suicides by children ages five to eleven. While emergency room visits for suicide attempts or suicidal thoughts bloomed from 580,000 in 2007 to 1.1 million in 2015, nearly half of those visits were by children younger than eleven.

Israel's teen suicide rates are among the lowest in the world—less than a third of the OECD average and less than a quarter that of the United States, Australia, Finland, and Canada. Israel and Greece are the countries with the lowest teen suicide rate in the OECD.

Many theories have been put forward to explain plummeting teen mental health—from social media and smartphones to an array of sources of stress. As Derek Thompson chronicled in the *Atlantic*, citing clinical psychologists, "in the last decade teenagers have become increasingly stressed by concerns about gun violence, climate change, and the political environment."

But these explanations do not explain why Israeli youth are seemingly immune to this epidemic: most have smartphones and access to social media, they are blasted with the same dire climate change predictions, they are exposed to an endless loop of polarizing political debates, and they have more direct exposure to violence, be it from rockets, terrorism, or direct combat experience. On the face of it, Israeli teens should be even more stressed than their peers in calmer countries.

Arguably, the data indicating rising despair are even more significant reflections of societal health than measures of happiness (or, rather, unhappiness). At the launch event for the 2022 *World Happiness Report*, Gallup CEO Jon Clifton pointed this out, based on a conversation he'd had with the Nobel laureate Daniel Kahneman, an Israeli whose groundbreaking body of work (together with Amos Tversky) on decision-making revealed the productive and counterproductive ways people make judgments.

"Increasing happiness and reducing misery are very different things," Kahneman told Clifton. "I would focus on the negative end. It should be the responsibility of society to try and reduce misery." Clifton noted that one of the "most concerning trends we've ever seen in the history of our reporting is that stress, sadness, physical pain, anger, and worry have now reached a record high." This could not be blamed on the pandemic, he said, because all five of the indicators had been rising for ten straight years.

Israel does not seem to have been as affected by these trends. According to Israel's Central Bureau of Statistics, loneliness, for example, dropped by 20 percent between 2002 and 2016. Why might this be?

Several studies point to Israeli "familialism" and "groupism" as key sources of social support. A joint UC Berkeley–Tel Aviv University study comparing social connectedness in the U.S. and Israel found "the Israelis' networks were significantly denser—more interconnected—than the Americans' networks." The study also suggested, based on similar research in the UK, Canada, and China, that the Israeli density of communal ties and friendships "is clearly higher than that of the other nations and may be among the highest in the world."

Some countries excel in fostering happiness, but not in reducing despair. Israel is exceptional in both. It is among the happiest and most optimistic countries in the world, while also having the lowest rate of deaths of despair among OECD members. At the same time, Israel's life expectancy is high, and a high birth rate ensures that Israel would remain young and keep growing, while the rest of the wealthy democracies are aging and shrinking. Something extraordinary is happening in Israeli society.

Our previous book, *Start-Up Nation*, described how Israel became the unlikely home to the highest density of technology start-ups in the world. At that time, not long after the 2008 financial crisis, governments and companies scrambled to become more innovative. Yet no one seemed to have noticed that Israel, this tiny and remote country, had built the world's second-largest innovation ecosystem. It was as if we had stumbled on an invisible mountain.

Now the world's affluent democracies seem to be caught in a vicious cycle of demographic collapse, accelerated aging, deepening pessimism, and loneliness. In these countries, the best days seem to be receding in the rearview mirror. While there is a natural human tendency toward nostalgia, today whole societies look ahead with a sense of unraveling, decline, and even doom. That feels like something new.

This book explores how Israel has shown surprising resilience against many trends that have been sapping affluent societies of their health and vitality. Measurable indicators suggest that Israelis are engaged in shaping their future, and even building it. Why is Israel so different? Once again, it feels as if we have stumbled on a mountain.

Understanding the Israeli example will help answer some of the most crucial questions of our age. Can we build societies with a greater sense of purpose? Can we rebuild community in an age of hyper-individualism and loneliness? Can we build guardrails of commonality to keep political divides from tearing apart democracy itself?

Israel shows that there is nothing inevitable about decline and despair. That striving for individual excellence and economic prosperity does not have to come at the expense of communal values. That there is a way to live with, and even thrive in, an age of rapid change and uncertainty. And that even a divided society can share something meaningful, and can argue and protest out of caring for the country, not just for one's self. The story of how this happened is the story of the genius of Israel.

Chapter One

UBER TO THE MOON

WHO WANTS TO GO TO THE MOON??

—Facebook post by Yariv Bash, cofounder of SpaceIL

It's not about being optimistic that things will work out.
It's about being optimistic about what happens when they don't.

—Kfir Damari, cofounder of SpaceIL

Three months after taking office, President John F. Kennedy huddled with his advisors in the White House. The Soviet Union had just stunned the world by sending the first man into space. It was the most daring of a string of Soviet space firsts. "Is there any other space program that promises dramatic results in which we could win?" Kennedy asked.

It wasn't just space that was at stake. In a secret memo a week later, President Kennedy's vice president, Lyndon B. Johnson, wrote that "other nations . . . will tend to align themselves with the country which they believe will be the world leader. Dramatic accomplishments in space are being increasingly identified as a major indicator of world leadership." Putting the second man in space wouldn't hack it. They had to come up with something so audacious, so impossible, that there would be no doubt who had won the space race and, by extension, who led the world in innovative power.

In 1961, America's GDP was, in today's dollars, less than one-fifth of its current size. The state-of-the-art computer weighed thirty-two tons, cost $66 million (in today's dollars), and had two megabytes of memory—less than the size of a single photograph today. Electric typewriters were cutting-edge technology. The idea that a human being could walk on the moon and return to earth safely seemed like science fiction. No one had a clue how it could be done. But was there anything that America could not do?

The United States had emerged from World War II as by far the world's dominant military and economic power. But it was not just power that characterized America in those years; it was also optimism, idealism, and belief in itself. Membership in communal organizations soared. There was the post–World War II "baby boom." There seemed to be a belief that the United States was rocketing toward a better, more prosperous future. What better expression of American exuberance than to send a rocket to the moon?

Bar Shot

They looked like any three guys in an Israeli bar, plotting their next start-up. But if you could see what they were sketching, it wasn't an app or a gadget. It was a spacecraft. Yariv Bash, Kfir Damari, and Yonatan Winetraub—all engineers in their late twenties—barely knew one another. They had come together in response to seven words that Bash had posted on Facebook on November 10, 2010: "WHO WANTS TO GO TO THE MOON??"

In the fifty-three years since Sputnik, the first satellite to orbit the earth, had launched the space era, only the largest nations had reached the surface of the moon. The former Soviet Union achieved the first soft landing with its spacecraft Luna 9 in 1966. The United States succeeded in landing the first human being on the moon in 1969. And in 2008, India was the next country to make it there, with a probe that intentionally crashed into the moon's south pole. China, by that time, had succeeded in sending an orbiter to the moon, but had not yet achieved a soft landing on its surface.

The three guys in the bar planned to add Israel to this short list of large nations. Their project had begun almost as a lark.

A few days earlier, Yariv Bash was walking home after midnight in Tel Aviv and had an idea. He was looking for an inspiring project for Mahanet, a three-day "creativity camp" that he had cofounded for soldiers serving in classified IDF technology and intelligence units. The event took place on an air force base in the desert. Everyone was encouraged to build something innovative. There was only one condition: it had to be useless. At the last gathering, one team built a waterslide simulator and another baked the largest pizza in the Middle East.

"Maybe I can get approval to build a rocket that will go to the edge of space, release a small plastic spacecraft and take a video," Bash suggested to a friend of his earlier that evening. His friend said, "You're thinking too small. Have you heard of the Google Lunar XPRIZE?" Google was offering $20 million to the first privately funded team to land a spaceship on the moon, move it five hundred meters, and send pictures back to earth. The competition sought to nudge the private sector into exploring deep space, a realm that had been the exclusive domain of a few national space programs.

Bash and his friend poked around the website. Registration had been open for about three years and was going to close in six weeks, on December 31, 2010. The registration fee was $50,000, and you had to submit a plausible plan for how you would do it. The project itself would cost untold millions of dollars.

Bash had told his friend that he was crazy to suggest applying for the Lunar XPRIZE. The teams in the competition were mostly big companies with large budgets. "But as I was walking home, I thought to myself, if I were to enter an Israeli team in the competition, what would I call it?" Bash later recalled. That night, he registered the domain name SpaceIL.com. ("IL" is the two-letter internet abbreviation for "Israel.") He also posted on his Facebook page, "Domain name. Check. Application. Check. WHO WANTS TO GO TO THE MOON??"

The next day, Bash received a text from Kfir Damari, a fellow engineer he had met at Mahanet. "If you're serious, I'm in," he wrote. Bash had also emailed Yonatan Winetraub, an acquaintance who worked in the space division of Israel Aerospace Industries (IAI). The three of them decided to meet at Carla Bruni, a bar in Holon, a city just south of Tel Aviv. The prize deadline was only weeks away.

Damari had grown up in Alfei Menashe, a small middle-class town in the center of Israel. He was studying computer engineering at Ben-Gurion University, having served in one of the army's elite intelligence units. Computers had been part of his life from an early age; he was six years old when he first began coding. "I wrote my first virus at the age of eleven. It was a really stupid virus, but it worked," he said.

Yonatan Winetraub had been obsessed with space since childhood. At sixteen he joined one of the first teams of high school students to design a CubeSat—a satellite just ten centimeters square on each side and weighing 860 grams. While still in high school, Winetraub published an academic paper about the altitude control of satellites. After his military service, while working at Israel Aerospace Industries, he attended a selective space studies program at the International Space University at NASA's Ames Research Center. That is when he met Peter Diamandis, the founder of XPRIZE Foundation, and heard about the Google Lunar XPRIZE.

The XPRIZE competition captivated him. On his own, Winetraub started working on a design for a CubeSat that could get to the surface of the moon. "When I returned to Israel," Winetraub said, "I tried to get people excited about my design and went around saying, 'Hey, let's build this.'" He felt ready. By his early twenties, Winetraub had already worked on half a dozen satellites, including as lead systems engineer on an IAI CubeSat. When he saw Bash's email, he jumped at the chance to put his plan into practice.

Over drinks at Carla Bruni, the three engineers did some calculations and sketches. How could they get to the moon as quickly and cheaply as possible? They speculated about the viability of a spacecraft the size of a Coke bottle, minus the thrusters and fuel tanks.

They would not have a superpower's multibillion-dollar budget. They wouldn't even have the paltry budget of Israel's national space agency behind them. The young Israelis would send a rocket to the moon under the auspices of SpaceIL, an educational nonprofit organization.

The first challenges the three young engineers faced were to find the $50,000 needed to register and to create a credible design for the spacecraft, both of which needed to be done by December 31. They understood that they had to pass the straight-face test. Who would take them seriously, three amateurs with no experience in space exploration and no money? A few weeks to cobble together $50,000 "is not trivial for guys who had one too many beers and big dreams," Danny Grossman told *Tablet* magazine. Grossman is a former Israeli Air Force fighter pilot who was among their first donors.

What followed was a classic demonstration of the feeling that most of Israel sometimes acts as one big family—an attribute that sets it apart from other advanced countries. Part of the reason these young engineers would even think about embarking on such a project is that they knew they would not be alone. They knew they could approach anyone to help, and there was a decent chance that others would be inspired to join a big project on behalf of their country.

"We emailed Isaac Ben-Israel, the chairman of the Israel Space Agency," Bash said, "and luckily he took the meeting." In Israel, everyone—no matter how important—responds to anyone, even to random cold emails and WhatsApp messages. Ben-Israel, a retired major general who had directed the Defense Research and Development program, was a two-time winner of the Defense Ministry's highest award, a former member of the Knesset, and a professor at Tel Aviv University. "The fact that three young engineers—an MBA student, an aspiring entrepreneur, and a junior employee at an aerospace company—could so easily reach the head of the space program would be hard to imagine in most countries," Damari said. "Especially when our pitch was 'We want to land a spacecraft the size of a Coke bottle on the moon in two years.'"

At this meeting Bash, Damari, and Winetraub began to focus on an immovable obstacle: geography. Satellites are generally launched eastward, to take advantage of the momentum provided by the earth's rotation. But if you look at a map of the Middle East, you'll see that nearly every country to the east of Israel did not have diplomatic relations with Israel, and most were in a cold war with the Jewish state that could turn hot from any accidental flash point. A crash landing or even a successful and peaceful launch could spark a geopolitical crisis. "That's why Israel is the only country that sends up [satellite] rockets against the rotation of the Earth," according to the journalist Armin Rosen. But launching against the natural force of the earth's rotation requires extra fuel, which meant the spacecraft would have to be even larger than the SpaceIL team had sketched out at the bar.

During the presentation, Ben-Israel commandeered Bash's laptop and flipped through the slides himself. "It won't be the size of a Coke bottle, it won't cost ten million dollars, and it won't take two years. It will be ten times bigger, cost ten times as much, and it will take ten years," he said gruffly. The three young men assumed that he was about to kick them out. But instead he said, "Guys, you're still not there, but I'm willing to be on your board and help you out."

The Hebrew word that Ben-Israel would likely have used instead of "guys" is *hevre*, a much more loaded term in Israeli culture. *Hevre*, which comes from the same root as *haver* (friend) and *hevra* (society), is not easily translatable into English. One's *hevre* can range from a group of lifelong friends to a group who have just met but are united by a common purpose. It's moving from "you" to "we." By calling them *hevre*, Ben-Israel was siding with their improbable mission.

Flush with Ben-Israel's encouragement, in the weeks leading up to the deadline, the three Israelis also secured the support of Daniel Zajfman, then president of the Weizmann Institute, one of Israel's premier scientific research institutions. Another crucial endorsement came from Arie Halsband, the head of the space division at Israel Aerospace Industries—and Winetraub's boss, three or four levels above him. "Arie started shouting at us when he saw our plans," Bash said. Then he calmed down and told them, "I have the only space facility in Israel. As long as I think you have a chance, I believe it's my obligation to help you." Years later, Halsband said, "They couldn't have done it without us, but we would never have had the audacity to do it without them."

As it happened, the Israel Space Agency was hosting its annual conference just a month later, a conference that attracts high-level representatives from NASA and other national space agencies. Ben-Israel called Bash and said that he and his group could have fifteen minutes onstage to announce their team's pursuit of the Google Lunar XPRIZE. It was a prestigious platform from which to launch their project. After the presentation, someone from the audience came up to them and asked, "Do you need money?" It was Morris Kahn, an Israeli telecom entrepreneur and private equity investor. Kahn, who was friends with the Apollo 11 astronaut Buzz Aldrin, was passionate about space exploration. "Come over to my office, I'll give one hundred thousand dollars to this project," he said. Kahn would become SpaceIL's main backer, eventually contributing $47 million.

The team entered the competition and spent the first two years developing their spacecraft before realizing that the design wouldn't work.

Two more years were spent on another failed design. Each time, they ran out of money and had to go back to their donors, saying that their plan had failed and they needed more funding. And each time, their key Israeli supporters came through. Each design made the spacecraft bigger, heavier, and more expensive. It was not until 2015 that they landed on a design that worked. In the end, just as Ben-Israel had predicted, it was much bigger, took almost a decade, and cost $100 million.

While $100 million sounds like a large number, it was a "bargain basement price" for a lunar mission, said Lee Billings, a senior editor at *Scientific American*. "No one has ever approached anywhere close to that before," he said. How did SpaceIL get the price so low?

Winetraub and his engineering team came up with two ways to dramatically cut costs. First, the spacecraft would have to be small—if not a CubeSat, then as small as possible. Second, SpaceIL would have to develop a completely new trajectory for reaching the moon.

One of the most expensive parts of getting to the moon is launching the spacecraft. By employing reusable rockets, SpaceX had brought the cost of launching payloads into space to a fraction of what it was for the Apollo space program. But the cost of a SpaceX launch was still $60 million—completely out of the range of SpaceIL's shoestring budget.

The only way to bring the launch price down was to build a spacecraft small enough to be just part of the payload of the SpaceX rocket, called the Falcon 9. *Beresheet* was much larger than originally planned, but still tiny for a moon mission. The whole vehicle, including legs and fuel tanks, was about the size of an electric golf cart. The SpaceIL founders called their moon lander *Beresheet*, meaning "In the beginning"—the first words of the biblical story of God creating the universe. These three secular, ambitious millennials viewed the mission of exploring the frontier of the future as connected to the larger story of the Jewish people and their Biblical heritage.

Because it was so small, *Beresheet* could share space with two satellites that were being launched on the same rocket. "This is the very first moon mission that has taken a rideshare—like an Uber—but I don't think it will be the last," said Leah Crane, a journalist for *New Scientist*. Sharing the rocket brought down the launch cost from $60 million to $20 million. And just as *Beresheet* hitched a ride on the rocket, NASA hitched a ride on *Beresheet* for a laser reflector to help guide future moon missions. "It's the first thing that NASA has sent to the moon in fifty years," Crane said.

Sharing the launch solved one problem, but created another one. The "Uber" that *Beresheet* was hitching on only went partway. The Falcon 9 was heading to launch satellites into earth's orbit, not spaceships to the moon. How could tiny *Beresheet* make it from there to the moon?

The Falcon 9 was a two-stage rocket. To get to the moon, you needed three stages, like the Saturn V. It was Saturn V's third stage that pushed the Apollo 11 astronauts from the earth to the moon. The third stage, though the smallest, was still about the height of a five-story building. Golf cart–sized *Beresheet* was dropped off in outer space with nothing. How was it supposed to get to the moon without a massive engine to push it there?

In theory, there was a way to do it. Apollo 11 rocketed directly to the moon in three days, three hours, and forty-nine minutes. *Beresheet* would have to swoop around the earth in increasingly elongated elliptical orbits until the orbit itself reached the moon, using the earth's gravity to propel the craft farther into space each time. This circuitous route required far less fuel, but it meant that *Beresheet* took forty-one days to reach lunar orbit and had to travel a distance fifteen times the length of Apollo's direct shot. No other moon landing had been attempted that way.

"Many experts at NASA didn't believe this could be done, and told me so," Winetraub said. None of the other teams competing for the XPRIZE chose to take SpaceIL's risky "slingshot" approach. But

Winetraub thought that future missions would follow the trail blazed by *Beresheet*. While it took much more time, the substantial fuel savings allowed the spacecraft to be smaller. It would be the only option for small spacecraft launched as "rideshares" on the same rocket with satellites destined for earth orbit.

According to former NASA administrator Charles Bolden, a onetime test pilot and astronaut himself, it was not just the low cost that was significant. "If a private organization like SpaceIL can put something on the moon, other entrepreneurs will dream about following in their footsteps," he said. "That would be monumental. It's a whole new ball game."

Jim Bridenstine, who would succeed Bolden as NASA's administrator, visited SpaceIL in Israel before the planned launch in the winter of 2019. Bridenstine told the three founders that if they were able to just *reach* the moon, without landing, for $200 million—twice what *Beresheet* had cost—that would usher in a new era in space exploration.

The SpaceIL team had not spent the preceding eight years in isolation from the rest of Israeli society. "Inspiring the next generation of scientists and engineers was a core purpose for us," Yonatan Winetraub said. "When we spoke to high schoolers, we were young enough to be their older brothers. We told them, 'We studied advanced math and science in school, and we got to be part of this moon landing. Maybe you can get to the moon, solve global warming, cure cancer, or whatever you want to do when you grow up.'"

SpaceIL had a team of volunteers who went to schools to teach about space. Winetraub credits SpaceIL's "*hevre* of volunteers" with encouraging one million young Israelis and kids around the world to create their own moonshots. Winetraub was surprised by the positive coverage of SpaceIL's mission worldwide. "Even the Iranian Space Research Center published a picture of our spacecraft," Winetraub told us.

The whole country followed the progress of the project. As the launch date grew closer, excitement within Israel grew. In many schools, from kindergarten through twelfth grade, classes learned about *Beresheet*. Astronaut costumes were a favorite on the Jewish holiday of Purim— when kids dress up in costumes like on Halloween—which happened to coincide with the planned mission schedule.

Beresheet launched on top of a SpaceX rocket from Cape Canaveral, Florida, on February 22, 2019. Kfir Damari and Yonatan Winetraub were there. Yariv Bash stayed in the control room in Israel. The launch went off smoothly. Within a minute or so the three founders had to hold their breath to see whether one of their cost-saving measures would pay off. *Beresheet* was attached to the rocket by a collar of spring-loaded bolts that would release simultaneously, pushing the craft into space. Usually these collars are custom-made, but SpaceIL bought one "off the shelf." It worked.

One of the founders of Israel's military satellite program told SpaceIL's leadership, "If you can communicate with *Beresheet* after it is released into orbit, hats off to you." According to Bash, it was clear that every step of the way was another opportunity for failure. All they could do was take it as far as they could. "We had an unspoken agreement between us: we won't stop unless something stops us," he said.

After traveling all that way, *Beresheet* had only one chance to jump from the earth's orbit to the moon's orbit. A mistake in one direction meant it would crash into the moon; a mistake the other way would send it off into deep space. The maneuver required the space equivalent of slamming on the brakes at a specific moment. It took about nine minutes for *Beresheet's* nine engines to turn the spacecraft in the right direction, and about six minutes for the engines to slow the spacecraft down to the correct speed.

After these tense minutes, the control room team could see that the maneuver worked. At that moment, Israel became the seventh nation, or group of nations—after the United States, the former Soviet Union, Japan, the European Space Agency, India, and China—to orbit a spacecraft around the moon. And in Israel's case, it wasn't even a national program, but a nonprofit started by three *hevre* in a bar.

On April 11, *Beresheet* began its descent to the moon's surface. Though it was late evening in Israel, the whole country was watching. In other countries, too, people watched to see if the first private mission to the moon could pass the toughest test of all: slowing down from six thousand kilometers per hour to zero before falling the last five meters to a soft landing on the lunar surface.

Israeli president Reuven Rivlin hosted a pajama party for kids who wanted to see the landing live. Public screenings were held around the country. Prime Minister Benjamin Netanyahu sat just outside the control room with Morris Kahn, SpaceIL's main philanthropic backer. A large screen depicted the status of *Beresheet*'s nine engines and various coordinates. One crucial number stood out: the rate of descent.

Failing Forward

It still wasn't clear to us what prompted Bash, Damari, and Winetraub to take on this enormous challenge in the first place. We asked Kfir Damari why a communications engineer who knew nothing about space would jump to answer Bash's original Facebook post.

"It wasn't really about space; it was about taking on a challenge that seemed impossible," Damari said. "The other part of it was Zionism— that is, doing something important for the State of Israel. For me, it connected to another moment in my life—when I graduated officer school and went to show my grandfather my new ranks. I knew that he would be so proud. So it was these two things, doing the impossible and doing something that would make me and everyone around me proud." Damari told us more about his grandfather, a Holocaust survivor from North Africa who had been imprisoned in a Nazi concentration camp in Tunisia. He later escaped, immigrated to Israel, and fought in the War of Independence. Damari's grandfather lived to attend the ceremony at which his grandson was commissioned as an army officer.

The journalist Armin Rosen surmised that a sense of national solidarity may have been an advantage that none of the other private teams had: "After all, the fate of the Jewish people on this planet has, until recently, been largely out of their own hands. The lunar mission would be a monument to a miraculous triumph over centuries of existential danger." With Damari's family journey in mind, Rosen wrote: "The idea of the citizens of a Jewish state attempting a moon landing would have contained many levels of science fiction–like absurdity until quite recently."

This attraction to the impossible is typically Israeli. Solving problems is something of a national sport. Israel's cultural operating system is based on repeated exposure to ever-increasing challenges, both before and during military service. This life trajectory produces people who become addicted to doing things that are difficult, important, and meaningful.

Yariv Bash also had experiences growing up that gave him the confidence to take on the seemingly impossible. "I was a couch potato during high school, mostly playing video games," he said. "Then they put me in an IDF special forces unit and I found myself doing crazy things. I didn't know that I could climb a ten-meter rope, carry a friend up a mountain, not sleep for two days, or hike seventy kilometers. You learn about yourself in those moments." Later on he worked as an electrical engineer in a government agency that he couldn't name, for security reasons. "We could produce anything, from a radio, to a computer, to an iPhone— whatever was needed," he recalled. "These two junctions in life taught me that I can basically do anything."

But what was it about the particular challenge of sending a rocket to the moon that inspired Bash? It was not just about the audacity of it. There was a deeper, more personal reason that Bash rarely spoke about.

In July 2013, Bash was invited to speak about SpaceIL at the Volkswagen headquarters in Germany, after some visiting executives from that company had heard him speak in Israel. After he had accepted, he wanted to learn more about the connection his grandfather, Yitzhak Bash, had to the company. Bash's grandfather had died when he was sixteen, so Bash talked to his family and managed to piece together the story. Yitzhak Bash, a Hungarian Jew, was sent to Auschwitz with the rest of his community toward the end of World War II. Germany was in a desperate effort to produce more armaments and was using Jewish and other forced laborers to increase production. Just before being sent to the gas chamber, Yitzhak was diverted along with a group of three hundred Hungarian engineers to work on Germany's V-1 rocket program. German companies were deeply enmeshed in the war effort. The company that had won the V-1 contract: Volkswagen.

At the Volkswagen headquarters in Wolfsburg, Yariv Bash stood in front of a group of their top management. His first slide was a picture of his grandfather. Bash said, "Seventy years ago my grandfather worked here as a forced laborer, twenty years ago he came to visit as a Holocaust survivor, and today I am here to tell you about how Israel will send a spaceship to the moon." Speaking about the visit to an Israeli newspaper, Bash said, "I guess you could say that rocketry is our family business."

Contrary to the stereotype of entrepreneurs, Israeli start-up founders tend to be surprisingly sober about their chances of success. It's not naive overconfidence that allows them to take risks. It is more about their ability to brush off, and even appreciate, failure. As Damari put it, "It's not about being optimistic that things will work out. It's about being optimistic about what happens when they don't."

In many places, the fear of failure stems not just from potential financial difficulties but from social stigma. If the chances of success are low and the consequences of failure are catastrophic, it is no wonder that entrepreneurs are harder to find. But in Israel, as Damari explained, "no matter what happens, it will be okay. The realization that the worst that can happen is not so bad gives you a lot of confidence."

Another critical advantage for the SpaceIL founders was that, as crazy as their idea was, and despite the fact that most people said so, there were enough people in senior leadership positions willing to give them a chance. Damari could not imagine any other country where three young engineers could launch a space program. "I think that this is probably the only place where there is such an accessible network of physical and scientific assets," he told us. That they could reach the heads of the space agency and one of the top universities in a few days had an impact. "They were drawn to the same sense of doing something big for the country that we were, and they weren't afraid to help us try."

Hevre

Yossi Klein Halevi is an Israeli author and an astute student of the Israeli psyche. He moved from New York to Jerusalem in 1982, where he married and raised a family. He has written a number of award-winning books, including *Like Dreamers*, which traces the history of Israel's defining political movements on the left and right through the eyes of six paratroopers who fought together in the battle to reunite Jerusalem in the 1967 Six-Day War.

There is something spiritual in the way Halevi speaks and writes, so it is not surprising that he is active in Jewish-Muslim and Israeli-Palestinian dialogues. He has a sharp eye for the cultural currents running through Israeli music and humor.

"Israel works on the basis of two essential social units," Halevi told us. "The family, which remains very strong here, partly because we're a small country, and you can't get away from your parents, and the Jewish family values that remain very powerful here. And the other extremely powerful social network in some ways even stronger than the family is the *hevre*, which functions as almost a supra-family."

Halevi, like Isaac Ben-Israel, was well attuned to the importance of *hevre*. He made the point that within a person's *hevre*, connections are constantly being added and strengthened as one goes through the different stages and experiences of life. He gave the example of when his own children were in high school during the dark years of 2000 to 2004, when the Israeli-Palestinian peace process fell apart and Israel was hit with the most intense wave of terror attacks in its history. More than one thousand Israelis were killed by Palestinian suicide bombings of buses, coffee shops, restaurants, and a nightclub.

Halevi told us about the bands of *hevre* that his children and their peers organically formed during those years. "They lost friends and some were wounded. But our kids didn't come to us at all. To this day I don't know what they were going through," he said. "They unpacked the situation in intense, impromptu therapy sessions where they all just got together. That's Israel. It's a society created by youth movements. Pre-state Israel was a youth society. And it has remained that way. That's one reason why there's so much vitality here."

In 2001, two Israelis founded a national website called *Hevre*. It had five banners you could click on:

Hevre from high school
Hevre from university
Hevre from youth groups
Hevre from the army
Hevre from work

At its peak it was among the five most popular websites in Israel. The categories traced the main Israeli social circles, and tellingly, it was designed more around group identity than individual identity.

When you ask Israelis why their country scores so high in the international happiness rankings, they have to think for a moment, because they are not used to the idea of their country as happy. But they don't reject the idea, either. And a common explanation they offer is "You're not alone." Or that there is a sense of belonging. Or a sense of *b'yachad*, which means "togetherness." *Hevre* are an important part of the sense of *b'yachad*.

This is the kind of social support that you get in small tight-knit communities. What's unusual about Israel is that this feeling also exists at the societal level. And it is this kind of support that can give people like Yariv Bash, Kfir Damari, and Yonatan Winetraub the feeling that they won't be alone if they embark on a crazily ambitious project. They'll find allies along the way. It also encourages people to identify with the country and contribute to it.

Ask Not

One thing we still did not understand was how something started by three young engineers could be so seamlessly adopted by the people and the State of Israel as a national project. In most places, private efforts stay private. The space endeavors of Elon Musk (SpaceX), Jeff Bezos (Blue Origin), and Richard Branson (Virgin Galactic) are private. None of them have sparked the national pride of their home countries. The other teams in the Google Lunar XPRIZE competition came from more than a dozen countries and might have inspired national pride if they had won. But the Israeli team, starting with its name, SpaceIL, saw themselves as pursuing an ambition on behalf of their country, rather than just themselves.

The national element was on display in the "selfie" that the *Beresheet* spacecraft took as it descended toward the lunar surface. The picture, broadcast back to earth live and in high definition, showed the gold-foil-covered leg of the spacecraft with the moon filling up the background. A small sign stuck out from the craft, showing the Israeli flag and inscribed with the Hebrew words *Am Yisrael Chai*—"The People of Israel

Live." Below that, in English, were the words "SMALL COUNTRY, BIG DREAMS." At the bottom were the logos of the Israel Aerospace Industries, SpaceIL, and the XPRIZE Foundation. When the picture was broadcast, a cheer went up across the country. It was a cheer for Israel, not just for SpaceIL.

Behind the flag sign, Bash, Damari, and Winetraub had also inserted a minuscule complete edition of the *Tanakh*—the Hebrew Bible—engraved into a disk the size of a coin. As Armin Rosen wrote, it contained "each Hebrew letter as small as a microbe, and part of a time capsule with over 10 million pages of data."

For many Israelis, one of the most meaningful experiences in their lives is to be entrusted with real responsibilities for securing the state, primarily through their military service. The threats they face are not abstract or thousands of miles away. They know that if they don't do their job, enemy forces could get through Israel's defenses and harm their families, friends, and neighbors.

In his inaugural address in 1961, President John F. Kennedy famously appealed to Americans' sense of duty. "Ask not what your country can do for you," he said, punching the cold January air with his finger, "ask what you can do for your country." His ringing exhortation inspired action rather than cynicism. Kennedy, like many in his generation, had fought in World War II. That one should sacrifice for one's country did not need explaining; it had been practiced. The consequences of not doing so were still fresh in people's minds.

Fast-forward to 2020, when a U.S. senator running for reelection in Kennedy's home state of Massachusetts seemed to capture a new zeitgeist when he declared: "We asked what we could do for our country. We went out, we did it. With all due respect, it's time to start asking what your country can do for you." In today's world of deepening individualism, doing something for your country feels like an increasingly alien concept. But not in Israel.

Landings Are the Hardest

Over the weeks that *Beresheet* was orbiting the earth in ever-widening circles on its way to the moon, the Israeli public did not pay much attention to it. But as the landing grew closer, the excitement swelled. Would the journey end in triumph or disaster?

Standing at the front of the observation deck filled with dignitaries and families, the heads of SpaceIL and the space division of Israel Aerospace Industries provided live commentary, with the large control room screen visible behind them. Of all the hurdles that the spacecraft had to overcome, landing was the most difficult. Kfir Damari recalled what an old space hand had told him: "Landing on the moon requires a million miracles."

Of course, none of this was known to the national audience watching the numbers on the screen, tracking the orientation and speed of descent. It looked like an overcomplicated dashboard of a car, only with a couple dozen engineers sitting in rows at their stations watching with great intensity. On the other side of the screen was an animation showing the progress of the spacecraft on a line that dipped downward toward the moon.

As the spacecraft neared the transition point from orbiting to landing, the hosts explained that it would autonomously determine whether everything was working. If not, *Beresheet* would abort the landing and make another four-hour orbit around the moon and try again. At the key moment, the control room went still as everyone waited to see if the maneuver had taken place. Finally came the announcement: "Descent has begun. We have passed the point of no return."

The descent from twenty kilometers above the moon to the surface would take seventeen minutes. Then problems started to happen in rapid succession. The numbers on the screen froze as telemetry—the communications stream from the spacecraft—was lost. Seconds later it came back. But then a voice said that the main engine had shut down. It was clear from the faces in the control room that this was not supposed to happen.

The main engine restarted, but it was not clear whether there would be enough time to avoid a crash. Then communications were lost again. A few painful seconds passed as no one wanted to reach the inevitable conclusion. Finally, the head of mission control announced that *Beresheet* had crashed into the lunar surface. A journey of more than eight years, culminating in a flight of 6.5 million kilometers over forty-eight days, had failed in the last ten minutes.

Successful Failure

Kfir Damari has often been asked how he felt at that moment. "Of course, I wanted a soft landing," he told us. "But I remember that one of my first reactions was relief." This was not the response we expected. "We sat down in a bar, and everything didn't work over and over again, the organization almost ran out of money so many times. And we got there. That's it. The journey ended."

Yonatan Winetraub pointed to the long-term effects from the excitement that *Beresheet* had built among young people. "Before *Beresheet*, if you were to go to investors and say, 'I'm going to the moon for one hundred million dollars,' they would laugh you out the door," he said. "Now an entrepreneur can say, 'Look, the Israelis did it, it can be done.'"

When Bash, Damari, and Winetraub founded SpaceIL, there were thirty-three teams registered for the XPRIZE. By the end, only SpaceIL and four others had persevered. And of these five remaining teams, only SpaceIL had launched anything into space.

Now that the doors are open to bargain-basement moon missions, better designs will be developed. "One day, someone will land a CubeSat on the moon," Winetraub told us. CubeSats are made of ten-centimeters-per-side cubes that can be assembled like Legos. There are some 1,200 orbiting the earth now. "Someday maybe a kid will be able to do it."

SpaceIL also opened new pathways for Israel to partner with countries once hostile to the Jewish state. The Falcon 9 rocket that carried *Beresheet* for the launch also carried a U.S. Air Force satellite and a satellite for an Indonesian telecom company. When stacked in the Falcon 9's payload bay, waiting for takeoff, *Beresheet* looked like a small gold ornament on top of the massive green Indonesian communications satellite. Indonesia, home to the largest Muslim population in the world, does not recognize Israel. But the Indonesian executives involved in the launch were happy to spend time with Damari and Winetraub at Cape Canaveral. "When we saw them at the launch site we congratulated each other and had a little celebration!" Winetraub recalled.

After *Beresheet* crashed into the moon, Bash, Damari, and Winetraub had no intention of starting over. There was no contingency plan. Their two-year adventure had stretched to eight years. But it wasn't just that. The pressure had been intense. "We had no Kennedy," Damari said. "It was on us. If we had failed at any point it wasn't just our start-up. We felt that we had the nation's hopes on our shoulders."

Within months, however, the sense of unfinished business gained momentum. Immediately after the crash, the Google Lunar XPRIZE team—which had come to Israel to watch the landing—huddled in a corner for a few minutes, and on the spot decided to award SpaceIL the first-ever $1 million "Moonshot Award." The ebullient chairman and founder of the XPRIZE Foundation, Peter Diamandis, explained the decision. He called SpaceIL's feat of getting to the moon for just $100 million and engaging fewer than fifty engineers "a leap forward towards affordable and accessible space exploration." Soon after, a

British-American philanthropist contributed another $1 million to the new effort.

And so *Beresheet 2* was born. Damari summarized the first challenge they were up against: "We knew that a lot of folks would say, 'You did this already.' We faced a difficult question: How could we make the new mission as inspiring as the first one?" SpaceIL decided to send an orbiter to the moon from which *two* landers will attempt to land on the surface. The orbiter will continue around the moon for months or years. And all this will be done for the same budget as the first *Beresheet*, and much faster—$100 million by 2026.

The *Beresheet 2* program also created an opportunity for SpaceIL's educational mission to go global. Students from other countries will be able to propose experiments and control the sensors on the orbiter themselves. "We've been going to countries and offering them an opportunity to have a space program," Damari said. In January 2023, NASA agreed that *Beresheet* would carry a NASA experiment that would measure radiation from the moon's surface.

In 2013, about three years into SpaceIL's journey, Yariv Bash had founded a start-up, Flytrex. Start-ups are almost by definition ambitious, but this one dove into one of the most hotly contested markets: on-demand drone delivery of retail goods to suburban homes. Bash believes that Flytrex is positioned to be a leader in part because it is the only start-up, as of 2023, to receive Federal Aviation Administration (FAA) approval in the United States. In March 2017, Bash suffered a tragic personal setback. He was paralyzed from the waist down in a skiing accident. Whether working in the *Beresheet* control room or presenting Flytrex at big tech conferences, Bash could be seen in a wheelchair. "I'm the same person, just half a meter shorter," he said. Indeed, it does not seem that his appetite for taking on impossible challenges has slackened in the least.

Yonatan Winetraub went in another direction after SpaceIL. He pursued a doctorate in biophysics, writing his thesis on a possible new optical method for revealing cancer cell communication. He went on to head a lab at Stanford University that is working on noninvasive cancer detection.

But Winetraub also had a "hobby," as he called it: developing a way to grow chickpeas and make hummus on the moon. Growing food on the moon is not a gimmick; it's going to be a critical element in NASA's plans for a permanent manned presence there. Freeze-dried space rations will only go so far. Bringing food from earth is not economical over the long run. And in any case, people need greenery and fresh vegetables to make life more livable.

Winetraub's dream is to combine the disciplines of biology, physics, and space to make hummus on the moon, maybe even with soil from Jerusalem and water from the Sea of Galilee. Like *Beresheet*, it is not just about personal accomplishment or advancing science. It is also about making an Israeli contribution to the world.

It is hard to imagine a few random engineers—without any university, company, government, or organization of any kind behind them—trying to launch a space program in any other country. What makes this audacity, or chutzpah, possible? Perhaps it is the feeling that you won't be alone on the journey. That you will pick people up along the way, swept up by the craziness of the idea. And that even ponderous institutions, like large companies, universities, and government agencies, will become inspired and help rather than obstruct.

Without the power of *hevre*, of a desire to be part of something bigger and doing things together, chutzpah wouldn't work. Or at least it wouldn't be as common. Or part of a national culture, not just the province of technology entrepreneurs.

The *Beresheet* technical team was based entirely on volunteers in SpaceIL's early years. These engineers were building a spaceship in their spare time.

"This spirit of togetherness was crucial to make progress early on and get to the level where we could get enough funding for a full-time team," Yonatan Winetraub recalled. Many of those volunteers went on to build start-ups, some of which became public companies.

While Israelis are notoriously chaotic, pushy, and rude in the eyes of outsiders, problem-solving is an Israeli happy place. It is a communal activity, something that you do with people who become one of your multiple circles of *hevre*.

But chutzpah and *hevre* cannot be manufactured or grafted onto a society. They emerge from deeper forces working among Israelis, which start early in childhood and persist for a lifetime.

Chapter Two

WHERE'S THE CLASS?

In Israel, contribution to the public good is still an ever-present major demand. Israelis are expected to take the national interest into consideration, not just to cater to their private careers and kin. They are supposed to make personal sacrifices for society, to volunteer for various tasks, to fight and to die if necessary for the country.

—Sammy Smooha

In 2011, Stanford professors Sebastian Thrun and Peter Norvig decided to put their course, "Introduction to AI," online for free. To their astonishment, 160,000 people signed up. This being Stanford, the faculty saw a commercial opportunity and founded the first two companies to offer what became known as Massive Open Online Courses, or MOOCs. Thrun founded Udacity, and two other computer science professors, Daphne Koller and Andrew Ng, founded Coursera.

The problem was that only one in ten of those enrolling in these free courses completed them. As we all learned only too well in the COVID-19 era, it's hard to sit for hours in front of a screen learning by yourself. But then something strange happened. Koller, an Israeli, noticed that in Israel some groups of people were completing the online courses at a rate of over 80 percent.

Upon investigation, she discovered that these were Israeli high school students taking college-level courses from several leading U.S. universities. They shouldn't have been finishing these courses at all, let alone doing so with stellar success rates. But it wasn't that these kids were so smart. They were typical students from regular schools. The difference was that they were taking the courses together using a method called "Team Classroom."

It worked like this: the whole class would watch a video from the course. Next, every student would hold up a sign with one of three colors. Green meant that they understood the material well enough to teach someone else. Yellow meant that they understood, but not well enough to teach. And red meant that they didn't understand the material at all. Then the whole class went at it with a single goal—that everyone would be able to hold up a green sign.

Rather than one against all, the students had to bring their classmates over the finish line. And the system worked so well that teachers with no knowledge of the subject matter but a knack for encouraging the students could help them excel. Using the Team Classroom method, a high school Bible teacher could teach college-level physics.

The Power of *Gibush*

Tamar Katriel felt as if she were in a time machine. As a doctoral student, it was strange, after all these years, to be sitting at a cramped desk in the back of a grade school classroom. She was there to research and promote a new method of personalized instruction in Israeli schools. The centuries-old mainstay of education—a teacher lecturing in front of a classroom—was beginning to be questioned.

Katriel was excited about the new technique: a learning plan attuned to each individual child's strengths and weaknesses. The more adventurous teachers were game to try it. They, too, were frustrated with one-size-fits-all education and its need to "teach to the middle," leaving the weaker students behind and the strongest ones bored and unchallenged.

The teachers could see that the new ideas worked. The students were scoring higher on tests and learning more, and they were more engaged. What could be better? But some of the teachers started going back to the old methods. As one explained, "It worked, but I felt I was losing the feel of the class."

This result mystified Katriel. At first she chalked it up to the difficulty of going beyond one's comfort zone. But these were the best teachers, the ones especially eager to improve learning outcomes. Eventually she got it. There was something even more important to them than their students' test scores. It was *gibush*.

Gibush (pronounced "gi-BOOSH") is another one of those Hebrew words for which there is no good English translation. "Bonding" or "cohesiveness" are closest. But neither of those concepts captures the emotional power of the word in Israeli society. *Gibush* is not just a process or description. It is a deeply held value.

Just as *hevre* refers to any group that a person is part of—close-knit friends from school, a youth scouting group, a community project, a military unit or workplace—*gibush* is the act of bringing people together with the goal of deepening the bond uniting them. You can say, "I went on a hike with the *hevre* for *gibush*."

Katriel saw the importance of *gibush* in the vehement response from one agitated teacher to whom she was explaining the concept of personalized education. "Where is the class in all this? Where is the *gibush*?" the teacher asked. In a parents' meeting, the mother of a seventh grader told Katriel that what she wanted for her daughter was a cohesive classroom. The daughter, for her part, complained, "We have a lousy class. It needs a lot more *gibush*." Another teacher said in his self-evaluation for the year that his class was a "total failure" because he had not succeeded at *gibush*.

It was clear that teachers, parents, and students all regarded the *gibush* of their class to be paramount—as crucial as any test score or other "objective" measure of achievement. In other countries, the metric of success is individual student performance; the class is just a functional vessel to achieve that end. Classes are not treated as living beings with their own independent character that needs to be nurtured, even at the expense of individual learning outcomes. That is not the case in Israel.

A teacher put it best. "I have thought about these things a lot," she told Katriel. "Some people say that students should come to school to learn, that's all. I don't agree. I think if we give up the goal of *gibush* in the class, the State of Israel will unravel. We can't afford that." To this teacher, *gibush* was not a nice thing to have. It was existential.

Historian and journalist Daniel Gordis was born in New York, but moved to Israel as an adult. He drew this contrast to illustrate the origins of this ethos: "According to the American myth, the wilderness was conquered by individuals or small groups. Daniel Boone. Davy Crockett." Gordis raised three children in Israel who have all served in the army, cofounded the first liberal arts college in Jerusalem, and has authored numerous books on Israeli history and society.

Gordis is inspired by America's origin story. But he believes Israel's founding myth—which goes back thousands of years—helps explain *gibush*: "The myth recounts that we were six hundred thousand people at Mount Sinai, crossing the desert en masse. The Jewish story isn't one of individuals or small families, but of a massive migration toward the Promised Land, a suggestion that only in the company of many others can we reach our ultimate destination. The image of our trek through the desert tells us one thing in particular: we're a people who need community."

In this way, school plays a much larger role in Israel than just the education of children. It has a clear function: to embody the value of the group, not just the individual, in Israeli society. Israelis start learning at an early age that "it's not all about you." They are part of something larger than themselves. And this group socialization doesn't just happen in school. If anything, it happens even more intensively outside the school walls.

Not for Adults

Inbal Arieli, a former officer in the IDF's 8200 intelligence unit, founded 8200 EISP, what may be a global first: a nonprofit start-up "accelerator" built around veterans of a military unit. Over its first thirteen years, the almost two hundred start-ups that went through the 8200 EISP program raised $1.4 billion in venture capital investments.

Arieli herself went on to become a serial entrepreneur, investor, and expert on the roots of Israeli innovation. In her book, *Chutzpah: Why Israel Is a Hub of Innovation and Entrepreneurship*, she writes about the pivotal role of youth movements in sowing the seeds of entrepreneurship at an early age. She gives the example of the printed message her son Yarden brought home from school in the third grade:

> On Tuesday, June 5, we will hold the first Tzofim [scouts] gathering for the third graders to prepare for next year. If your son or daughter is interested in joining, we will pick them up at the school gate at 4:00 p.m. and walk together to the scout troop's center. Alternatively, they can meet us there at 4:30 p.m.—Thanks, The New Counselors

What this terse message doesn't say, and what didn't happen, says a lot about Israeli culture. First, scouts is a neighborhood thing. When there is more than one troop within walking distance, kids decide which to join based on where their friends are going or where their older siblings went. Sometimes it's a family tradition—their parents went to the same troop. Second, the note made no attempt at persuasion. It is assumed that most kids will want to join. For most kids, part of reaching the age of nine or ten in Israel is joining the scouts or one of the many other youth movements. Third, though the unidentified counselors are probably all of fifteen or sixteen years old, parents are expected to trust them to shepherd their child, along with a couple dozen other kids, to their destination. There is no elaborate "first day of camp" send-off. The signal is clear: *We kids are in charge, trust us, your child is in our hands.*

Giving children responsibility has been at the core of scouting since the founding of the movement by the British army officer Robert Baden-Powell in 1907. "Expect a great deal of your Patrol Leaders and nine times out of ten they will play up to your expectation," Baden-Powell wrote about the teenagers who were put in charge of about eight younger scouts. "But if you are going always to nurse them and not trust them to do things well, you will never get them to do anything on their own initiative." To Baden-Powell, the character-building aims of scouting hinged on giving young people responsibility. "The patrol system is not one method in which Scouting for boys can be carried on. It is the only method."

But Baden-Powell, and scout movements around the world today, also believe in an important role for adult scout leaders. "Association with Adults" is one of eight essential scout methods, on the principle that "Scouts learn a great deal by watching how adults conduct themselves." There, Israeli youth movements break ranks with their international counterparts. For Israeli youth movements, learning from adults does not seem to be valued or practiced. One reason for maximizing separation from adults is to give more responsibility to the campers themselves. But it also reflects a more profound difference in goals.

In Israel, as elsewhere, youth movements are designed to produce better members of society. "We must change boys from a 'what can I get' to a 'what can I give' attitude. . . . In Scouting you are combating the brooding of selfishness," Baden-Powell said. Accordingly, volunteering is a cornerstone of youth movements in Israel as it is elsewhere. So is learning about the value of the group and of teamwork, and even of serving your country and the wider world. But the difference in Israel can be seen even in the name: youth *movement*. The youth are supposed to not just join society, but to shake it up.

The youth movement that gave birth to many of Israel's kibbutzim was Hashomer Hatzair (Young Guard). Like other pre-state youth movements, it organized Jewish youth in Europe to move to British-ruled Palestine and become pioneers who would build the new state. This youth movement still exists today. In harkening to its history, Hashomer credits Baden-Powell's scouts, but also describes how it differs.

The goal of Baden-Powell's scouting was to turn the youth into good and loyal citizens who follow the path paved for them by their parents, but the goal of Hashomer Hatzair was to strengthen the qualities of a person who rebels against his fate, who acts in his life and the life of his people. Hashomer drew from scouting, refreshed and adapted every aspect of it to the Zionist ambition to create a new Jewish person.

Hashomer describes its founding ethos as "a rebellion against the pale and meaningless society of adults, a rebellion against the fate of the Jew in the diaspora." The goal was to replace generations of passivity in the face of the oppression of European Jewry with "belief that everything is possible, that human history can be changed, and that youth is invincible and its path is not paved before it."

Hashomer's vision was secular and socialist, as epitomized by the ultimate communal utopia, the kibbutz. What was striking, however, is that the premier *religious* youth movement was also revolutionary. On March 7, 1929, in Jerusalem, thirty-eight grade school boys gathered to form the first troop of Bnei Akiva. They did so despite the opposition of Mizrahi, the umbrella movement of religious Zionism. Mizrahi's rabbis worried that Bnei Akiva was not led by a prominent religious figure, and that its activities might distract the youth from their religious studies. But their first concern was that "a youth movement by its nature rebels against the status quo. Religion and rebellion are opposed to each other, because religious education must be conservative in its relation to the present and the past." Mizrahi eventually embraced Bnei Akiva, which grew to become the largest religious Zionist youth movement in the world, with about 125,000 members in forty-two countries, and to found most of the religious kibbutzim.

In many other countries, scouting is recognized as a nice youth activity, but not a common stage in life integrated into the nation's history. Israelis recognize youth movements as not just good for building individual character, but for learning the value of *gibush* that is so central to the culture as a whole. As in the classroom, where the teachers thought that *gibush* was more important than learning different subjects, in scouts the key value is that *the group is no less important than the individual.*

The strong youth movement tradition also contributes to bonds between generations. Many Israeli parents have their own memories of being a scout and a counselor as they were growing up, and they encourage their own children to embrace the *gibush* of Tzofim or other youth organizations. It is an endless rite of passage: awestruck fourth graders grow up to be counselors by the time they graduate high school, running the whole youth program. The few adults who supervise this self-replenishing system are there to be seen and not heard, as the young people themselves are in charge.

For immigrants to Israel who did not have this formative experience, watching their children go through it can be bemusing. Every summer, what seems like a thousand scouts from troops across the country take over a forest, evoking a happier version of *Lord of the Flies*—scores of encampments with sweaty kids milling about, with hardly an adult in sight. The lethargy that parents may see on visiting day is misleading. Their children are preserving their energy for the nights, which they spend jumping around with their faces painted with the troop's colors and trying to belt out their troop chant louder than their neighbors. Another favorite activity is building massive wood structures with the troop name spelled in oil-soaked rags that they burn in the night, perhaps to sear the tribal belonging into their collective consciousness.

Anyone watching these kids in the forest might think they were witnessing chaos, but they would be wrong. Embedded in these activities are deep and powerful socializing forces. The first is to instill in young people a sense of responsibility for one another. For many Israelis, becoming a youth movement counselor is their first experience managing projects and people. The second is to learn what *gibush* is and how to create bonds between people that can last a lifetime.

On Their Own

In April 2018, the leading Israeli Hebrew-language news provided a rare window onto a scenario the IDF is planning for: fighting Iran's proxy force, the Shiite terrorist group Hezbollah, far from Israel's borders, in Lebanon.

The force from the 101st Paratroopers Brigade advances by the light of a full moon in southern Lebanon. The soldiers are attacked at close quarters. Some are wounded and the battalion doctor is treating the injured. The orange lights blinking in the far ridgeline, south of them, are not in Israel. There is no reassuring sound of evacuating helicopters on the way. There is no other unit in the area. As their adrenaline subsides and the dawn breaks, the paratroopers start realizing: they are deep inside of Lebanon. They are on their own.

The last time Israel squared off in a full-scale war with Hezbollah was in 2006. Back then, Hezbollah was closer to a guerrilla force than an army, though it was armed with thousands of missiles that it rained on the towns and cities of northern Israel. In the years since, Hezbollah has become one of the strongest armies in the Middle East. And its fighters now have combat experience in Syria.

Hezbollah reportedly has more than 40,000 fighters and as many as 120,000 missiles in Lebanon, many with enough range to reach Israel's major population centers. And Iran is the primary weapons supplier, funder, and commander of Hezbollah.

In the next war, as always, intelligence will be critical, and not just to locate missile launchers. Before those launchers can be rooted out, there is a crucial need for even more granular intelligence to solve a thorny problem. How will Israeli ground forces (who will have parachuted or rolled deep into enemy territory with not much more than what they can carry on their backs) survive and fight for days and weeks?

A deciding factor in this conflict is whether these troops will be able to operate independently. The soldiers will have to find the food, medicines, and fuel they need in the local towns and villages around them. For that to happen, they will need to know where the markets, pharmacies, and gas stations are. Looking at aerial photos is not enough. They need to know which of these places are operating and stocked.

This problem presents an almost impossible intelligence challenge, one that in the summer of 2013 confounded Avi Simon, the officer in charge of a satellite imagery intelligence analysis unit. The Chief of Staff's General Headquarters, the most senior command in the Israeli army, had assigned Simon the job of scanning 80 percent of northern Lebanon by the end of the year, to identify sources of supplies for troops on the ground. Six months into the job, Simon was nowhere near finishing the task and had nothing to show the high command.

Simon was a lieutenant colonel in Unit 9900, the full name of which is the Terrain Analysis, Accurate Mapping, Visual Collection and Interpretation Agency. It's a mouthful but, in short, this unit trains analysts to make sense of the microscopic details in the millions of images gathered by

Israeli satellites, airplanes, and drones. Given the overwhelming amount of visual data, the unit's engineers code algorithms to train computers to process and interpret the reams of data into actionable intelligence—everything from long stretches of desert to dense urban areas.

But there was a limit to what computers could do. Simon explained: "We are constantly scanning huge areas and trying to understand them—if there's some orchard in Lebanon that's not on the map or isn't easily identifiable in the aerial footage, and you didn't know about it and therefore didn't plan around it . . . suddenly your tanks can't maneuver around it."

He rattled off other examples: "There's a small stream that you thought was uncrossable for a vehicle, but then you realize that it is sometimes crossable. My normal analysts see the stream and just think, 'It's in the way.' It takes an entirely different level of concentration to make sense of the tiniest degree of change—depending on the day or the hour of the day—in the size of the stream that may make the difference."

Staring at aerial images for hours at a time and studying the minute details sitting in plain sight was too boring and too difficult for Unit 9900's analysts. Then a new cadre of cadets finished their training course and joined Simon's unit. "I was getting a lot of heat from the general. We thought there was no way we'd finish on time," he told us. "But then, four months later, it was complete. My commanders were astounded."

Senior brass from different intelligence units started visiting, wanting to meet the team that had pulled this off. "The commanders didn't realize they were talking to a special group. All they knew was that one minute we were flailing and the next it was done," Simon said. The special group was part of a program called Roim Rachok, which in Hebrew means "to see far." The Roim Rachok soldiers didn't understand what the fuss was about; they had been given a mission and they did it. But as Simon told us, "All these cadets that solved the impossible had one thing in common: they were on the autism spectrum."

The Right to Serve

"It's a very Israeli story," Tal Vardi began with a wry smile. "For my part, it started at the *shloshim*." A *shloshim* (from the Hebrew word for "thirty") marks the end of the traditional thirty-day mourning period following the death of a close family member. These gatherings often bring together an eclectic group who share a connection to the deceased, but have never met each other.

This *shloshim*, in February 2011, became a reunion of about thirty members of an elite paratroopers reconnaissance unit who had served together in the 1970s. They came to mourn Nadav Rotenberg, a twenty-year-old soldier who had been killed by friendly fire on Israel's southeastern border. Nadav's father, Omer Rotenberg, had served on Tal Vardi's team. The unit had three teams, each led by an officer, and almost all of them were at the *shloshim*. Some had flown in from outside the country to support their grief-stricken comrade.

The Rotenbergs lived in Ramot HaShavim, a collective farming community known as a "moshav"—another Israeli social invention like the kibbutz. This moshav was founded in 1933 on farmland that used to be far from Tel Aviv, but has since become a suburb abutting the expanding metropolis. It still clung to its agricultural roots.

"We all sat around in a circle on the grass," Vardi said. The unit reflected almost every corner and stratum of Israeli society. "There was Dror, who came from Yemen," one of the poorest, most isolated Jewish communities in the world. (From 1949 through 1950, 49,000 Yemenite Jews were rescued by an Israeli emergency airlift called Magic Carpet, which was the first time they had seen an airplane, much less flown on one.) One was a Russian immigrant, another had come from the ancient Jewish community in Cochin, India. As the men went around the circle, they learned that since their army service, one had become a professor, another had gone to look for oil in Siberia.

As they sat in the sun with the aroma of the surrounding orange orchards wafting about, Vardi could still picture each of them in their youth, before they added a paunch and lost some hair. With one another, they reverted to their old roles—the strong one, the brave one, the smart one, the funny one. And Vardi, though only about one year older than the rest, still retained an aura of leadership.

"Many of them had served together in *miluim* for decades, but as an officer, I was sent somewhere else," he observed. *Miluim*, or reserve duty, is a uniquely Israeli institution. Due to Israel's growing population and the changing nature of warfare, the need for Israelis to serve in *miluim* has gone down over the years, although 5 percent of Israelis continue to return to their units into their forties. In Vardi's generation, it had a bigger impact.

Back then, many Israelis would return to their units for weeks at a time to train and for active duty. This annual ritual would continue well into their forties. When *miluim* was still part of the fabric of daily life, it was not uncommon to look for someone in a company, ministry, or university and be told, "Oh, he's in *miluim*." And that was it; you had to wait until he returned.

Miluim was born of necessity, but it also produced profound social benefits. It intensified and maintained bonds of trust across diverse economic, ethnic, educational, and religious divides. You could have a taxi driver and a business executive who had served in the same unit in their late teens still glued together through decades of their adult lives because of *miluim*.

"As we went around the circle, when it came to me I said that Ronit and I together have seven kids and we both teach yoga," Vardi said. After his experience as a commando—he fought in the Yom Kippur War and in the raid on Entebbe—he had served in intelligence. He had recently retired young, as is common in military careers. Along the way, he decided to study biology, then international relations. Israeli "careers" tend to be eclectic.

"When it came to Boaz's turn, it was a very different kind of story," Vardi recalled, speaking of Boaz Keinan, another member of the unit. "He said simply, 'I have two kids. One is sixteen and was born deaf, and after two years, we found out he was autistic. And his fourteen-year-old brother is autistic, too.'"

Vardi hadn't seen Keinan since they served together, but after the *shloshim* he invited him on a two-day hike in the desert. They had a lot of time to talk. "I asked him to tell me more about his life. He lived in the U.S. and had a software company. He told me about their daily hardships," Vardi said.

Israelis tend to skip small talk. The typical Western sensitivity over not being too "intrusive," "nosy," or "prying" doesn't exist in Israel. You talk about real life, certainly with people you served with, even if you haven't been in close touch for more than three decades. People expect you to ask and you expect to share. It's natural. Not with everyone, of course, but this unguardedness is evident to newcomers to Israeli society.

Keinan told Vardi that "people with autistic kids have one overriding fear: what will happen the day their child turns twenty-one, when the institutional support runs out." The parents are left with the responsibility of their adult child and need to figure out a way for them to lead a relatively normal, independent life. The reality is that adults with autism are all but universally consigned to a life of joblessness.

Keinan had decided to sell his software company and start a foundation. He wanted to build a new life model for adults on the spectrum. "And he asked me to run it," Vardi said. Why would Keinan ask someone who knew nothing about autism to run his foundation? And why would Vardi take up a cause with which he had no connection except for his chance reunion with a former army buddy? It speaks to a tremendous amount of trust.

No one had solved the problem of the cliff that faces people with autism when they reach age twenty-one and want to work and live independently. Vardi and Keinan did not know the solution, but they knew what they wanted to create—a new life model for people with autism that would allow them to reach their full potential and lead independent and fulfilling lives.

Keinan's foundation started its work by gathering experts in autism from Israel and around the world for three days in the quaint northern town of Safed, the birthplace of Jewish mysticism centuries ago. The idea was to come up with a research project, and to explore technological solutions. But something happened that upended the entire effort.

"I got a call from my old friend Tamir Pardo, who was then the director of the Mossad," Vardi told us, giving a hint as to where he had served within the intelligence community. Pardo wanted to know if Vardi was the person he had heard was working on autism. Seemingly out of nowhere, Pardo told Vardi that he would give his organization "a blank check" from the Mossad.

Why would the head of the Mossad be interested in helping? For years, even the name of the Mossad chief was a secret. In the newspapers he would be referred to by the first letter of his first name. Former intelligence chiefs rarely give interviews, but on this subject Pardo was happy to talk to us.

"The idea came from my wife, Omrit. She gets all the credit," he said. Omrit Pardo was a speech therapist who worked with kids with autism. She was aware of the dire need to find a way for them to become independent as they moved into adulthood. In school, many of these children needed almost daily professional support. How could they possibly function in real jobs and navigate life's challenges on their own?

Omrit had been consulting with a scientist at the Weizmann Institute of Science who had been researching the special capabilities of youth on the autism spectrum. "I thought that there must be a way that these unique skills can be used," Omrit said. "I started pushing Tamir to create a unit in the IDF or Mossad." When Tamir Pardo was deputy director of the Mossad he would tell his wife that he couldn't get the budget to look into it, "but the minute I became chief she told me, 'No more excuses, you're in charge.'" Pardo knew who to call.

In addition to Tal Vardi, Pardo also reached out to Leora Sali. She was a graduate of Talpiot, one of the most elite programs in the Israeli military, where only sixty soldiers each year are admitted, out of ten thousand who are invited to try out. They go through paratrooper basic training, then a specialized three-year course during which time they complete a compressed university degree in physics, math, and sometimes computer science. They then disperse around the military and intelligence services as crack problem solvers. There is stiff competition among various branches to receive *Talpionim*, as graduates of the program are called. After completing their long course, Talpiot grads serve in the IDF for another six years.

"I held a number of different technological positions, then managed teams, then departments," Sali told us. "My husband and I have two kids. When the older one turned three, we discovered that he had autism. He's twenty-six now. So I have known about autism for the last twenty-four years."

Tal Vardi and Leora Sali—each with a deep interest in young adults with autism—knew each other through military intelligence circles. They shared the view that people on the spectrum might have a talent for analyzing visual intelligence. She suggested doing a study to explore the concept. Vardi responded, "That's nice, but I think we should do it for real. *Yalla*. If it works, it works." It would be hard to find a more Israeli word than *Yalla* ("let's do it" or "let's go").

The potential for impact was clear. For Israelis, military service is a calling card; it shows potential employers what you can do. It is also a membership card to Israeli society. While other countries see the advantages of national service, but struggle with the notion of requiring it, in Israel the situation is almost the opposite: service is seen as a right, not just a requirement. This is particularly true for people who are exempted from service because of a disability. It was obvious to Vardi and Sali that the dream of youth with autism, and their families' dream for them, was to be able to serve in the Israel Defense Forces.

The first step was to present their idea to the commander of 9900, the highly classified unit handling visual intelligence. The commander told them two things that still frame their basic approach, Vardi said. "First, the amount of visual data is essentially endless. It comes from satellites, planes, drones—and as technology progresses it increases all the time." The second point surprised them: "I don't see a computer replacing people doing this kind of job for the next twenty to thirty years." The commander told them that if they could figure it out, he was open to it—but the entire training program had to be run outside the military, before the future analysts enlisted and arrived at the unit.

Through a friend, as it usually goes in Israel, they connected with Ono Academic College, located in a town called Kiryat Ono, not far from Tel Aviv. Ono had departments of speech therapy, occupational therapy, and physiotherapy, all of which would be needed for soldiers on the spectrum. They met with the rector, Dudi Schwartz. A couple months later they agreed with the management of Ono to launch a pilot program, funded fifty-fifty between the college and the foundation. "We started recruiting people and built a special place, all with no paper signed, just shaking hands," Vardi said.

Vardi and Sali wanted to begin with just twelve young adults, but they had trouble finding candidates. They created a steering committee that included senior representatives of the Ministries of Education and Welfare and the commander of Unit 9900. The Welfare Ministry representative said that they may be struggling to find people now, but the prevalence of autism has, for some unknown reason, been increasing. In the 1990s, the World Health Organization declared that autism had become an epidemic.

We have seen a pattern repeat itself. Big Israeli bureaucracies, like government ministries and the military, often move at a glacial pace. Yet these same organizations can move quickly if they get caught up in the atmosphere of innovation around a mission. Under the right circumstances, where a common national cause is involved, bureaucratic rules bend. It happened with the *Beresheet* moon mission, and it happened here.

In 2013, Avi Simon got a call from his commander, the head of Unit 9900, asking him to meet Vardi and Sali. They told Simon they were looking for real intelligence analysis problems for youth with autism, and they didn't want any special treatment.

"If it is mandatory for our young people to enlist," Simon recalled thinking as he listened to the pitch, "then it's mandatory for us to *allow* everyone to enlist and maximize their potential. This is what we mean by an army of the people. And here was a group of people that were being left behind, but had something real to offer."

In other words, there is a deep social relationship between the military and the citizens. Serving is both a *requirement* and a *right*. It can be a terrible blow for a young person if the military tells them that they cannot serve. In our conversations with Simon, he kept invoking the vision of David Ben-Gurion, Israel's founding prime minister, for the IDF to be a tool not just of national defense but also of societal health. The mission of the IDF, Ben-Gurion wrote, was "to be a melting pot of the diasporas gathering in Israel, a school of civic education and a cradle of a renewed nation." It was not just about securing borders and fighting wars, but "the army must convert this mix of tribes with their various languages into one national unit, teach them Hebrew, and the fundamental values of the state and prepare them for the task of pioneering and making the desert bloom."

Think about that for a moment: the military as a *school of civic education* for Israelis in their preparation for *making the desert bloom*. Simon saw the kids on the autism spectrum as part of this continuum: "That's where we came up with the name for the unit, Roim Rachok ('see into the future').

We were looking at it—from day one—as a holistic plan: from training, to enlistment, to becoming contributing citizens after their service."

As Noam, a young adult with autism who served in the IDF as part of the program, and who now works for Intel, described it: "In other countries with mandatory service, you would think that getting exempted means getting a head start on learning a job rather than losing years to the army. But in Israel, it's the opposite." He added, "You want to serve your country because it's a key to your career, and you don't want to be left out of that national experience."

At first these soldiers had their own separate room, commander, and missions. But Simon wanted them down in the "engine room" with the other soldiers. After a year, pairs of soldiers with autism were put in with the regular image analysts. "Suddenly you would walk in and see soldiers wearing the same uniform and that was it. Sometimes the soldiers from Roim Rachok were not the weirdest guys in the room," Simon said with a smile.

An example from the conflict in Syria made their talents clear. "When things started to unravel in Damascus, as the civil war there began in 2011 and 2012, we wanted to understand if day-to-day life was continuing," Simon said. "So one of the Roim Rachok analysts noticed two images of the swimming pools at the Damascus Hilton Hotel, in the heart of the Syrian capital," which provided the answer. As Simon explained, "Can you see if the sunshade umbrellas move around at the swimming pools? If the umbrellas don't move from day to day, it means that it's not business as usual," he said. Simon then instructed the Roim Rachok imagery analyst to look at the entire city of Damascus and come up with a taxonomy for everything that he saw. "He may not have an intuition for the operational application for this kind of intelligence, but he won't miss a single detail. And that detail can be a critical piece of intelligence—sometimes life and death."

The Roim Rachok program was so successful that other imagery analysis units—in the air force, navy, special operations, and so on—started trying to persuade these analysts to come work for them. And a pattern began to emerge in which different IDF commanders began to come out of the shadows to recruit Roim Rachok analysts to serve in their respective units. Over time, the program's participants have come to serve in over thirty military units. This range of occupations has been reflected as each cohort transitions out of the army into the workplace, including jobs in major technology companies.

As groundbreaking as Roim Rachok was, it could only serve a fraction of the people with autism who had the potential to serve in the IDF. There was a structural problem that no outside organization could solve. When their eighteen-year-old peers were all receiving their draft notices, teenagers with autism automatically received a notice saying they were unfit to serve. Roim Rachok took advantage of the fact that people who receive such exemptions can still try to be accepted to the IDF as volunteers, but this was like putting your foot in a door that was closing in front of you. For most, that door was tightly shut.

On July 28, 2021, the door opened. On that day, the first fifty-three soldiers with autism started their service not as volunteers but as draftees. They were part of a new program called Titkadmu (Move Forward), founded by Udi Heller, himself a soldier with autism. Heller was unusual in that his parents did not reveal his autism to the military, so he was drafted like any other eighteen-year-old.

By the time Heller had finished his army service, his commanders knew that he was neurodivergent. In 2019, after Heller's regular army service, Colonel Dan Goldfus, the commander of the Nahal Infantry Brigade, called Heller back for a mission: figure out how to integrate three soldiers with autism into the brigade. Heller had no idea how to approach this mission. He didn't even know about all the organizations that were helping young adults with autism volunteer in the IDF, because Heller hadn't gone that route. Heller was shocked to discover that the IDF automatically exempted even the most talented people with autism from the draft at age sixteen, without even testing them.

"I started a war," Heller said, "against this blind policy." He presented the brigade commander with a study recommending to flip the current policy: create a tailored evaluation process for *all* teenagers with autism to determine their eligibility for service. Heller also described a new unit that would give these soldiers the support they needed to reach as high as they could in units throughout the military.

Those first fifty-three soldiers were just the beginning. In the first two years of the program, five cohorts were drafted and over three hundred soldiers from the unit served in the IDF. Heller believes that the IDF today employs, on an absolute basis, more people with autism than any other organization in the world. He may be right, and this is just the beginning. "This project opens the doors for thousands," Heller told the *Jerusalem Post*. "Parents write me that their child now has a future."

"The way to change the stigma against autism is to draft those on the spectrum into the army," Heller said. "There's room for everyone in the IDF." The word *gibush* usually refers to bonding people within small groups. But can this be done on a national level?

Simon credits the education system and the scouting movement for beginning to give young people the sense that they are part of a national project. But, he says, "it's the army that's the one last institution that shapes most of the population before they go out into the real world and injects some of that special sauce that keeps society together." This is *gibush* on a national level. In other words, the Roim Rachok program and now Titkadmu were enveloping more and more young people—including those with autism—in *gibush*.

Roim Rachok and Titkadmu are not just breakthroughs for Israelis, they potentially point the way toward solving a global problem for people with disabilities in general and with autism in particular: employment. In the United States, almost half of twenty-five-year-olds with autism have never held a paying job. According to the Office for National Statistics of the United Kingdom, at only 22 percent employment, people with autism are the least likely to be employed of any other disabled group. According to the A. J. Drexel Autism Institute at Drexel University in the United States, among all categories of disability, adults with autism have the highest unemployment rate.

There are many advocacy groups tirelessly working to raise awareness of the often impressive benefits of employing people who are on the autism spectrum.

"Sometimes I can do what it would take somebody a week to do in a couple of hours," Morgan McCardell said cheerfully to *CBS Mornings* in April 2022. "That's the advantage to being able to hyper-focus." Before she was recruited to participate in a small pilot program at the National Geospatial-Intelligence Agency (NGA), McCardell had spent almost ten years living on disability payments. CBS interviewed her at the desk where she had just been poring over satellite imagery of a Russian military base near Alaska.

Yet, despite much talk about the need for neurodiversity and the high satisfaction of employers who do hire people with autism, the dismal unemployment statistics have barely budged. Initiatives to employ those with autism at major companies continue to grow in number, but even combined they impact a very small percentage of adults with autism. According to Autism at Work, a high-profile initiative that includes over twenty of the largest companies in the United States, those employers reported that a total of about eight hundred adults with autism had been hired by them by the end of 2020. An additional eighty or so major employers have their own autism hiring initiatives, but together they employ only about 1,500 workers.

The real breakthrough, according to Heller, is to show that "autism is the new normal." That is, to consider people with autism across the full range of employment according to their abilities. With relatively modest accommodations to job interviews and the work environment, the status quo could be flipped—from a large majority of people with autism being unemployed to a large majority working.

As Heller puts it, "Autism organizations often market their employment initiatives as excellence programs. It's easy to place a tiny percentage at the top. But autistic people may be excellent in specific areas, but very regular in other areas. The innovation of Titkadmu is that it opens the door for large numbers of autistic people to any profession." Like many of us, people with autism just need their first big break. "It's a lot like finding where I fit in finally," Morgan McCardell said.

Chapter Three

PERPETUAL BOOM

*All over the world, countries are confronting population stagnation
and a fertility bust, a dizzying reversal unmatched in recorded history
that will make first-birthday parties a rarer sight than funerals,
and empty homes a common eyesore.*

—Damien Cave, Emma Bubola, and Choe Sang-Hun,
"Long Slide Looms for World Population," *New York Times*, May 22, 2021

*Israel is operating in a completely different dimension
than all other developed countries.*

—Alex Weinreb, demographer, Taub Center for Social Policy Studies

In Israel, youth is interwoven in the country's founding myth. It was the young people who, in the years before the state, settled the land. With their daring, sweat, and blood, they played a critical and romantic role in building the Jewish state from nothing—draining the swamps, settling the land, and defending the country.

In 1946, two years before Israel declared independence, there were almost no Jewish development projects in the Negev, a triangle-shaped swath of desert that stretches over half of the territory of Israel today. In July of that year, a British-American committee announced a proposal to divide British-controlled Palestine into Jewish and Arab states. The plan did not include the Negev in what would become Israel and prohibited

Jewish residential development there. David Ben-Gurion believed that the Negev desert was essential for Israel's existence and flourishing. "It is in the Negev that the creativity and pioneer vigor of Israel shall be tested," he said.

The reaction of the Yishuv—the pre-state Zionist community in Palestine—to the British-American plan was swift and, as it turned out, decisive. On the night of October 5, 1946, a few hundred young people fanned out to eleven barren spots in the Negev and built "Tower and Stockade" development communities. According to a fortuitous loophole in British regulations, once a structure had a roof it couldn't be torn down, even if it had received no building permit. So, under cover of darkness, a handful of these pioneers slapped together prefabricated pieces into a tower with a fence around it big enough to protect a few small houses.

The outposts had no road, water, electricity, or telephone, just a few people willing to stick it out there. But it was enough. By morning, there was nothing the British could do. If not for these and other Tower and Stockade outposts that popped up overnight, the Negev would likely not be part of Israel. Though still populated sparsely, today the Negev is home to Israel's fourth-largest city, Beersheba, which has become the nation's leading cybersecurity cluster, combining multinational companies, start-ups, a major university, and the IDF's technology units.

Yossi Klein Halevi argues that Israel is "a society created by youth movements." The pre-state Yishuv was a youth-centric society. In other countries, youth culture remains largely a mystery to older generations, for whom so much has changed since they were young themselves that they have little shared experience with the younger generation. Not so much in Israel, Halevi says: "Army service helps create an intergenerational common experience where parents know what their kids are going through. There's at least some shared language. There's a comfort and ease in the cross-generational relationship. And that has helped keep Israel a very youthful society as well."

A Shrinking World

On November 15, 2022, in a major milestone for humanity, the world's population officially hit eight billion. Just before this, the United Nations issued a projection: the global population would peak at 10.4 billion around 2080 and start to decrease. But this may be too high an estimate. According to what is perhaps the most comprehensive population study to date, published by the Institute for Health Metrics and Evaluation (IHME) in the *Lancet*, the peak will arrive around 2065, at 9.2 billion, and drop to 8.8 billion by the end of the century.

The IHME study also found what lead scientist Christopher Murphy called a "jaw dropping" result: the population of twenty-three countries—including Japan, Italy, Spain, and Thailand—would drop by at least half by the end of the century. Many wealthy countries have launched expensive programs to cajole their citizens to have more children. The German parliament passed a law guaranteeing day care for all children at least twelve months old, in addition to the $265 billion a year the government currently appropriates for family subsidies. Some Swedish and German kindergartens are open twenty-four/seven to accommodate parents who work at night.

By 2050, Russia's population is expected to be one-third lower than it was in 2020. In 2006, President Vladimir Putin called the demographic crisis "the most acute problem in contemporary Russia" and announced large cash incentives for families having more than one child. The government even installed curved park benches to get couples to slide closer together. In Ulyanovsk, the city where Lenin was born, the local government took the directive even further, declaring September 12 "National Conception Day." On that day, couples could take half a day off work to do their patriotic duty. Anyone who gave birth nine months later could win a grand prize—an SUV. These incentives have had only limited effect; in 2020 Russia's fertility rate was about 1.5, well below replacement, and may fall further.

But the fertility promotion program that scores highest for creativity (and chutzpah!) belongs not to a government but to a travel agency in Copenhagen. In March 2014, the Spies Rejser agency launched an ad campaign called "Do It for Denmark." In addition to various seductive images of champagne, oysters, and lingerie, the ad featured a Danish "psychologist and sexologist" testifying that vacations release endorphins that cause couples to "see each other in a new light." Another ad in the campaign, also filled with statistics and innuendo, was titled "Do It for Mom" and featured hopeful potential grandmothers waving as their children flew off on their reproductive vacations.

These efforts, however, have failed to move the demographic needle. None of the campaigns, no matter how expensive, offensive, or creative, have succeeded in restoring fertility rates even to replacement levels. But all this effort and expense raises the question, *Why are they trying so hard?* What's wrong with a dropping birth rate?

The answer has to do not so much with the size of the population as with its composition. The real problem with lower birth rates is not that the population shrinks, but that it ages. The combination of shrinking and aging sets off fiscal alarm bells: fewer young people means a growing "dependency ratio," the ratio of working-age people (eighteen to sixty-four) to non-working-age people (under eighteen and over sixty-five).

But the even bigger problem is harder to quantify. While people are increasingly staying fit and active for much longer, on balance, study after study has shown that an aging society tends to be less productive, less optimistic, less innovative, and less energetic than a youthful one.

The Young and the Innovative

In the 1970s and '80s, the Japanese economy was growing so rapidly that many economists predicted that it would surpass the United States in GDP per capita. In 1970, a book titled *The Emerging Japanese Super-*

state began to sound the alarm. By the 1980s, with an increasing number of Japanese cars on U.S. roads and Japanese purchases of iconic U.S. landmarks like Rockefeller Center, the prospect of *Japan as Number One* (another book title from this era) was a genuine concern for many Americans. But it was not to be so. The 1990s turned out to be a lost decade for Japan. While there are many explanations, one tends to be overlooked: the aging of Japanese society.

While there are many creative people at all ages, the peak of inventiveness tends to tilt toward youth. Studies show that a scientist's output— including the work of Nobel Prize winners and great inventors—usually rises steeply in the twenties and thirties, peaks in the late thirties or early forties, and then trails off through later years. A 2014 study by economists James Liang, Hui Wang, and Edward P. Lazear comparing Japan and the United States noted that half of the top ten high-tech companies in the United States were founded after 1985, and their founders were young, with an average age of only twenty-eight. By contrast, in Japan, none of the top ten high-tech companies had been founded in the previous forty years.

But it's about more than just the sheer number of young people. The researchers found that from 1976 to 1994 the number of young department chiefs in the Japanese companies had dropped by half. Older managers had taken over, and they weren't going anywhere. This blocked younger workers from gaining the experience they needed to strike out and found their own companies.

The upshot is that it's not enough to be young to be dynamic and innovative; you need to be young *in a young society*. The same 2014 study analyzed surveys of 1.3 million people from over eighty-two countries and found that entrepreneurship is strongly correlated with age, both on the individual and societal levels. The authors suggest reasons for this correlation. "The young may generate more ideas as a result of higher levels of social interaction when young. They may be more able to think in novel ways and thereby break away from products and production methods of the past. Alternatively, the young may be more willing to take risks, perhaps because they are less constrained by family expenses." While it is hard to know the exact reasons, the authors argue that what matters is the finding that entrepreneurship declines as societies age. They found a clear "inverted U-shaped" relationship between age and entrepreneurship. Young countries (median age thirty-seven or below) had an entrepreneurship rate that was about double that of old countries (median age forty-one or above). Israel's median age is about thirty and growing slowly, while the European Union's median age is over forty-four and growing faster.

The data show that a young worker in a young workforce will on average be more entrepreneurial than the same-age worker in an old workforce. This insight has profound implications for understanding the success of Israel's innovation sector and its growing competitive advantage in an aging world.

Morningburg vs. Twilight City

In an essay in the *Atlantic* titled "Europe's Real Crisis," the American journalist Megan McArdle offers a helpful illustration to understand the difference between young and aging societies. She imagined two neighboring towns that are almost identical except for one difference: their median age. In the one she called Morningburg, the average resident is twenty-eight. In the second town, which she called Twilight City, the average householder is fifty-eight.

The age gap gave the two towns very different complexions. Morningburg is bristling with artisanal coffee shops, where budding entrepreneurs sit with their laptops open, plotting their next venture. They are at an unencumbered stage in life, when they feel most driven to take risks, put in long hours, make their name in the world, and try to build something new. Some neighborhoods cater to singles and others are popular with young families.

In the town next door, it's another story: "In Twilight City, time horizons are shorter—people aren't looking for projects that will make them rich or famous 20 years from now." They are trying to keep what they have, rather than build the future. According to studies that McArdle cites, "older people worry more than younger ones about losses and are therefore especially averse to risk. Twilighters also tire more easily and need more time off for illness, so hours worked slowly decline each year."

Life in Morningburg feels different from life in Twilight City. University towns feel different from retirement communities. Young countries feel different from old countries. Morningburg has energy and promise, and people gravitate toward it. Twilight City has the pizzazz of a bowling alley and the urgency of a golf course.

In Twilight City there is a lot of wealth sloshing around because people in their fifties are at the peak of their earning and spending power. On the other hand, the town also has a lot of older retired people living mainly on their savings. By this description, Europe is already in Twilight City, or as the Harvard social scientist Arthur Brooks puts it, "Europe is a blend between an amusement theme park and an assisted living facility."

The United Nations estimates that by 2030, the number of people globally who are older than sixty will be growing *three times faster* than the general population. In 2018, just thirteen countries had an over-sixty-five population higher than 20 percent; by 2050, eighty-two countries will cross that threshold.

In addition to its tiny fertility rate, South Korea is the fastest-aging country in the world. By 2040, there will be 60 percent more Koreans seventy and over than twenty and younger. In Israel, it's almost the inverse: by the same year, there will be three times as many under-twenties as over-seventies. And it's worth noting that 2040 is not far off. While the difference in age composition between Israel and South Korea will be extreme, it represents the wider trend. Israel is already younger and growing faster than all the other wealthy democracies, a gap that will continue to widen.

Four Is the New Three

Aya Peterburg was eighteen years old when she was drafted into the IDF. She was assigned to work in the office of the chief of intelligence, but she wanted a position where she could work more with people. One of the commanders in an intelligence unit offered her to join his unit in a role where she would interview high-ranked people who were coming back to serve in the most secretive positions.

"My job was to talk to them about their whole lives," she recalled. "Some of them had tough stories. But we weren't trained to be psychologists, we were trained to figure out if they were truthful and reliable." By the time she was twenty years old, she was commanding the unit to which she had been assigned.

Following her army service, Peterburg spent nine months backpacking around India, and then returned to Israel to earn a combined degree in business and law at the Interdisciplinary Center in Herzliya. After practicing law for long enough to know it was not for her, she joined an enterprise software start-up company. The founder of Sequoia Capital, a leading venture capital fund in Silicon Valley, offered her a position. In 2018 she and her Sequoia colleague launched a new fund, S Capital VC. "In our fund, we do everything just the two of us," she said. "There's no investment committee. We spend a lot of time with each company."

Peterburg told us that the skills from her days interviewing people for intelligence positions have come in handy when sizing up entrepreneurs. "As investors, we look for founders who can lead people and withstand the pressure of hitting wall after wall. That's what you have to do in a start-up."

In 2014, just before Peterburg joined Sequoia, and while already in a high-pressure job, her first children were born—twins, a boy and a girl. Three years later, she had another son as she was working on cofounding S Capital VC: "I always say that the fund was his twin."

When we spoke to Peterburg in 2020, her fourth child, another boy, was five months old. But her cofounder wasn't concerned about the impact of Peterburg's growing family on their business. "He kept telling me you should have as many kids as you want," she told us.

Most people around Peterburg had three children. "If you have two children," another working mother in tech told us, "sometimes you get questions like 'Are you sure you want to stop at two?'" Others, though, brushed off these concerns, saying that two was enough for them. But, generally, Israeli society seemed to regard two kids as a small family. In fact, Peterburg added, "four was becoming the new three."

Still, the decision was not simple. "Every mother has guilt," she said. She worried whether she gave the kids enough attention, given how hard she worked. "I was thinking, although I want a fourth child, will it be better for the kids because they have another sibling, or worse because I will have even less attention to give them?"

According to the Israeli sociologist Darya Maoz, "Today the status symbol in secular Israeli society is getting married early and having four kids." Amit Aronson, a well-known restaurant critic, told us that, among the secular crowd in Tel Aviv, "you know successful people in high-tech have 'made it' if they have a lot of children. They have four kids and are proud of the fact that they can afford it. Yachts, private planes, and fancy cars are not the symbol here. . . . It's the number of kids."

Aronson's perspective showed how unaware Israelis seem to be of how anomalous they are. They don't realize that their normal number of kids, three, is about twice the European average. Or that everywhere else, greater wealth and education is associated with *lower* fertility. Within Israel's secular elites there is a noticeable social trend in the opposite direction. Even if small in numbers, that such a phenomenon exists at all is remarkable. It is rare in other wealthy countries that having a larger family is considered a status symbol.

In Israel, the social and cultural winds encourage young families to have more children. It is considered a positive good that is to be admired, celebrated, facilitated, and encouraged. In other countries, if there is pressure it is in the opposite direction. The social and cultural trends are toward having fewer children.

Essentially, Israel and the rest of the wealthy world are on different paths: one toward larger families, the other toward smaller ones. This is not a difference in degree, but in direction.

To understand *why* Israel diverged from the rest of the world, it is helpful to trace our way back to the fork in the road, back to *when* the paths diverged. Revisiting a time when the United States, and to some extent Europe, was going through a time of high fertility can shed light on where Israel is today.

Above the Line

A single picture symbolized the end of World War II: a returning American sailor kissing a nurse, a total stranger, in New York City's Times Square on V-J Day. The exuberance of what became known as the Victory Kiss seemed to mark the beginning of a boom that swept over nearly every aspect of American life: marriage, jobs, housing, education, transportation and, perhaps most of all, babies.

The "birth quake," as the demographer Diane Macunovich called it, came out of the blue. During the 1930s, amid the Great Depression, birth rates plummeted, leading to dire warnings that the political and economic power of the West would decline. Then suddenly, starting during the war years and exploding afterward, birth rates nearly doubled within just a few years. This "totally unexpected, earth-shattering, and groundbreaking event," as Macunovich put it, happened not just in the United States but in the entire West throughout the 1950s and '60s.

Buoyed by a strong economy and optimism for the future, Americans made up for lost time building families. By the time the baby boom was over in the mid-1960s, the generation born after the war made up almost 40 percent of the U.S. population.

And then there was Israel. In 1950, Israel's fertility rate was a very high 4.5, more than one child above the rate in the United States, which peaked at 3.8 in 1957. By then, Israel's fertility rate had dropped, but it was still above the U.S. level. What happened in Israel next defied all demographic logic.

For more than a decade and a half, from 1958 to 1974, Israel's fertility rate barely budged, remaining close to four children per woman. It was as if Israel had slammed on the brakes, halting the plunge in fertility happening in every other wealthy country and through much of the developing world as well. During this same period, the U.S. fertility rate plummeted from its baby boom high of 3.8 to 1.8, below the replacement rate.

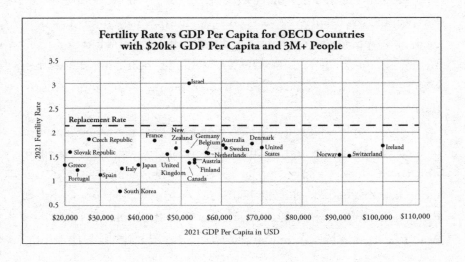

77

When Israel's fertility resumed its drop around 1975, an even bigger anomaly happened. Instead of continuing down to the levels of the United States and Europe, Israel leveled off again around 1990 and stayed at about three children per woman for the next three decades, where it remains today. Israel's baby boom, in the sense of fertility far above the rest of the OECD, has continued for the last seventy years.

It is hard to overstate how much of an outlier Israel is. Countries that account for more than half the world's population have crossed the line to below-replacement fertility. Israel is the only wealthy country that has not fallen below replacement. Even much poorer countries, such as India, have fallen below replacement. Indeed, Israel seems to be the only country in the world that has broken the iron law of demography that links rising economic development with below-replacement fertility rates.

Today, Israel's fertility rate remains nearly double the rate of the United States and Europe and triple that of wealthy Asian countries like Japan, South Korea, and Singapore. In cultural terms, the norm in Israel is three children, in the United States and Europe two children, and in Japan, South Korea, and Singapore, one child.

In every other country except Israel, fertility rates drop as incomes, women's education, and women's participation in the workforce go up. But over the last twenty-five years, incomes in Israel have more than doubled, and women's participation in the labor force and education levels are among the highest in the OECD. While in most countries women with university degrees have fewer children than those without, in Israel the levels are the same.

Some people assume that Israel's high fertility rate must be explained by the fecundity of the "ultra-Orthodox" community, also called Haredim. This community is known for its extremely large families—on average more than six children. But the Haredim constitute about one-eighth of the population and their fertility rate has been dropping (as has that of Arab Israelis, another community in Israel with historically high fertility rates)—so they cannot be the primary reason that the national fertility has stayed high. Secular Israelis—the ones in cafés with the laptops and tattoos—are having 25 percent more children than their counterparts in Europe and other wealthy countries. And the group categorized as "traditional but not very observant," which is a large part of the Israeli mainstream, has a fertility rate 55 percent higher than the OECD average.

But you don't need to study the statistics to see the difference. It's obvious to anyone living in Israel. If you look around, you see many families with three children. Four is still in the "normal" range. The most common number of children among secular women born in Israel is three, a full 43 percent. If you add in the percentage who have four or more children, that proportion rises to 50 percent. In Europe and America, the situation is reversed. One or two children is more the norm. About 70 to 90 percent of women there have two or fewer children.

The contrast becomes even greater if you ask women about their ideal family size. Among native-born secular Jewish women, 55 percent say that their ideal is three children. Another 26 percent say that four or more is ideal. This is much more than the 18 percent of women who prefer two children. And only around 1 percent voted for zero or one child. Again, these are secular Israeli women, who have the lowest fertility rate among native-born Israeli Jews.

Walk around Israeli neighborhoods, sit in a park, go to the beach, look at friends—even look at advertisements with a stock photo of an Israeli family—and you see three-child families. You will find this nowhere else in the developed world, and it sets up Israel for a host of accompanying social benefits and challenges. Whereas in other wealthy countries, policies have been put in place to try to increase the fertility rate, in Israel it is the organic needs of a high fertility society that drive family-friendly policies. Israeli society is pro-natalist from the bottom up, rather than the top down. Everything must bend to accommodate having children. One of the places where this can be most clearly seen is the workplace.

Chapter Four

THE KIDS ARE ALRIGHT

Is that a child? I hear a child. This is terrible, they have no humanity here at Waze. They are putting children to work.

—Comedian Conan O'Brien stumbling upon toddlers playing
in the Waze Tel Aviv headquarters

As we have seen, many high-income countries are going to great lengths to reduce the cost of raising children in order to reverse collapsing fertility rates. But it is not just about the cost of day care or education. The largest factor is harder to quantify and is only marginally addressed by countries' "baby bribes." It is the tension between career and family. Part of this tension is the never-ending struggle to strike a "work-life balance." But perhaps the greatest force pressing on birth rates is the choice that women, primarily, feel forced to make between having a career and starting a family.

These tensions exist in Israel as well. For young families especially, the combination of demanding work, making ends meet, and raising small children can require seemingly superhuman stamina. The difference is that Israel, perhaps uniquely among high-income countries, has a society that is much more accommodating to pursuing both tracks, career and family, simultaneously.

• • •

"I tried to convince her to join us for about two years, but she wasn't ready to commute from Tel Aviv to Jerusalem. One of the reasons we moved the company to Tel Aviv was to recruit Sarah." Yossi Pollak had always been on the hunt for the top people in the country to work at his start-up, but Sarah Levy Schreier, the company's chief technology officer, was his most crucial hire.

The company that Pollak cofounded, Sight Diagnostics, was trying to solve a big problem at the intersection of health care diagnostics, artificial intelligence, and computer vision—three Israeli specialties. Pollak and Schreier met in Talpiot (the "genius program" in the IDF we described earlier). Pollak needed a team that combined the highest level of mission orientation and talent, which usually could be found in his former program. *Talpionim*, as members of the program are called, had years of not just technological experience but of tackling project after project with multidisciplinary teams. Pollak wanted to attract as many of them as possible. Sarah Levy Schreier was not only in Talpiot, but she had also been Pollak's superior there.

"I had never heard of Talpiot," Schreier told us. She was asked to go through the long selection process and was accepted. "Later on I found out that there were five thousand people trying out for forty spots. At the time, it was a difficult decision for me because I wanted to do many other things. I wanted to sing in an army band, or maybe to be a trainer in a combat unit."

The Israeli military's filtering process is hardly perfect. But often it has an uncanny way of discovering skills that draftees don't know they have and puts them on a different path than they expected. "I never knew I had a talent for physics," Schreier said. In the end, it seemed like a big commitment—six years—but too big an opportunity to refuse. So at eighteen, she decided to join.

"We were the first three women to train at Mitkan Adam, a base famous in Israel for combat training," Schreier recalled. They did their basic training for four months with two Duvdevan platoons (the same unit the Netflix series *Fauda* is based on), one Oketz platoon (an elite canine commando unit), and Schreier's Talpiot platoon of thirty-seven men and three women.

Since this commando training base had never operated with women, the IDF had to improvise the living arrangements. "All one hundred sixty men shared one set of bathrooms and showers, and we had the same number for just the three of us," she told us. They spent two months in the field, sleeping in the desert during the week and returning to the base on weekends. This arrangement led to an unexpected accommodation. Schreier explained that when you are sleeping in the field you don't get to shower, "but apparently there was an IDF regulation requiring that women be given the opportunity to shower daily. So a special army truck would come pick us up in the middle of the desert every day, drive us to the base, give us seven minutes to shower, and drive us back to the field to join the rest of our platoon."

But when it came to the physical part of the training, Schreier and the other two women had to go through the same regimen as the men. "It was difficult," she said, "but I was in good shape. I left basic combat training with just a few stress fractures." Schreier finished the training at the top of her class. Her nonchalance in describing all this was striking. On the one hand, she wasn't shy about laying out her extraordinary achievements. On the other, she wasn't bragging about it, just telling us her story without minimizing or exaggerating.

We have found that many Israeli entrepreneurs have a laconic style that may have carried over from their military days. They can come off as unsentimental about what they are doing, so much so that it is hard to get them to talk about the vision of their companies. It was refreshing to feel Schreier's unselfconscious excitement about taking on tough but meaningful challenges. She seemed to see her work as a continuation of the mission-driven environment of her military service.

"When I was in the military, it was obvious that we were doing something important, something big and difficult," she said. That's what she was looking for in the field of innovation.

Tolerating Toddlers

But there was another aspect to Sarah Levy Schreier's career path and recruitment to Sight Diagnostics that was unlikely to have occurred anywhere but Israel. Whenever we asked Israelis whether it was considered acceptable for them to bring their children to work or dash off early to pick up the kids from school, they looked at us as if they didn't understand the question. It is just the norm. And this is not because there is a leisurely pace at the workplace. On the contrary, these are people who work hard.

Despite this intensity, in Israel work is not a time-gobbling monster that throws the remaining scraps to be spent with the family. The time at work is not off-limits to family. There is a distinction, but it is not an impermeable wall.

"When I first interviewed for a job at Sight Diagnostics, I was three months pregnant," Schreier recalled. "Yossi was asking me to join as vice president for research and development—a critical job. And now I had to tell him that in six months I'd be taking my maternity leave." (In Israel, fifteen weeks of paid maternity leave is mandatory.) "So I came out and said it and held my breath," she said. "And he was like, 'It's fine. It's part of life here.' It just wasn't a big deal."

Sight Diagnostics grew to 130 employees under Schreier. At any given time, there are many people having babies, mothers taking maternity leave, and fathers taking paternity leave. "It's everywhere in the company," Schreier said. "It's actually everywhere in the country."

Israel is not the only nation where the line between work and family is more permeable; countries range on this measure. According to the prominent organizational psychologist Adam Grant, "Countries with a Protestant work ethic have a very strong expectation that work should be task-focused, efficient, and professional, and relationships should be kept outside." If you compare the United States with India, he told us, "we are much less likely to invite our coworkers over for dinner or go on vacation with them."

Israel feels more like India in this regard. A measure of this distinction is how much coworkers know about one another's families. Israel is such a small, interconnected place that there is usually some tie via schools, youth movements, military service, kinship, or mutual friendships. Just knowing how many children a coworker has and their children's stage in life—are they preschoolers, in elementary or high school, or in the army—is common. This kind of mutual awareness is itself a form of work-life integration.

The notion of work-life balance assumes that these two central spheres of life—work and family—are in a perpetual conflict where work has the upper hand. In Israel it is more like a marriage, where each spouse learns to compromise and find a way, however imperfect, that is livable for both. In Israel, society does not just allow people to build families, but encourages them to do so. After all, if your boss has three or four kids, having the same is a cause for admiration, not resentment or concern.

A Drop of Milk

Alexandra Benjamin moved to Israel from England and decided to have children on her own. She first had her son, Ivri, and two years later she gave birth to identical twins, Ella and Alma. She told us of an experience in an appliance store. The salesman, who was religious, saw that she was pregnant and asked if her husband would be joining her. She responded that she was a single parent by choice.

"His immediate response was not even neutral—it wasn't 'Oh, that's interesting.' It was more like, 'Wow, that's such an incredible thing to do.' And that's been my experience since. I definitely attribute this to how pro-family the culture is."

Benjamin also found it striking that fertility treatments were available not only to couples with fertility problems but also to single women on the same terms. Israel is an extreme outlier in fertility treatments, over five times the European average.

She also pointed us to one other aspect of Israeli society that illustrated to her how welcoming it is of single mothers by choice: some years ago, Mother's Day was renamed Family Day—a deliberate effort to include nontraditional families. The day chosen was also highly symbolic.

When Israel established its version of Mother's Day in 1951, a children's newspaper launched a contest to pick a date. Nechama Frankel, an eleven-year-old from Herzliya, suggested a date in memory of Henrietta Szold, who had headed Youth Aliyah, an organization that had rescued thirty thousand Jewish children from Nazi-occupied Europe. Szold had also founded the Jewish women's organization Hadassah and was a pioneer in reducing infant mortality in Jerusalem in the pre-state period, when it was among the highest in the world. She founded *Tipat Halav* (A Drop of Milk), a network of neighborhood clinics for pregnant women and for new mothers and their infants. What made the choice poignant was that Szold never had any children herself.

"I find it incredibly beautiful," Benjamin said, that Szold "was chosen to be honored through Mother's Day, as someone who didn't have children, because of how central and expansive the idea of family was. As the creator of *Tipat Halav*, in a sense she was the mother of all the babies in Israel. That's a nice little thing that's always moved me."

The flip side of the high degree of social support in Israel for raising families and the high birth rate is increased social pressure on couples, particularly women, to have children. Sharon Geva, a historian and the author of *Women in the State of Israel: The Early Years*, told *Haaretz*, "I don't know if there's another country where people ask, 'Only two children?' Why 'only'?" As we explained in the previous chapter, it is rare in Israel, compared to other affluent countries, for women or couples to choose not to have children, or to have just one child.

Even in countries with low fertility rates, it can feel uncomfortable and isolating for women (and men) to be childless. Indeed, the word "childless" has a somewhat negative, or even stigmatic, connotation. Some people who cannot or choose not to have children prefer the word "child-free," thereby flipping the judgmental tone into an aspirational one.

Paradoxically, alongside the "four is the new three" trend discussed in the previous chapter, there are very small but growing numbers of Israelis joining the "child-free" trend. There is little doubt, however, that it is socially harder, whether by choice or circumstance to be without children in Israel. As Maya, a woman who manages a Facebook group for Israeli women who don't want children, told the online magazine *Tablet* under a pseudonym, "It's really hard to be the one who doesn't want to be a mother in a country where there is a straight path from kindergarten to high school to the army to marriage to children."

Free-Range Responsibility

Many developed countries, seeking to solve the problem of low fertility rates, have offered generous subsidies for childcare in the hope that this will remove or reduce financial pressure on prospective parents. In Israel, this policy is less necessary, in part because many Israeli parents can lean on two sets of grandparents, making it easier to have the larger families they want while strengthening family bonds. Generally, this arrangement is met with a sense of relief by new parents and anticipation by new grandparents.

It is perhaps no coincidence that two of the countries where grandparents play the largest roles in childcare are the Netherlands and Israel, compact countries where it is logistically simpler to do so. Parents can often rely on their own parents to take care of the kids at least one day a week. Raising three or four kids, while both parents have full-time jobs, as many Israelis do, is a challenge on all fronts—not least financially. Having grandparents taking a day on a weekly basis helps. In Israel, among all women aged 25–39 with at least one child, 71 percent receive grandparental assistance, while among native-born secular Jewish respondents, 82 percent report receiving help from their grandparents.

According to Shmuel Rosner, a prominent Israeli journalist, everything in Israel is built around the children. "In other countries, you don't see many children in trendy restaurants. There are not as many playgrounds and fewer kids are in them. When you see lots of families with three kids around you on a Saturday night date at a nice restaurant, you are more likely to want to have three children yourself."

There is another way that it's just easier to raise kids in Israel: children have more freedom to go out on their own. When immigrants or temporary residents from the U.S. arrive in Israel, they are often gobsmacked by the difference. There is a much more open attitude toward autonomy for children in Israel.

In his presentations to U.S. audiences, the urban designer Victor Dover asks three simple questions: *Did your parents walk to school? Did you? Do your children?* The differences across generations are dramatic. In the first generation, 86 percent walked to school, in the second 61 percent, and today only 10 percent.

In Israel, letting your children walk to school is as common as it has become rare in many other countries. For most Israelis, it would be awkward for their children to be the oddballs escorted to school. These norms are powerful. If the norm is *not* to let your kids walk alone, you can get in real trouble if you go against that norm.

"Across the U.S., parents are getting harassed and even arrested when they let their kids leave the house without a security detail," Lenore Skenazy told us. She is the author of the book *Free-Range Kids: How to Raise Safe, Self-Reliant Children (Without Going Nuts with Worry)*. One mother in Maine was arrested for letting her seven-year-old play alone in a park within sight of her house. A Canadian father is mounting a legal battle to allow his kids, ages seven to eleven, to take the city bus alone to school. A Utah congressman felt it necessary to try to amend federal law to protect parents from "civil or criminal charges for allowing their child to responsibly and safely travel to and from school by a means the parents believe is age appropriate."

What's most peculiar is that while the incidence of kidnappings has been dropping for decades in the U.S., Canada, the UK, and elsewhere, the perception of "stranger danger" has been on the rise. "Statistically, kidnapping by a stranger is so rare in the United States that a child would have to stand alone at a bus stop for over a thousand years for it to happen," Skenazy told us. "Meanwhile, we are depriving our children of the experiences they need to develop into confident, resilient, and independent adults."

The Israeli psychologist Danny Hamiel described the dichotomy as the difference between *safety* and *safeness*. "Safeness is a feeling or a psychological state," he pointed out, observing that Israeli parents give their children more freedom—as people in other countries did a generation ago—because they have this feeling of safeness.

"In Israel, I trust my neighbors," Hamiel continued, moving from the general to the personal. "I know they will help me. Although we are a crazy country—lots of wars, lots of things happening—we feel safe. I think this is related to the culture of being together."

The main reason is that parents know that if their kids are in any trouble, strangers will intervene to help. Israelis may not be good at standing in lines, avoiding arguments, or being polite, but if someone is in trouble they will rush to help.

In essence, the situation in Israel is the opposite of what one finds in many other developed countries. Rather than seeing strangers as a threat, Israelis see strangers as a layer of safety that they can depend on because everyone is part of the same community. It is not considered an intrusion to intervene if there is a child, or anyone, struggling.

We were having coffee in a Tel Aviv park with Ami Dror, a seasoned entrepreneur, as he narrated the scene we were watching to make this point: "Look, you see random groups of kids playing together, not just families in separate groups. People aren't watching their kids like hawks. They are not watching them at all. There's a belief that it is good to give kids more freedom."

Dror explained that Israelis assume that everyone is looking out for everyone else's kids. "Like if I see two kids fighting, I will walk over—I will not even look for their parents—and I will tell them to stop. And that's totally normal," he said. He then drew the contrast with the West: "Imagine if you did that in other countries? They would say, 'Why are you harassing my child?' But here I would naturally do it because I feel responsible for these kids. I've never seen them before, but I feel responsible for them. Why? I don't know! But I do."

There is a saying from the Talmud that is deeply embedded in Jewish culture and is often invoked by Israelis: "All of Israel [referring to the Jewish people] is responsible for one another." While this ideal may seem to be hardly evident in the midst of the bustle of daily life or divisive political debates, if someone is in trouble it kicks in. A culture of mutual responsibility produces a feeling of *safeness*, which in turn translates into a feeling of family-friendliness. It's also easier to raise children when you don't have to chaperone them all the time, which in turn—studies show—adds to their happiness and self-confidence.

The psychologist Peter Gray studies the effects of giving children more freedom to take responsibility for their own lives. He calls this parenting style "trustful parenting, the most natural and least stressful form of parenting, for both parent and child." Gray showed us his own research on young adults who were raised by this parenting style: "Trustful parents are not irrationally afraid for their children's lives. Trustful parents have faith in their children's capacities, and that faith becomes a self-fulfilling prophecy. The enemy of trustful parenting is fear, and, unfortunately, fear runs rampant in our society today." In Israel, there are fewer "helicopter parents." (Incidentally, the term "helicopter parent" was coined in 1969 by the Israeli clinical psychologist and former schoolteacher Haim Ginott in his classic bestseller *Between Parent and Teenager*.)

That raising "free-range kids" is the norm in Israel is a big part of the country's family-friendliness. Another is that Israeli life revolves around spending a lot of time with the family, not just after work, but for a sacrosanct time of gathering every week.

Chapter Five

THANKSGIVING EVERY WEEK

*During my first 18 years, I spent some time with my parents during at least
90 percent of my days. But since heading off to college and then later
moving out of Boston, I've probably seen them an average of only five times a
year each, for an average of maybe two days each time. 10 days a year. About
3 percent of the days I spent with them each year of my childhood.*

— Tim Urban, author/illustrator, *What's Our Problem?
A Self-Help Book for Societies*

*Even if you live on the other side of the country from your family in Israel,
it's still very close. And if you don't come home for every Shabbat, or at least
every other Shabbat, you're in deep trouble.*

—Noa Tishby, Israeli actor and producer, *In Treatment*

On the fourth Thursday of every November, something unusual happens
in the United States. If you could look into each American home on this
day you'd find a surprisingly similar scene: families gathering for Thanksgiving dinner. Few traditions cut so seamlessly across America's divides of
religion, ethnicity, politics, and class. Scattered families gather from far
and wide. At its best, this annual culinary ritual combines the intimacy of
the home with the communal power of shared national experience.

Indeed, in many countries there is a holiday, religious or not, that is
the traditional time for families to converge and reconnect. Multitudes

struggle through swollen airports and highways. During the Spring Festival in China, the entire country is on the move as people return to the homes of their youth. In numerous countries, Christians celebrate with family gatherings on Christmas, as do Muslims during the holy month of Ramadan.

Jews also have their traditional family holidays. Around the world, the Passover meal, or Seder, is famously such a night, with extended families gathering for an hours-long feast that comes at the end of winter. In Israel, it's not only Passover. Every Jewish holiday is a time for family gatherings, even among secular families. And every season has its holidays. There is Sukkot in the fall and Shavuot in the spring, both of which are national as well as religious holidays. The Jewish High Holidays of Rosh Hashanah and Yom Kippur come as summer departs.

These holidays multiply the number of times that Israeli families gather compared to most developed countries, but the biggest difference is this: if you were to look into most Jewish homes on an ordinary Friday night, you would see something similar to that American Thanksgiving scene. Friday is the time for Shabbat, the Jewish Sabbath, for which Israeli families gather as if it were a major holiday. (Shabbat, like all Jewish holidays, begins at sundown the previous day.) In some homes, Shabbat is "brought in" with singing, blessings for children, prayers over wine and bread, and a set table. But even in secular homes it is the occasion for an unrushed sit-down dinner with not only the whole household but also grown children living outside the home, including those who have their own families.

In essence, on Friday the natural centripetal force that sends grown children away reverses and brings them back for one evening. Married children can't be at both sets of parents' homes every week, but the usual practice is to be with one or the other, so that parents have at least some of their children (and grandchildren) back home.

In many other countries this would be logistically impossible because the distances are too large. But Israel is a small country, and even smaller when you consider that more than half of Israel's population lives within a triangle about one-seventh the size of New Jersey that includes the cities of Jerusalem, Tel Aviv, and Haifa. It's likely that every family member is within an hour's drive and almost certainly less than two hours away.

Israel's small size facilitates such weekly gatherings. But just being nearby is not enough to explain why Israelis have a mini-Thanksgiving nearly every week. Without the gravitational pull of a holiday tradition, it wouldn't happen. That weekly holiday is Shabbat.

According to Micah Goodman, one of Israel's leading public intellectuals, Shabbat is so powerful that it has become ingrained even by those who seem to have no connection to religion. "What does it mean for society when over half do kiddush?" he said, speaking of the blessing on the wine that is offered at the beginning of Shabbat dinner. "Rituals are one of the most powerful parts of culture because humanity never invented a better technology for gluing people together." He added, "Even those who do none of the blessings still gather the family for Shabbat dinner. It's an Israeli institution."

This particular family-centered ritual seems to have protected Israelis from the dislocation that has eroded the social fabric in other countries. In his article (later expanded into an influential book) "Bowling Alone," the Harvard political scientist Robert Putnam documented how Americans were participating less frequently and less actively in communal organizations than had been the case a generation or two earlier. He also found that they ate meals together with their families far less regularly, as well as watched TV together and went on family vacations less frequently. "Virtually all forms of family togetherness became less common over the last quarter of the twentieth century," he wrote. This trend has only worsened in the twenty-first century.

The early twentieth-century Hebrew essayist Ahad Ha'am was not exaggerating when he said, "More than the Jewish People have kept Shabbat, Shabbat has kept the Jews." According to Goodman, "communities do not create rituals; it's more that rituals create communities. And the simplest way to describe a community is a group of people that are witnessing each other's lives, in the most supportive and non-instrumental ways."

Throughout the centuries, keeping ("guarding" in Hebrew) the Sabbath became one of the most distinctive rhythms of Jewish life. Jews were prohibited from driving, turning electricity on or off, spending money, or using any kind of screen, including phones: anything that burned energy or distracted from reflection, prayer, and family and communal time. Shabbat helped create community because Jews had to live close together to be walking distance from a synagogue.

The unifying idea was to imitate God, who "created the world in six days and on the seventh He rested." The Jews would "create" all week, while Shabbat was for appreciating and contemplating what all that creating was for. Shabbat should be a palpable refuge from earthly pursuits, not just a day off. "A palace in time," in the words of Rabbi Abraham Joshua Heschel. In the ancient, pagan world, there were holy places and objects, but Judaism, according to Heschel, invented holiness in time.

More than 70 percent of Jewish Israelis have a traditional Friday night dinner with family and friends each week. If most Israelis are so secular, why do they "religiously" observe the tradition of Shabbat dinner? And why is it so widely observed among secular Jews in Israel, when it is not so rigorously celebrated by secular Jews in Diaspora countries?

Secular Israelis, despite appearances, practice a new set of rituals that have emerged in just the last generation or two. In some ways, it is a "civil religion" like those that have emerged in other countries. National customs, such as eating turkey on Thanksgiving, watching the Super Bowl, and barbecuing before fireworks on the Fourth of July, can be seen as part of America's civil religion. Friday night dinner is at the bedrock of Israel's civil religion.

Amit Aronson is a leading Israeli restaurant critic and television personality. He belongs to Tel Aviv's seemingly hyper-secular elite. Yet his Jewishness is natural, even though it is far away from Judaism as conventionally defined. "The way I define it is all cultural," he explained. "I speak Hebrew, live my life in Hebrew, consume Hebrew movies, books, television, poetry—everything. I don't need to light candles on Friday to know it's Friday. I don't really say kiddush. I went to my grandmother's, because it's Friday. It was always like that. And it's now that way for my own family. It's what my young kids know about Friday nights. Three generations together, every Friday night."

The multigenerational aspect of this weekly ritual is its own outlier; especially at a time when a variety of studies highlight the growing trend of young people not spending meaningful time with grandparents, great-aunts and -uncles. What's important about the regular interaction across generations is the unique form of teaching, learning, mentoring, and nurturing in both directions, for youth and the elderly.

According to a *Boston Globe* article, "senior citizens [in the U.S.] live in nursing homes where they mainly see other very old people, while new retirees now often buy condos in age-segregated communities. . . . Adolescents, who in a previous era might have spent significant time around adults while farming, apprenticing, or helping with the family business, spend their after-school hours on social media, talking mostly to one another." And in contrast to the intergenerational relationships that are a staple of Israeli life, especially each week over Shabbat, "it is possible, today, for a middle-aged [American] office worker to go to sleep on a Friday having interacted all week with not one person more than a decade older or younger."

The *Globe*'s reporting was based on a study in the *American Sociological Review* that found that, for most Americans, family and genuine friendship networks consist of only two confidants. As recently as the late 1990s, the average was three confidants. Even more worrisome, the number of Americans who do not have any confidants has tripled. And

Americans over sixty years old reported that only 25 percent of the people they discussed "important matters" with were younger than thirty-six. When the study removed relatives from the count, only 6 percent of elderly Americans discuss serious matters with much younger people. One government has gone so far as to offer financial incentives for young families to live within four kilometers of their grandparents.

The institution of Friday night dinner doesn't just bring together families across generations, it bridges across Israel's diverse cultural mosaic. Not just who is *at* the table, but what is *on* the table.

"You know, we Israelis are all very different—where we are from, the way we look, our accents or our parents' accents," Aronson explained to us. "But then there is this idea that we are usually united. Everyone sees it through their own lens. I see it through food."

Food? Where was he going with this?

"As a country, we celebrate the same holidays at the same time," Aronson went on. "Even if you don't celebrate in the same way, everyone is preparing a Seder for Passover and it always involves refraining from eating bread, so everyone's got to be creative. . . . People start comparing notes. Or it's Hanukkah, and we all need to eat something fried, or it's Rosh Hashanah and we need something sweet, or it's Yom Kippur and we're all preparing a meal to break the fast."

Israel's culinary symphony also plays weekly, on every Shabbat. "Why do people make cholent on Fridays? Because you're not supposed to cook on Shabbat. . . . You need to make something that can be kept warm for twelve hours and then you eat it."

Cholent is common in Ashkenazi and, later, Sephardic kitchens (roughly speaking, Ashkenazi Jews originate from Central and Eastern Europe, Sephardic Jews from Spain and the Arab world.) It's often also referred to as *chamin*. Universal ingredients include meat and potatoes. Ashkenazi recipes mix in beans and barley and Sephardic recipes often throw in rice and chickpeas. This distinctive stew can be traced back to the Second Temple period, but over the centuries different Jewish communities around the world have contributed their own twists on the ancient dish. The cholent pot is brought to a boil on Friday before Shabbat comes in, and kept warm on a hot plate (or comparable device) that stays on through the next day's lunch because observant Jews cannot cook fresh hot meals during the Sabbath.

"So a Ukrainian immigrant here smells the *chamin* being boiled in her Moroccan neighbor's apartment below," Aronson continued. "She knocks on the neighbor's door to ask what's in the recipe—spices like harissa and coriander and ingredients that the Ukrainian Jews would never use. But she could relate to the idea, despite the fact that the flavor was very strange to her," Aronson now describing images he had seen firsthand. "She'd try it out. Perhaps the first way to communicate with your weird neighbor who speaks Arabic or has a Persian accent is preparation for Shabbat each week. You both have children coming home from the army base for Shabbat, and you're always looking for new takes on their favorite comfort food. You don't even have to speak the same language, you just open the lid of the pot and smell. . . . And so began many relationships."

We sat with Aronson in a café at the bustling and very modern headquarters of Start-Up Nation Central—a nonprofit organization that is a convening spot and nerve center in Tel Aviv's high-tech scene. But the dishes we were devouring were anything but modern—an Austrian-Israeli recipe for chicken schnitzel and a Mesopotamian recipe for freekeh-based mujadara with black lentils. The café, Asif ("Harvest" in Hebrew) is a mix of restaurant, rooftop vertical farm growing rare herbs, and museum with revolving exhibitions and cooking workshops. There are some 2,500 culinary titles in Asif's library.

Asif is a project of the Jewish Food Society, founded by Israeli culinary expert Naama Shefi and philanthropist Terry Kassel, and their broader effort houses digital archives of many more thousands of Jewish recipes from all corners of the world. "I think about it like an art gallery, like a collection of artifacts. The library is quite literally a collection, an *osef*," Shefi told us (*osef* comes from the same Hebrew root word as *asif*). "And when you're here in Israel, these recipes tell you a lot about the far-flung diversity that are the people in Israeli society."

It's not just the range—or cholent—of nationalities. "People think about Israel as a desert, but it is actually made up of many microclimates," Shefi explained to *Vogue* magazine. "It's a tiny place, smaller than New Jersey, but it has green mountains, a beautiful coast, lush valleys—and also a desert. When you have that kind of density, creativity, and immigrants from seventy nations, ideas and recipes travel at a very rapid pace, and then they transform and combine in very interesting ways. Toss that into the Mediterranean climate and what you have is the perfect culinary storm."

Aronson said that if he asked ten Israelis what they make for Shabbat, he would get ten different answers, but they would be variations on a common idea. "As different as their cultural backgrounds are, they don't look at each other as foreigners anymore. Food is a really easy way to bridge barriers in that it takes the sense of strangeness out of people."

Perhaps this blend of diversity and unity helps explain a paradox: Why are Israelis so high on the world happiness rankings despite being so different from the other countries topping the list?

Tucked in the Dutch province of South Holland is the headquarters of the World Database of Happiness (WDH), run by Ruut Veenhoven at Erasmus University Rotterdam. For his book on the happiest places on earth, former National Public Radio correspondent Eric Weiner describes the WDH as "the secularist's answer to the Vatican and Mecca and Jerusalem and Lhasa, all rolled into one." During his visit, Weiner stumbles upon a "secret" of happiness research: the homogeneity of happy populations. According to Veenhoven, the "happiest places don't necessarily fit our preconceived notions. Some of the happiest countries in the world—Iceland, and Denmark, for instance—are homogenous, shattering the American belief that there is strength, and happiness, in diversity."

If homogeneity makes a country happier, what about Israel? Maybe Israel shows that a diverse population coupled with a robust civil calendar and cultural elements that bind people together could be the best of both worlds. If variety is the spice of life, eliminating it cannot be good for happiness. But without something in common, those same differences can be a recipe for strife and polarization.

Another binding force is a new form of Judaism that is emerging in Israel. Journalist Shmuel Rosner and the statistician Camil Fuchs call this amalgam "Israeli Judaism" in their book of the same name. In its practice, Israeli Judaism is different from Judaism in the West. Some practices are in, others are out. As we have seen, Friday night dinner is in. Prayer and synagogue attendance are less common. By contrast, the synagogue plays a central role in Diaspora Jewish life. For many American Jews, synagogue membership is their primary connection to Jewish life, much more so than Shabbat dinner.

One might think that traditions left over from Jewish history might be evaporating from Israeli secular culture, but the opposite is the case. "Over the last decade and a half," Rosner told us, "Jewishness has become more and more part of Israeli secular culture," but in ways that would be hard for Jews elsewhere to imagine. "You see swarms of young and seemingly hedonistic Israelis dancing at a concert and belting out the lyrics that the musician—with nose rings and tattoos—is singing onstage. And the lyrics are from the book of Psalms, or the eleventh-century Jewish poet Ibn Gabirol."

Ishay Ribo, who grew up Haredi and still wears the black kippah of an Orthodox Jew, is one of the most prominent of a wave of religious singers on Israel's pop music scene. In 2021, Ribo's song "Cause of Causes" (*Sibat HaSibot*) was the most played song of any kind on Israeli radio. In the song's music video, Ribo is seen standing alone in the desert, playing his guitar and looking up to the heavens while singing, "We don't have any king, other than you, creator of the universe, cause of all causes. . . ." His songs are deeply religious and, at the same time, pleas for understanding between the religious and secular worlds. The song calls for accepting "the black and white with all the colors of the rainbow," saying that they are all "beloved people created in God's image."

The proportion of the population who adhere to this secular religious, Israeli-Jewish hybrid is growing, drawing from the more religious community on the one side and from the more secular population on the other. "Israeli society's shared cultural touchstones appear to be growing more and more Jewish, and traditional lines between the secular and religious populations are fading, particularly in the realms of music and art," Sarah Rindner, an Israeli educator, wrote in *Mosaic*. This hybrid provides a mixture of meaning, community, and freedom, and for many Israelis it satisfies a need not to miss out on the creative energy and opportunities of modernity while still benefiting from the warmth of belonging that rituals provide. "It's becoming more and more natural for everybody," Rosner said, speaking of the integration of Jewish themes in Israeli secular culture.

A Matter of Meaning

William Breitbart is the founder and director of the Psychotherapy Laboratory at the Memorial Sloan Kettering Cancer Center in New York. Breitbart's lab developed a counseling program called meaning-centered psychotherapy (MCP) to address the profound loss of meaning that cancer patients often experience. This technique was inspired by the famed Viennese psychiatrist Viktor Frankl, author of the classic book *Man's Search for Meaning*, based in part on his own experiences in the Auschwitz concentration camp. Frankl observed that those who survived were not necessarily the prisoners who were young and strong. The key factor, he claimed, was whether they had a clear purpose to live for, such as reuniting with a spouse. In his own case, he wanted to finish a book that he had been working on before the war. The one possession he had tried to save was the only copy of the manuscript, but it was confiscated.

Frankl argued that there is no single "meaning of life"; each person can discover something that gives life purpose. Breitbart and his colleagues developed a series of readings and exercises designed to tease out what mattered most to the patients. The researchers then studied the effectiveness of MCP in four separate studies, and showed that MCP "reduces despair, enhances meaning, and as a result reduces hopelessness, depression, desire for hastened death, physical symptom distress and improves quality of life" of cancer patients, as Breitbart wrote. As Frankl himself succinctly put it: "Despair is suffering without meaning."

Family is one of our greatest sources of meaning, and most people instinctively understand that their family is their strongest anchor in difficult times. In September 2017, the Pew Research Center asked 4,867 U.S. adults, "What about your life do you currently find meaningful, fulfilling or satisfying? What keeps you going, and why?" The result could not have been more clear: family came in first by a wide margin (69 percent), mentioned twice as often as career (34 percent), the second-place answer.

The studies also found that the closer these young adults felt to their family and friends, the higher they rated life as meaningful. Other studies have shown that a sense of belonging is a "strong predictor" of meaning in life, and that family is often the core source of that feeling. As human beings, we crave meaning and belonging, and the two are entwined. Evolution has made us crave social connection almost as much as we need water and food. And just as thirst and hunger impel us to find sustenance, loneliness and depression impel us to find social connection.

As countries become wealthier and more modern, family-centered life tends to fade away in favor of more contingent relationships. What is unusual about Israel is that it somehow combines the autonomous, liberal values of modernity with the family-centric values of more traditional cultures. Israelis treasure both their independence and their families.

This, of course, is true for many people in other advanced countries, but the difference in Israel is that the families are larger and closer, both geographically and in the time and frequency spent together. In addition, the Israeli family maintains a higher priority with respect to work compared to other wealthy countries. But unlike in traditional cultures, where there can be tremendous pressure on children to conform to family or cultural norms, Israelis have a great deal of freedom and autonomy to find their path.

After the Family

In just the last half century, humanity has been conducting an unprecedented global experiment among billions of people: *What would our societies be like without families at the center?*

This new world is already taking shape at a rapid pace. A 2012 report by the Civil Service College of Singapore observed, "Increasingly, family no longer serves as the central organizing feature of society. An unprecedented number of individuals—approaching upwards of 30 percent in some Asian countries—are choosing to eschew child bearing altogether" as well as other family relationships. Even more surprising, similar studies show that among those choosing not to start their own family, there are growing numbers of adults also choosing to allow extended family ties to weaken—withering relationships with siblings, cousins, aunts, uncles, and parents. Family relationships across the board may not be as central in some places as they once were.

The report notes that the post-family era is most advanced in the high-income world, particularly Europe, North America, and the wealthier nations of East Asia. But it is also taking root in emerging countries like Brazil. The reasons are varied, from economic pressures to the retreat of religion to the influx of urbanization.

If there is a standard-bearer for this new era, it might be Sweden. In Stockholm, a staggering 60 percent of households consist of people living without any connection to immediate or extended family. In his book *Going Solo: The Extraordinary Rise and Surprising Appeal of Living Alone*, the sociologist Eric Klinenberg argues that the city has become something of a paradise for singletons who have mastered the art of creating community with non–family members. "We're actually quite social, and we've learned how to be okay when we're on our own," he writes. "Solitude, once we learn how to use it, does more than restore our personal energy; it also sparks new ideas about how we might better live together."

On the individual level, there are many reasons why family might not be a viable source of connection and meaning. Not everyone has or wants a family or children. When people say that their friends or community are "like family," for many this is not just an expression, but a reality. "Friends are the family you choose," it is said. There are many sources of human connection, and it could be risky or unhealthy to depend too much on any one of them.

The societal level is another story. Compared to similarly modern countries, societies with larger, closer families have an advantage. With greater connection to other generations comes more meaning in life, less despair, more happiness, longer life spans, and deeper social connections.

Bruce Feiler has written seven *New York Times*–bestselling books, the first of which was *Walking the Bible*, chronicling his ten-thousand-mile journey through the five books of Moses. "I wanted to explore the greatest stories ever told, in the settings where they actually occurred," he recounted for us. His expedition followed Abraham's path from the banks of the Tigris and Euphrates (now part of Turkey), through Egypt, and ultimately to Jerusalem.

Later in his writing career, Feiler pivoted to writing about lessons at the intersection of families, careers, and happiness, with books including *Life Is in the Transitions*, *The Secrets of Happy Families*, and *The Council of Dads*. We thought that his switching from writing about biblical stories to personal happiness was abrupt. But he saw it as a logical extension. "Our brains are wired to process the world through story," he told us.

In the early 1980s, a small cohort of academics began to write about the importance of narrative to human identity. "They created a field called narrative psychology, which at the time was a fringe academic discipline," Feiler explained. Two decades later he began meeting these psychologists. Marshall Duke is a professor of psychology at Emory University and an expert on the role of rituals in human resilience. Duke hosted Feiler at his home for a Shabbat dinner with his wife and the Duke children and grandchildren.

Over a traditional Friday night dinner, Duke unpacked his research on how a child's knowledge of the story of one's family can be a predictor of emotional health. "The more children knew about their family's history, the stronger their sense of control over their lives, the higher their self-esteem, and the more successfully they believed their families functioned," Feiler recounts in one of his bestsellers. "Children who have the most balance and self-confidence in their lives do so because of what . . . [Duke] called a strong intergenerational self."

There are plenty of occasions for the ritual of storytelling: Thanksgiving, Christmas, annual family vacations, the Fourth of July, "or any other ritualized activity that brings different generations together," Feiler added.

And Duke's research highlights that the most impactful storytelling for developing a durable intergenerational identity is around stories that involve hardship. "Most of the breakthroughs in the Bible come in the moment of hardship: when Abraham leaves his father's house and goes down to the land and he doesn't even know where he's going; or when the Israelites are in Babylon when they invent Shabbat."

The biblical story of the *Avot* (Fathers—Abraham, Isaac, and Jacob) and *Imahot* (Mothers—Sarah, Rebecca, Rachel, and Leah) is the epic intergenerational story of a family that became the Jewish people. To be a Christian, Muslim, Hindu, or Buddhist is to be an "adherent" of their creeds, meaning that they share certain beliefs. By contrast, to be a Jew is to be a "member" of the Jewish people, which means being part of the Jewish family. Anyone can become Jewish. The difference is that, with other religions, the convert is joining a *faith*, while in Judaism they are joining a *family* and becoming part of that family's ancient story.

This means that Jewish Israelis have three interwoven strands of story anchoring them to their "intergenerational self"—the stories of their people, their country, and their own personal family. And for most Jewish Israelis, their family story includes the intergenerational story of how their parents or grandparents came from near or far to bind their fates to Israel.

Chapter Six

TOUCHING HISTORY

We are a people that likes to quarrel with each other all the time, but in the
end, our shared two thousand years of exile is a very powerful story.

—Tzvika Fayirizen

You don't realize it when you are there, but Jerusalem is on the edge of a
desert. Sometimes, when it's cold and rainy in Jerusalem, you can go over
a hill into the desert and the sun will be so bright that you have to squint.

Micah Goodman came to his door to meet us. "You won't need those
jackets, we're going for a hike," he said, smiling at his bundled-up guests.
Goodman liked to do interviews while showing off the spectacular views
and fresh desert air around his home. Once we started walking we could
see in one direction the mountains of Jordan through the clear desert sky,
and in another direction the road snaking down to the Dead Sea, with
the spires of Jerusalem on the ridge behind us. Dry canyons dropped on
either side, with a shadow of green on their slopes that had sprung up
after too-rare rain.

Goodman, whom we met in the previous chapter, is a public intellectual and polymath, having written books on everything from biblical commentary to Israel's geopolitics. Not only have all his books been
bestsellers, but he also created a new genre: books that bring core texts of
Jewish thought to a general, secular audience. Classics like Maimonides's
The Guide for the Perplexed had never crossed the divide between yeshivas
and secular Israelis. But Goodman changed that.

He was also a cofounder of a new kind of Yeshiva (Jewish seminary) focused on Israelis in their twenties, after their army service. The immersive program recruits Israelis who are secular and religious, politically right and left, and has them studying together the great works of Western and Eastern traditions, and also the Jewish tradition.

During the COVID-19 lockdowns, you had to hustle to secure a spot in Goodman's Zoom classes as they hit the five-hundred-person limit. He is a popular speaker because he has a way of presenting big ideas in a mischievous way, with enthusiasm and humor. He teaches Jewish thought with the bravura with which Richard Feynman taught physics.

"When you live in Israel, you feel like something big is happening all the time," Goodman told us. "Here, every Israeli feels like history is happening and we can touch it, like we can push it a bit. Meaning comes from two aspects: one, you feel there's something bigger than you, and two, you feel you have a role in that thing that's bigger than you.

"Big countries, like America or China, have really big stories. But they are too big to push. Small countries have really small stories—so, okay, I could touch history, but there's not much to touch," he said with a shrug. "Israel is a small country with a big story. So its story is big enough to give you meaning and small enough for you to have influence on it.

"What do I mean by big things happening?" Goodman continued. "Let's say you open the Bible and you see, wow, the Jews were kicked out of the Land of Israel and fled to Babylon. They should have disappeared. Instead they came back and completely reinvented Judaism.

"So that's a big story. But is it bigger than opening the newspaper this morning?" he asked rhetorically. "Day to day, we're living in a drama in history of biblical proportions. It's not like we're talking about tax reform here, right?" He was getting animated. "Look at the big debates in Israel. Where are the borders? Who is part of the Jewish people? What does it mean to have an army of the people—universal military conscription?

One in five Israelis is Arab, how can we best live together in a Jewish state?"

While other countries may have border disputes with their neighbors, Israel's neighbors have resisted its existence for the better part of the past hundred years. Israel's borders await definition by an agreement that formally accepts Israel's place in the region. The main political divide—the issue over which elections are debated—has historically been over Israel's strategy toward achieving peace and security.

The issues that tend to dominate politics in other countries, such as the economy, are barely debated in Israel. Instead, fundamental controversies have remained in play since the founding of the state. These include the exemption of the Haredi community from military service; whether there should be a formal constitution; who is Jewish for the purposes of marriage, conversion, and citizenship; and, of course, many other fraught questions concerning peace and security.

"These are not debates about the quality of our lives; it's about the essence of our lives. And you feel like it's ours to decide, it's really ours," Goodman said. "People feel that they have a role to play, that they are necessary. That's a piece of what gives us meaning."

Now It's Your Turn

Tzvika Fayirizen has the close-cropped hair and unlined face of a career military man. In the summer of 2020, he retired after thirty-five years in the IDF with the rank of brigadier general. He lives in Rehovot, a venerable suburb of Tel Aviv, is married with five children, and at age fifty-three, is already a grandfather. He jokes that the Hebrew word for grandfather (*saba*) is an acronym for "authority without responsibility."

His last position was doubly odd: he commanded the IDF Education Corps and had served in the air force as a navigator in F-15I fighter jets, a squadron commander, and an air force base commander. Why did the IDF have an Education Corps, we wondered. And why would they ask a former air force base commander to lead it?

Fayirizen had these same questions before accepting the command. "It's not really obvious why the IDF should deal with education at all," he said. "Isn't this the job of parents, schools, and youth movements?" When he asked for examples of education corps in other Western countries, he found out that there are none. So why does the IDF think it knows better than the British, German, French, and American armies?

These questions led him to a monthslong personal inquiry before accepting the new command, the final one to cap a distinguished career. It came down to the core social contract between the military and the people. "The deal is, you, the IDF, protect me, and in exchange I give you the whole people. We are yours."

And it is not just the gift of the whole people. It is what everyone eligible for compulsory service is expected to give. Putting yourself or your children in the hands of the state is brought home in no uncertain terms when soldiers take their oath upon enlistment. Saul's brother Alex moved to Israel after university and volunteered for the army, where he served in the paratroops. He wrote about the experience in a letter to a friend back in the U.S. "At the ceremony I promised to give my life (even) for this country. That was pretty odd, and saying it really brings into focus what I have done."

Already in their junior year of high school, Israeli youth receive an envelope in the mail that calls them to show up at an enlistment center. "The question is," Fayirizen said, "what causes a sixteen-and-a-half-year-old, when they ask him, 'So, do you want to be a combat soldier?' to say, 'Yes'? It's not logical. We are taught to love life. Something here needs explaining."

Fayirizen then laid out three possible answers. "The first is the classic answer: they become comrades-in-arms. I am willing to give my life for my brother and I know he will give his life for me," Fayirizen continued. "But that teenager hasn't gone in the army yet, he has yet to meet the people for whom he will be willing to die. So that can't be the whole answer."

Fayirizen then pointed to the power of sharing a connection to recent military history: "The second layer is what we call the 'heritage of battle.' My four sons all served in the Golani Infantry Brigade. The youngest is serving now. They all go up to the Hermon, Israel's highest mountain, right on the border with Syria and Lebanon. The soldiers who fought there tell the new ones, 'Here, behind this rock, I lost my hand; behind this rock I lost my friend.'"

Fayirizen summed up the impact of what he called the *second layer*: "Their message of these stories is clear: 'It was my turn to protect the country so you could grow up here, now it's your turn so that I can grow old here.' Every brigade has its place where it fought and where the new soldiers come to learn that it is their turn to protect the country. But again," Fayirizen said, "all this doesn't lead a teenager to choose a combat role," because they don't know what unit they will be in when they are filling out their registration form.

The third answer is unique to the State of Israel, Fayirizen said, using his own story as an example. Fayirizen is six feet, two inches tall. But he said that his grandfather was taller and stronger than him. "He was a construction worker. We knew that he and my other grandparents were Holocaust survivors."

When Fayirizen turned eighteen, his grandfather took him on a walk and told him his story. It was the first time that his grandfather had told it to anyone. His two daughters, Fayirizen's mother and her sister, had never heard it. "It turned out that he was an officer in the Polish army. When the Germans took him prisoner, he was lined up on the edge of a pit, about to be executed. He dropped himself into the pit, waited there until they killed everyone, and then escaped into the forest." Fayirizen's grandfather became a partisan, fighting from the forest through the rest of World War II.

"Then he said to me, 'During those six years I had many dreams. I dreamed of food, I dreamed of my wife and son.'" Fayirizen's grandfather learned later that they were murdered in the Holocaust. But until this walk, Fayirizen didn't know that his grandfather had a wife and child in Poland before the war.

Fayirizen remembers his grandfather saying to him, "I had a lot of dreams, but I could not dream of one thing. I couldn't dream of it because a man can only dream of something he is able to imagine, and I never imagined that I would walk unbowed as a Jew in the State of Israel and that this country would be mine. Do me a favor. Make sure that it does not fall apart."

Fayirizen dwelled on this *third layer* as the best explanation. "That's how he ended our conversation when I was an eighteen-year-old boy. I think that today, after Israel has existed for seventy-five years, that everyone still has this historical feeling that seventy-five years is nothing, we are a speck of dust in history."

And then Fayirizen put the *third layer* in the context of the larger sweep of Jewish history: "We are a people that likes to quarrel with each other all the time, but in the end, our shared two thousand years of exile is a very powerful story. Even if their family has not personally experienced the Holocaust, they have experienced the story of two thousand years of exile. They know, even at a young age, that this is the only place that is theirs to nurture and protect, that their home is here. Deep down, this is what best explains why a sixteen-and-a-half-year-old would say that he is ready to fight for his country."

In many places, patriotism—feeling a personal connection to and responsibility for your country—is not necessary. It is considered quaint, primitive, even immoral. Nations, it is widely believed, are just a construct that separates people and causes conflict. The world would be better without them. Nationalism is the problem; universalism is the solution.

To Israelis, the nation is neither abstract nor assumed. Without it, as has been tragically proven throughout history and in the present, there is no life. Israelis are socialized to understand this because they will be called upon to sacrifice years of their lives, if not more, as their turn comes to protect the palpable vessel that they personally must continue to build. And in doing so, they gain a sense of belonging not only to a people and a project that is larger than themselves, but to a shared purpose.

Belonging and purpose are not luxuries. They are fundamental human needs without which it can be difficult to flourish, or even to avoid despair. By necessity and perhaps more than any other wealthy and free nation, Israelis have instinctively structured their society to meet these needs on many levels.

Fifteen Seconds

We stood looking at a large semicircular construction site, trying to imagine its promise. The area looked big enough to hold four or five apartment buildings. It was just an expanse of dirt next to a newly paved street. It wasn't hard to imagine what the buildings would look like because on the other side of the street there was a row of unfinished apartment buildings being built.

Roni Flamer, our guide, brandished a large laminated map of the complex like a construction foreman. He gestured toward the horizon and then pointed to the cluttered area on the map. "Our buildings will be about two minutes' walk from this high-tech office park and four minutes' walk from twenty-five municipal buildings, including schools and kindergartens."

Israel's population is growing rapidly, so new developments like this one can be found in dozens of locations across the country. But we had come to see this one with our own eyes. It was in a place that people should have been fleeing: the town of Sderot.

Sderot was established in 1951, one mile away from Israel's border with the Gaza Strip, a narrow, densely populated rectangle one-third the size of New York City, stretching along the Mediterranean Sea and ruled by Egypt at that time. In the wake of the 1948 War of Independence, in which the new state of Israel lost one percent of its population, the state was flooded with Jewish refugees from Europe and the Arab world, doubling its population within three years. The government sent many of these immigrants to "transit camps"—squalid collections of tents. Sderot began as such a camp, with eighty families, mostly new immigrants from Iran, Iraq, Syria, and Turkey. By 1961, North African immigrants, mostly from Morocco, comprised almost nine-tenths of Sderot's population. Starting in the 1990s, Sderot's population doubled as the town absorbed another wave of immigrants, this time from the former Soviet Union and Ethiopia.

Israelis take for granted that Sderot's crazy ethnic quilt is somehow normal. Extreme multiculturalism has defined the country from day one. Two out of every three Israelis are immigrants, the children of immigrants, or the grandchildren of immigrants. It is not unusual for young people to have parents from different countries so that three languages are spoken in the family, especially with the grandparents, whose Hebrew might not be great.

As a result of the 1967 Six-Day War, the Palestinian population in Gaza went from living under Egyptian occupation to Israeli occupation. For a decade or so after that war, Israelis from Sderot went to Gaza to shop, hang out at coffee shops, and enjoy musical performances. The traffic went both ways; Gazan musicians performed alongside Israeli musicians in Sderot's small theaters and nightclubs. This natural flow of people allowed the largely North African population of Sderot to reconnect to the Arabic culture in which so many of them had been raised.

The calm in Sderot did not last. In late 1987, the first Palestinian intifada—violent protests demanding an Israeli withdrawal from the territories captured in the 1967 war—erupted. In 2000, following the collapse of peace negotiations between Israeli prime minister Ehud Barak and PLO leader Yasser Arafat, mediated by U.S. president Bill Clinton, Arafat launched a wave of suicide bombings in buses and cafés in Israeli cities. Then, on April 16, 2001, the first Qassam rocket was fired from the Gaza Strip into Sderot.

The Qassam is an erratic, homemade affair. It looks like a pipe with fins. But it has become increasingly deadly. The first Qassams carried about a pound of explosives; the current generation carries a bomb twenty times more powerful. In 2005, under Prime Minister Ariel Sharon, Israel unilaterally pulled its forces out of Gaza and dismantled the small Jewish settlements there. Less than two years later, the Islamic fundamentalist group Hamas took over the Gaza Strip, leading to a major escalation of attacks. Within six months of the Hamas takeover, more than six thousand rockets had fallen on Sderot.

The bombardment started taking its toll. About one-quarter of the population left the town, leaving mostly those who could not afford to move elsewhere. In 2008, 2012, 2014, 2021, and 2023, Israel launched large-scale military operations into the Gaza Strip to suppress the terrorist groups launching rocket attacks against civilian areas. During the operation in 2014, an average of seventy-seven rockets *per day* were shot at Israeli towns, over the course of fifty days. An Israeli-made defense system called Iron Dome intercepted most of them, but many still got through.

When earsplitting sirens sounded, blaring the words "Code Red" throughout Sderot, residents had ten to fifteen seconds to take cover in a nearby bomb shelter. As the *New York Times* described it, "Residents have grown accustomed to—though hardly comfortable with—the constant sound of a town-wide alert produced when [a radar] blimp detects an incoming rocket." During these flare-ups, Israelis would watch on the nightly news scenes of parents grabbing their kids and racing into bomb shelters. Because they would struggle to make it to a bomb shelter within fifteen seconds, many kindergarten children were kept inside their school building all day. Volunteers from all over the country came to help the residents.

We assumed that embattled Sderot was not a place that anyone would want to move to. So when we heard that new neighborhoods were being built in Sderot—and that there was demand to live in them—we had to see for ourselves.

"There are neighborhoods here where people bought land for one hundred thousand shekels [approximately $32,000]. Now it goes for a million. Not a bad deal!" Alon Davidi, the long-serving mayor of Sderot, told us. We saw that the town had attractive middle-class houses, parks, and tree-lined boulevards. It didn't look like a shabby town of people who couldn't afford to live elsewhere, or a place under siege. It was hard to imagine everyone we saw in Sderot's tranquil neighborhoods running for their lives for the safety of bunkers.

"People don't just come here for affordable housing. Sderot is considered among the most developed places in the region. Kids in our schools get the highest scores in the area," Davidi said. "Most of all, there is a sense of community. People help each other."

As we stood looking out over the site where Roni Flamer's new development would be built, he, too, was confident that he would have no trouble filling the new buildings. But it wasn't just because it was a good real estate investment, or even because of the sense of solidarity that characterized Sderot. There was another ingredient—a social innovation that, if successful, could have great ramifications throughout Israel and beyond.

Flamer is the CEO and cofounder of OR Movement ("or" means "light" in Hebrew), an organization that over the last twenty years has created new communities in the less-populated north and south of the country. By 2022, OR Movement had established seventy-four communities totaling fifty thousand people—nine new developments, fifty-two in kibbutzim, and thirteen in working-class towns. But Flamer felt that the organization was still a long way from achieving its goal of making Israel the best place to live. The key to fulfilling that ambition was to create a new way to build communities, particularly in an urban setting.

Flamer brought us to see an empty stretch of dirt on the edge of Sderot, within sight of the Gaza border. "This neighborhood will be the first of a new model that incorporates everything we learned over the last twenty years," he told us. On the outside, it would look like any other apartment complex. But there were subtle differences, designed for community-building.

"The development will have parks, communal spaces, play areas for kids, coworking spaces, coffee shops, and spaces to rent for residents who want to start a business," Flamer explained. "Everything needs to be within flip-flop reach—that is, close enough to walk in your flip-flops."

In essence, Flamer had stumbled on a hot new concept in urban planning called the "fifteen-minute city." The idea is that everything you need should be within a fifteen-minute walk or bike ride from one's home. As *New York* magazine explained, "The virtuous city will fragment into a collection of villages that entices residents to stay put." During the COVID-19 pandemic, Mayor Anne Hidalgo of Paris made the fifteen-minute city her flagship project, closing many streets to cars. Indeed, the restrictions imposed during the pandemic gave the quest for "hyper-proximity" a big push. As Padden Murphy, the policy head for the urban spaces company REEF Technology, put it, "We're entering the big bang of proximity."

OR Movement's plan was to take the "fifteen-minute city" to another level. The new neighborhood in Sderot would be a pilot for creating something almost unheard of in wealthy countries: a true community among apartment residents who would normally have no connection with one another.

"Israelis are good at community because they think in terms of groups, not just individuals," Flamer said. "For many, when choosing a place to live, community tops their list." And why in Sderot, of all places? "Nobody wants to be under attack, but living with a shared threat does bring people together. And refusing to let that threat destroy a city gives people an added sense of contribution and meaning."

Roni Flamer was not always so public minded. He started OR Movement with three friends from high school—his *hevre*. At the age of seventeen, the four of them joined a class trip to Poland to visit the Auschwitz concentration camp. "The truth is," Flamer admits, "we did not travel for the right reasons. We thought it would be fun to travel and have a week off from school. It was a boys' school. So this was a chance to travel with girls. And if you are a troublemaker, then it's easier to get away with it in a foreign country."

The trip changed the four boys' lives. They couldn't fathom how the Holocaust could have happened to people that to them, as Israelis, seemed so strong and that was able to survive everything. Then Flamer remembered a declaration coming out of his mouth:

"'When we finish the army, we will establish an organization and call it Light (Or) and make Israel the best country in the world to live in.' At first my friends laughed at this. But something in the darkness of Europe and the Holocaust brought out from within us the feeling that we must bring light. So we committed ourselves: you don't fight the darkness, you add light. That's how OR Movement was born."

In the modern world, cities are associated with the loss of community. The theme song of the long-running 1980s television series *Cheers*, "Where Everybody Knows Your Name," symbolized the yearning for a lost communal connection. For the last two centuries, there has been a constant global migration into cities, driven by culture, convenience, and commerce. But the price to pay was that, unlike in a small town, no one knows your name.

Is there a way to have the best of both worlds? To have a true sense of community *and* the benefits of urban life? If that is possible, it will be a major contribution to human happiness and social cohesion. Social experiments like those in Sderot—coupled with the shared sense of history from countless family stories like that of Tzvika Fayirizen—combine to show that touching history is not just some intellectual exercise, but manifests on a practical level.

What does it mean to touch history? It's to live in a city that's at the edge of chaos and war and decide not only to stay there but to build something innovative. The story of Sderot is a metaphor for Israel as a whole. Israelis instinctively feel that their mission is not just to survive, but to create something better that will contribute to the world. That is why the feeling of Israelis that they can, and must, push history matters far beyond the patch of dirt on the outskirts of rocket-battered Sderot.

Chapter Seven

PEOPLE OF THE STORY

The great leaders tell the story of the group, but the greatest of leaders,
Moses, taught the group to become a nation of storytellers.

—Rabbi Jonathan Sacks

We don't do science fiction.

—Danna Stern

"Look around. Stories are everywhere in this country. It's how we cope. It's how we make sense of things. It's cathartic to talk about them, especially with guys from the unit." Lior Raz was telling us about a time in 2010 when he and his colleague Avi Issacharoff were in their late thirties, hanging out on an army base near Ramallah during their annual reserve duty. "The unit" was Unit 217, popularly known as Duvdevan, an elite counterterrorism program within the Israel Defense Forces. That's when the two friends began exchanging stories that still haunt them.

Issacharoff talked about an incident from January 1994. He and his Duvdevan team were summoned to the headquarters of the IDF's Hebron division, about fourteen kilometers east of the Green Line separating pre-1967 Israel from the West Bank. Having just completed an operation earlier in Idhna, another West Bank town, they thought they were done for the day and would be heading home to Jerusalem for the night.

But the commander informed them that he had just learned of some terror suspects who needed to be apprehended in Hebron, one of whom had been wanted by the IDF for some time. "Go fast," the commander told Issacharoff and his team. "Surround the house and call on them to surrender."

Duvdevan's primary mission is to operate undercover in Palestinian urban areas, blending in by fluently engaging with the population in Arabic, always in the correct local dialect and accent, and looking like locals to avoid suspicion. Like method actors, these soldiers study everything from a neighborhood's social networks and powerful families to its history, rituals, and daily rhythms. Duvdevan means "cherry" in Hebrew, as in the cherry on top of the IDF's conventional military capabilities.

As with many Duvdevan soldiers, Issacharoff had some background in Arabic. His grandmother had immigrated to Israel from Qamishli, a Syrian Kurdish city on the country's border with Turkey. He learned Arabic and Kurdish as second languages growing up.

When his team arrived at the house in Hebron, Issacharoff positioned himself so he could see the roof terrace of the building where four of the suspects were sitting and talking. He flipped on the light from his M16, directed the beam at them, and—in Arabic—instructed them to raise their hands and surrender. Moments later, he saw a flash of fire. The primary target of the mission had shot him in the back of his left leg.

Issacharoff fell to the ground, but still managed to return fire. For about fifteen minutes, the shooting went back and forth until his rifle malfunctioned. Another member of the Duvdevan team sprinted to Issacharoff, threw him on his back, and evacuated him to the IDF's headquarters. Medics stopped the bleeding, but his recovery took months.

Raz's story was even more wrenching. His father had immigrated to Israel from Iraq (he would later serve in the Shin Bet and the Mossad, Israel's domestic and foreign intelligence services, respectively) and his mother from Yemen. "When I was a kid, I spoke Arabic before I spoke Hebrew," he told us. On the morning of October 21, 1990, while Raz was serving in Duvdevan, his girlfriend, eighteen-year-old Iris Azulai, was walking home from the grocery store in Jerusalem when a Palestinian terrorist stabbed her to death.

Omar Said Salah Abu Sirhan, from a village near Bethlehem, had gone on a rampage in a quiet Jerusalem neighborhood, knifing Iris and several others with a sixteen-inch blade. He tried to murder a thirteen-year-old boy before being shot in the legs by an off-duty policeman. As the officer went over to apprehend him, Abu Sirhan screamed, "*Allahu Akbar*," and stabbed the officer to death. He was arrested and ultimately given three life sentences.

A year after Raz and Issacharoff exchanged stories during their 2010 reserve duty rendezvous near Ramallah, the Israeli government negotiated a prisoner exchange with Hamas that was controversial for its lopsidedness. Israel released 1,027 Palestinian prisoners in exchange for a single Israeli soldier, Gilad Shalit, who had been kidnapped at the border with the Gaza Strip by Hamas. Two hundred eighty of those prisoners were serving life sentences. According to Hamas leadership, the prisoners freed had been responsible for murdering 569 Israelis, including Iris Azulai. Omar Said Salah Abu Sirhan, Iris's murderer, became a free man. (He is reportedly working for Hamas television, has since married, and lives in Gaza with his new family.)

Twenty years passed before Raz could talk about the killing. The catalyst was a project that began that night on reserve duty in 2010, when he and Issacharoff began brainstorming about a television show inspired by their experiences in Duvdevan.

"Every Israeli has a story," Raz told us. The show they imagined became *Fauda*, and it first aired on Israel's YES network in February 2015. (*Fauda* means "chaos" in Arabic, and it's the Duvdevan radio call sign when an undercover operation has been exposed.) It was an instant hit in Israel—the most viewed series in the country—and then Netflix bought it, when it began attracting record-breaking audiences in North America, Latin America, Europe, Asia, and several Arab countries such as Lebanon and Kuwait. *Fauda* has even developed a following in the Palestinian market.

In the opening scene of the first episode, a Duvdevan leader is shot in the upper leg by a character with the same name as the man who shot Issacharoff in Hebron back in 1994. The third episode explores the relationship between one of the unit's operatives and his girlfriend; she is killed in a terrorist attack. The episode is dedicated to Raz's deceased girlfriend, Iris Azulai.

"We say something in Hebrew, that this show was written in blood. The blood of our friends, my girlfriend. There are so many stories in this show that are based on true stories that happened to us. That's what's different about Israeli television," Raz says.

The co-creators of *Fauda* had no formal experience or training in acting or filmmaking. They didn't have to study counterterror combat scenarios to make their story realistic. Raised by immigrants who fled from Arab countries, they spoke Arabic and had immersed themselves in understanding Arab culture. So they could accurately dramatize characters on both sides of the fighting.

Israel's television industry has transformed from a backwater into a hotbed of critically acclaimed programming. In just over fifteen years, Israeli TV content has become a global export with dynamics similar to Israel's tech industry. Among the Israeli television series that have become international hits are *Homeland*, *In Treatment*, and, more recently, *Fauda* and *Tehran*. There are several explanations for this success, but one stands out: the tradition of storytelling.

The Jewish people were forged from a story that began with the family of Abraham and Sarah, a story that is sacred also to Christianity and Islam. As this story continues in the Hebrew Bible, soon after the Jews first entered the

Land of Israel, they converged on Jerusalem to bring the first fruits of their harvest to the Temple. Each Jew was commanded to recite this declaration:

> My father was a wandering Aramean, and he went down into Egypt and lived there. Few in number, they became a great nation, powerful and numerous. But the Egyptians made *us* suffer, subjecting us to harsh labor. Then we cried out to the Lord, the God of our ancestors, and the Lord heard our voice and saw our misery, toil and oppression. So the Lord brought us out of Egypt with a mighty hand and an outstretched arm, with great terror and with signs and wonders.

All religions are communicated through stories because, as humans, stories travel the well-worn path into our hearts and minds. What is different about the Jewish story is that it is told in the first person. *My* father. *We* cried out. God brought *us* out of Egypt.

The Passover Seder is almost universally practiced by Jews around the world, including most secular Jews. Certainly among almost all Israeli Jews. And the Seder is an act of memory, of reenacting the story of the Exodus from Egypt. As the Talmud puts it, "Each person must see themselves as if they personally left Egypt."

"Stories give the group a shared identity and sense of purpose," said Jonathan Sacks, the late Chief Rabbi of the UK. "Churchill told the story of Britain's indomitable courage in the fight for freedom. Gandhi spoke about the dignity of India and non-violent protest. Martin Luther King Jr. told of how a great nation is color-blind." But there is a difference, he went on: "The great leaders tell the story of the group, but the greatest of leaders, Moses, taught the group to become a nation of storytellers."

Andrew Marr, a prominent BBC journalist (who is not Jewish), described the reach of Jewish storytelling: "The Jews have always had stories for the rest of us. They have had their Bible, one of the great imaginative works of the human spirit. They have been victims of the worst modernity can do, a mirror for Western madness. Above all they have had the story of their cultural and genetic survival from the Roman Empire to the 2000s, weaving and thriving amid uncomprehending, hostile . . . tribes."

Israel is a country built on a story. It is the bookend of the story of exile, of the return of a people to their ancient land and language, and to sovereignty over their own fate. Every country has its story, but only a few have an animating myth without which they would not exist.

The United States is such a country. America is not just a piece of territory that broke away from another country. It was founded on new principles that still infuse what it means to be an American. Similarly, it is impossible to be an Israeli without in some way absorbing the country's story. This is true even for Israelis whose identity is in tension with, or even opposition to, that story.

Israel is a particularly story-rich environment because, as a nation of immigrants, almost every family has its origin story. Other families have a story of living in the land over many generations.

Another reason why Israel is a petri dish for stories is that it is messy and contentious. Israelis live and work in close proximity to one another. Conflicts erupt daily. As the Israeli television executive Danna Stern pointed out, "We're very open. We're very verbal. We overshare. We go into details. There is no sense of privacy and there are no boundaries between work and home. Mix all those ingredients together and you have a recipe for love and conflict." Israeli viewing preferences reflect the fervor within the country: "Israelis are probably the world's most neurotic TV audience," says the Israeli actor Ron Leshem.

"We don't do science fiction," said Stern. "We do hyperlocal stories about our lives and the life of the nation." And while they are local—such as Netflix's *Fauda* and *Shtisel*, HBO's *Valley of Tears*, Amazon Prime's *Srugim* and *The Band's Visit*, and Hulu's *Hatufim* (remade in the United

States by Showtime as *Homeland*)—they nonetheless focus on universal themes such as love, fear, redemption, and familial tension.

The Israeli formula is working. At the end of 2019, the *New York Times* published a ranking of what it identified as "The 30 Best International TV Shows of the Decade," and Gidi Raff's *Hatufim* was named number one. There were more Israeli shows on the *Times* list than shows from Canada, Spain, or India. *The Band's Visit* went a step further. It was adapted to the theater and became one of only four musicals in Broadway history to win what are called the "Big Six" Tony Awards: Best Musical, Best Book, Best Score, Best Actor, Best Actress, and Best Direction.

And then there are the adaptations. American studios have a long history of purchasing international films and television shows, or formats, in order to adapt them for an American audience. The biggest source has traditionally been the UK, which supplied the early versions of *Survivor*, *Big Brother*, and (in an earlier era) *All in the Family*. Israel is now second to the UK for American-purchased adaptations, and is very competitive with the UK on scripted adaptations. According to the *New York Times*, Israel has become "a kind of global entrepôt for creative TV, has prompted producers in other countries to look for Israeli partners to package their shows for international markets."

By any metric, Israel is home to one of the most dynamic creative arts ecosystems in the world. In the decade beginning in 2010, Israelis produced more than 350 feature films and 2,500 hours of original scripted television series. Most of this content is in Hebrew, for a market of only two million homes.

On a per capita basis, that's more original produced content than comes out of the UK, Canada, Germany, or France. Head farther east, to India's Bollywood, which is a TV and film juggernaut, serving a population of more than one billion people and 200 million television-viewing homes—a hundred times the size of Israel's market. Yet when it comes to comparing the volume of content, tiny Israel is on par with Bollywood.

Israel is home to about 120 independent production companies, eight accredited—and internationally recognized—television and film schools, and more than ten annual film festivals (including one in Sderot, just a mile from the Gaza Strip). But it's an industry that's still young.

Blockbusters on a Shoestring

When Danna Stern first took the Netflix acquisitions team through the *Fauda* budget, the Americans were stunned to learn that the cost of producing the entire first season of *Fauda* was just $2.5 million. This was the approximate budget for producing a single episode of a typical Netflix series. Gidi Raff, the creator and showrunner of *Hatufim*, made the same observation: the cost to produce the entire first season of his show cost less than one episode of Showtime's adaptation of it, *Homeland*.

Issacharoff and Raz had found all sorts of ways to keep costs down, like forgoing expensive professional stuntmen: "Our army buddies performed the stunts as a favor," Raz told us. Since Israeli television and film has historically had minuscule commercial market potential (reflecting the small size of the Hebrew-language market), there were no funds to finance blockbusters. But far from being a liability, Israelis have turned the limitation to their advantage.

Hagai Levi is the creator of *BeTipul* (*In Treatment*), which first aired in Israel in 2005. Levi is the son of two therapists and studied psychology at university. *BeTipul*'s format is one of the most innovative in TV history: the entire series was shot in one room—the therapist's clinic—and follows each patient through a nine-week period of treatment.

"I didn't have money to make a show, so I needed to do it on the cheap," Levi told us. "One room is cheap." Each night of the week for that nine-week season, the therapist would see a different patient. So the viewer could choose to track the weekly therapy session of their favorite patient on the same day every week, as though the viewer were part of the regular weekly appointment with that patient.

One psychology journal described *BeTipul* as "the most significant convergence of the realms of drama and therapy to date." Previously, according to the historian and writer Shayna Weiss, "when psychoanalysis was portrayed in TV or film in the US and Europe . . . it often focused on the juicy bits such as shocking revelations about one's past. *BeTipul* breaks from this pattern and focuses almost exclusively on the process of therapy."

BeTipul was the first Israeli show to be purchased and adapted internationally. HBO's *In Treatment*, which was almost a word-for-word English translation of the first season of the Hebrew-language show, had banner years at the Emmys, Golden Globes, and Writers Guild Awards. It's since been seen in more than twenty international markets.

"We have such small budgets that if I want to convince the audience to watch [*Hatufim/Homeland*] and not *Breaking Bad*, we really have to be special," Gidi Raff told us. Echoing Danna Stern's point, Raff then zeroed in on how going local is the key: "What the most successful Israeli shows have done is to be extremely Israeli. Be very, very local and in making it as personal as possible, somehow there you find the universal themes that an international audience can enjoy."

According to Keren Margalit, the creator of Israeli television hits, "We don't have money for anything. If you can't go wider, if you can't go big with special effects, you need to go inside. To go very, very deep and find real characters. I think a lot of Israeli television developed from this understanding."

Israelis also approach development very differently. Ideas for shows are not subjected to repeated focus groups to determine if they will hit a nerve in the market. There is no "pilot episode" in Israel, where the studio tests a representative audience's reaction and then creates the rest of the series to meet the audience where it's at.

• • •

Samuel "Shmulik" Maoz fought in Israel's 1982 war with Lebanon, spending thirty days as a gunner in a four-man tank. Following the war's conclusion, he wanted to tell his story. He tried to write a screenplay, but it took him twenty-five years. (His writing was so stressful that while doing it he would often vomit.)

Maoz had no experience as a creator, writer, or director—he had spent his entire post-military career as a cameraman—nor did he have any funding. So he had to innovate. The entire film was shot from the perspective of being inside a tank—he used the chassis of an old tractor— and the total budget was just $1.4 million.

The film was released in 2009 with the simple title *Lebanon*. The *New York Times* called it "an astonishing piece of cinema." The British film critic Roger Clarke noted that the "intensely personal grasp of the subject-matter is projected through a dark lens of claustrophobia: we never really leave the tank throughout the entire film, and are hemmed in with the conscript crew of four, who spend their time either frozen with fear or quarreling among themselves and especially with their commanding officer."

Lebanon won the most prestigious prize at the Venice International Film Festival—the first for an Israeli film. It also received a twenty-minute standing ovation. Israeli films have won numerous awards at the Tribeca Film Festival, Sundance, and others, and Israeli series feature prominently at almost every major television festival. As Avi Issacharoff told us, there are plenty of people like Maoz writing or directing Israeli TV and film by happenstance: "They didn't choose this career. They wound up in it because they had a story to tell." After leaving the military, Issacharoff worked as a journalist, and Raz in a succession of odd jobs, including as Arnold Schwarzenegger's bodyguard; but Issacharoff and Raz, too, had stories to tell.

While "quality" can be subjective, Danna Stern told us, "We try to make shows that are going to spur a meaningful conversation." Keren

Margalit's experience raising a child with autism drove her to create the series *Yellow Peppers*, about a family with a son with autism living in a small village in the Negev desert. It was adapted into English as *The A Word*—set in the Lake District of England—and was the first foreign-language series to be adapted by the BBC.

Yellow Peppers catalyzed a national dialogue in Israel about autism and led to a new genre. *On the Spectrum*—licensed by HBO Max—was a series about three adults with autism living on their own, and has won the most awards ever at Israel's version of the Emmys. Applications from Israeli tech companies to a foundation that places workers with autism in jobs skyrocketed by one thousand percent after the series first aired.

And even as Israeli programming has attracted interest from global buyers, the commitment to locally themed quality remains sacrosanct. "We're not going to cast someone because we think they might have more international appeal. That's not what we're doing here," Danna Stern told us. "We're making great television for ourselves. And then selling it to the world."

That helps explain the recent growth in television about orthodox religious themes. "[You used to] be able to count all the religious characters you'd seen on two hands," journalist Liel Leibovitz wrote in the journal *Sapir*. But since the 2008 hit *Srugim*, a television show made by and about religious Jews, "scores of Israeli actors, directors, writers, musicians, and entertainers have traveled some way down a path, growing more pious and producing works that reflect their spiritual journeys." And, as Leibovitz told us, it goes in both directions: the Haredi community is also "increasingly swapping its reticence for full-on engagement with the culture at large." Through streaming services, shows like *Srugim*, *Shtisel*, and *The New Black* have found large non-Jewish audiences around the world.

"Increasingly, Israelis think of Judaism not as a stubborn rejection of progress," Leibovitz wrote, "but as a rightful return to a tradition that continues to be an engine of creation, of growth and change and hope." There is even a television and film school in Jerusalem, Ma'Aleh, "devoted to exploring the intersection of Judaism and modern life," as described by its mission statement. It's a school with a religious orientation whose graduates have won awards at secular film and TV festivals throughout the U.S., UK, and Europe.

International blockbuster movies and television shows tend to be escapist. Whether they are about superheroes or science fiction, their attraction is that they are far from real life. What is the job of entertainment if not to transport us to another place and take us away from the day-to-day?

But sometimes there is a need to escape from escapism. The real world can also be captivating. The question is not *Which is better, reality or fantasy?* The point is that Israel specializes in producing slices of reality. And there is a surprising relationship between closeness to reality and happiness.

The young professor looked the part, except for being too athletic: slim and bespectacled, with a quiet intensity and a slight accent. "This course is not merely about information. . . ." The professor paused for emphasis. "It is about transformation." So opened Positive Psychology 1504, which became—with 855 students enrolled—among the most popular courses in Harvard's history. Over some twenty-two lectures in the course, the professor promised to explore what he called the Question of Questions: How can we help ourselves and others—individuals, communities, and societies—become happier?

Tal Ben-Shahar's path to becoming a rock star of happiness was not an obvious one. Growing up in Israel, he had been obsessed with playing squash. By seventeen, he was Israel's national champion, and went on to win the U.S. intercollegiate championship. It seemed like Ben-Shahar was living the good life—on a path toward making a living doing what he loved. Yet he noticed that the relentless effort needed to meet the next challenge quickly erased the exhilaration of winning. Playing began as a source of joy. Now he felt guilty whenever he was not training.

Ben-Shahar became interested in one of the great paradoxes of life: If we are doing what we love and getting what we want, why are we still unhappy? How should we live our lives if, as the great longshoreman-philosopher Eric Hoffer put it, "the search for happiness is one of the chief sources of unhappiness"?

After his military service, Ben-Shahar earned a degree in philosophy and psychology at Harvard, and then a PhD in organizational behavior at Harvard Business School. His thesis was about self-esteem. The Twitter version of his thesis: "We have two types of self-esteem, one is contingent on other people's praise and evaluation, the other on our own," he said.

When he was thirty-three, Harvard invited him to teach. His famous course on happiness began as a seminar with eight students, two of whom dropped out. The following year, the course had three hundred students, and the year after that almost nine hundred. "It just spread by word of mouth," Ben-Shahar said. "The students told their friends that the course helped them become happier."

We asked Ben-Shahar, as a prominent expert on happiness and an Israeli, why he thought Israelis were happy. He began somewhat face-tiously. "There are three secrets to happiness, and I'm going to give them to you. So the first secret to happiness is reality. The second secret is reality. And the third secret to happiness, you got it—reality."

What does reality have to do with happiness? "Because when you face reality, you learn how to better deal with it," Ben-Shahar explained. "And Israelis live in reality. At an early age, you have this army experience, which is so real, sometimes way too real for comfort. But it puts life into perspective. You have been in difficult situations. It was tough but, look, you survived. That's reality."

Micah Goodman thinks that closeness to reality makes Israelis less prone to conspiracy theories and more trusting of state institutions during a crisis. For Israelis, the notion of a "deep state" that is secretly scheming against the unsuspecting public is less believable. When a nation is fighting a common enemy, there is no separation between the people doing the fighting and the state that is organizing them. And due to all the forms of national service that most Israelis participate in directly or indirectly—especially during peacetime—the government is not an abstraction: it's part of almost everyone's daily life.

This sense of unity is expressed in the name of a popular and poignant song, "I Have No Other Country." Its first verse begins with: "I have no other country / Even if my land is burning / A single Hebrew word can / Pierce my veins, enter my soul."

Israeli patriotism is not bombastic. It is often tinged with protest, sorrow, and hope. The song continues: "I won't be silent because my country / Has transformed herself [lit. 'changed her face'] / I will sing in her ears / Until she renews her glory days."

The song, written in 1986 and revived many times, including by a who's who of artists in the early days of the pandemic, captures the Israeli tendency to, in times of trouble, appeal to the sense of solidarity that characterized the precarious founding decades of the state. But the word "until" carries with it the confidence and hope that the country returning to its better self is a matter of when, not if. It's never too late, because giving up is not an option. Israelis view their country as a continuing project, and being part of a project is a form of contact with reality, as a collective and as individuals.

It may seem paradoxical that the Israeli way to stay close to reality is through stories. Real stories from military service as a common stage in life, from the cloistered world of ultra-Orthodox communities in Jerusalem, from families living with autism in the Negev desert, to name a few local television themes. Israelis have self-confidence, born of experience, that they can deal with an unpredictably changing reality. Indeed, they seem to be drawn to it. Grounded optimism is an important part of the Israeli secret to happiness.

Chapter Eight

VACCINATION NATION

The most important ingredient in all vaccines is trust.

—Barry Bloom, Harvard T.H. Chan School of Public Health

Israel is not a disciplined place. This can be seen on the roads, in the supermarkets, and even in government offices. There is a somewhat cavalier attitude toward peacetime rules. High income and sales taxes make for a large "gray" economy where many transactions are made with cash, without receipts. The culture bristles against the idea that some people can tell others what to do. Everyone and everything is questioned. The combination of a lack of hierarchy, an inclination to improvise, and a comfort with chaos means that Israelis are difficult to train for jobs that require deference and attention to detail, like hospitality service in fine hotels and restaurants. An international luxury hotel chain opening in Israel went so far as refusing to hire any Israeli who had worked in the local hospitality sector, preferring instead to train its staff from scratch.

Nothing works like clockwork. Except when it does. It's as if Israelis have a split personality. There is the *balagan* (somewhere between "chaos" and a "mess") of daily life. Then there is crisis mode, in which Israelis know how to work together seamlessly and single-mindedly. The *misimatiut* (mission orientation) that they learned during their military service provides focus, coolheadedness, and discipline.

A key difference between daily-life mode and crisis mode is the level of trust. In daily-life mode, the attitude is "Why should I listen to you?

Who says you know best and not me?" This works when the stakes are low, but not in a crisis, when you need concerted action. Israelis learn that to succeed in a crisis, they must act together, and that teamwork inherently requires trust in leaders and in each other. In crisis mode, they can suspend their distrust of anyone who claims to be above them. They can assume that the same government bureaucrat or politician they disrespected in regular life could be trusted because they shared the same mission.

Most often, the crisis in question has to do with national security. But this ability to switch into crisis mode was also evident when the threat came from an unseen virus. In essence, Israel benefited from an ability to switch on trust in their political leadership, on top of the foundation of trust that already exists in the health system and medical science, at a time when, internationally, trust in all three was in short supply.

Ran Balicer was looking for something to do. At twenty-five, he had just finished up as the chief physician of the 77th Tank Battalion, a unit famous in Israeli history for saving Israel from invasion by Syria in the 1973 Yom Kippur War. It was now 2002, and he had taken up the position of deputy director of the epidemiological section of the medical corps headquarters. Not exactly the center of the action. For the top brass, epidemiological planning was like working on lowering your cholesterol in the middle of a knife fight.

As part of his training, Balicer had to make a presentation to his new colleagues. Searching for a topic, he stumbled on an obscure event from five years earlier—the 1997 outbreak of the H1N1 avian flu in Hong Kong. An influenza virus that normally infected birds had jumped into a human. It infected only eighteen people, but six of them had died. The entire Hong Kong poultry market had to be shut down and the flocks culled. The outbreak was quickly forgotten.

Balicer could not understand why no one was paying attention to this. "I said to myself, 'Who says it's not going to come back?' The same virus, but contagious, like the flu. If an exceedingly lethal agent becomes transmissible, it could be 1918 all over again."

The "Spanish flu" pandemic of 1918 was something many people had heard of but had no idea how bad it was. This influenza virus infected an estimated 500 million people—one third of humanity at that time—and killed approximately one in ten of them. More American soldiers died from the flu than in all of World War I. Children age five and young people aged twenty to thirty-four were hit hard. Life expectancy in the United States dropped by twelve years. The pandemic came in three waves, the most severe being the middle wave in the fall of 1918, but continued to come around in a mild form for the next thirty-eight years.

Over eighty years later, most people assumed that the disease had rampaged unfettered because people didn't have access to modern medicine. Today would be different, surely. In truth, the toolbox for fighting a pandemic had not changed much. Until a vaccine came along, which could take years, the main line of defense was still thought to be masks and isolating the sick.

There were some drugs that could help with treatment or prevent infection, but what would happen if the whole world needed them at the same time? "It would be the richest come first, not the first affected come first," Balicer said. There would be a desperate scramble for an insufficient supply.

The clear answer was for a country to stockpile large quantities of antiviral drugs. But governments are not big on planning beyond the next election cycle. What minister wants to spend real money now on some rare theoretical event in the future? He would have to figure out a financial reason to justify such spending.

Sitting in his small office, Balicer fired up an Excel spreadsheet and made some calculations. The costs of even a "minor" epidemic can escalate quickly. Indeed, just a year later, in 2003, the SARS epidemic in Canada would cost the country more than $1 billion, even though the virus infected only 251 people and caused just 44 deaths.

Crunching the numbers, Balicer found that for every dollar spent stockpiling drugs, the Israeli government would save $3.68 and many lives. And this calculus was just considering the costs of lost workdays and to the health system, not the value of the lost lives themselves. If you added the cost of shuttering the economy during a lockdown, the numbers would be staggering. Indeed, when the COVID-19 pandemic hit almost two decades later, Israel's economic growth shrank by about 6 percent.

Balicer decided to try to publish the idea as an academic paper. But he had never written for an academic journal. His boss suggested that he approach the big ones, like the *New England Journal of Medicine*, the *Journal of the American Medical Association* (*JAMA*), and the *British Medical Journal* (*BMJ*). These were some of the most prestigious peer-reviewed medical journals in the world, unlikely to accept a young doctor's first paper. But he was encouraged to push ahead.

As Balicer wrote up the idea, he realized it wasn't a full academic paper, just a rough calculation. But then he noticed that *BMJ* had a feature called "Editorials"—short articles endorsed by the editor. That should be sufficient for his somewhat simplified financial model for stockpiling antiviral drugs. "I only realized later that you usually had to be invited to submit an editorial, and that they were for big-time policymakers. But I sent it in and they accepted it!" Balicer marveled.

Armed with a published editorial, an Excel spreadsheet, and the support not only from his immediate superior but also from Itamar Grotto, his boss two levels up, Balicer pitched his idea to the head of the medical corps. He was intrigued and said, "Let's take it to Avi [Yisraeli], the director general of the health ministry," who said, "That's interesting, let's take it to the health minister." The health minister was intrigued and said,

"Let's take it to the finance minister." The finance minister at the time was Benjamin Netanyahu.

Six years earlier, in 1996, Netanyahu had swept into office as Israel's youngest prime minister ever (he was forty-six), but by 1999 he had become so politically toxic that he was not only run out of office but temporarily retired from politics. In 2002 Netanyahu retained a following within the Likud party and was contemplating a challenge to Prime Minister Ariel Sharon. He then made a deal with Sharon: a free hand in the finance ministry in exchange for not opposing Sharon's defense and foreign policies. Laser-focused on reclaiming the prime minister's office, Netanyahu became the most radical economic reformer the Finance Ministry had ever seen.

Balicer wasn't sure how the obscure issue of pandemic preparedness would fit into Netanyahu's ambitious agenda. The Finance Ministry was notorious for vetoing new programs, particularly under Netanyahu, whose signature policies were lowering taxes, slashing spending, and privatizing state-owned companies. But Balicer was determined to keep marching into offices with his spreadsheet and see how far he could go. "I was very young, I didn't know any better," he recalled. "I thought that if you showed people a good idea, they would be open to it."

While Balicer's idea for new spending had no political attraction for Netanyahu—if anything, the opposite—Netanyahu also had served in Israel's most elite commando unit, Sayeret Matkal, which reports to the IDF chief of staff. As a participant in many risky operations, the idea of preparing for every contingency, particularly unlikely but catastrophic ones, was familiar to him. Just as important, during his student days at MIT, Netanyahu had studied the power of exponential growth. So, when he was briefed on the inevitability of a pandemic and the need for a pharmaceutical stockpile, he said, "Interesting. Let's take it to the cabinet."

An enormous oval table made of lustrous light brown wood dominates the cabinet room. At the table for this meeting sat the most swollen government in Israeli history: twenty-six ministers. Briefing books, papers, notebooks, and bottles of water for each minister covered the table. The ministers were lazily shuffling through the three-ring binders bulging with more memos than they could possibly read.

In the middle, on one side of the table, in the oversized chair reserved for the prime minister, sat Ariel Sharon. Short and bulky, he filled the chair like a house. Exuding tremendous energy, Sharon was part farmer, part general, and part politician. He was a born decision-maker and leader, and one of the most powerful prime ministers in Israel's history. Not the kind of person around whom you'd want to be caught unprepared.

Balicer sat near the corner along the wall, between Grotto and Avi Yisraeli. He was more excited than nervous. Just being in the room and watching all these ministers talk about his idea was a new experience. Maybe he would do some whispering in the background—the higher-ups would do the talking.

Sharon made it to the end of the agenda. "Okay, what's this about stockpiling for avian flu?" he said, looking over reading glasses that made him look less the general and more the stern schoolmaster. Yisraeli stood up and started to explain. "The IDF medical corps has done a study on how we should prepare for a national emergency caused by a pandemic," he said. Yisraeli knew his customer. Using the words "national emergency" was like pressing a hot button.

"Sharon was a general, and generals prepare for the unlikely by design," Balicer explained to us. Dealing with emergencies is what generals do. The emergency is usually called war, but there are others. Whatever it is, the mentality is to always be prepared.

Sharon started to pepper Yisraeli with questions. *How likely is this? How bad could it be? What good are the drugs? How much will it cost? How much will it save?* Yisraeli gestured at Balicer to speak up. Balicer was shocked. It hadn't occurred to him that he would be called on to speak to the prime minister at a cabinet meeting.

"Are you absolutely sure you want me to talk?" he whispered to Yis-raeli, who just kept motioning for him to stand up. The ministers turned toward him. The prime minister looked at him.

"Someday an avian flu will mutate into something more contagious, more deadly, or both," Balicer replied. "It is likely that it wouldn't start here, that we would be hit as part of a global pandemic, like the 1918 Spanish flu. It has happened before and it will happen again—any day, without warning. The hospitals would start to fill up. The system would be overwhelmed. The economy would tank. If we have drugs ready, it could greatly reduce the pandemic's human and economic toll and would buy time until a vaccine is developed."

Now everyone in the cabinet room was paying attention. "We have to remember that there would be a desperate international struggle to obtain antiviral drugs during a pandemic," Balicer went on. "The price would go sky high, but that's not the worst of it. There is not enough manufacturing capacity in normal times to handle demand during a pan-demic." His point was that there wouldn't be enough medicine to go around at any price. "Our mathematical model shows that, compared to the costs of a pandemic, stockpiling is a bargain. Just looking at health system costs and lost workdays, there's almost a four-to-one ratio in sav-ings for every shekel we spend."

These arguments seemed to satisfy Sharon the general. But now Sha-ron the farmer tuned in. "The chickens are all in cages," he noted. "How do they catch avian flu from another country?"

"Well, Prime Minister," Balicer responded, "it seems that we are the promised land not just for people but for birds. Twice a year, five hundred million birds come through here on their way between Africa, Europe, and Asia. Israel is one of the first places to expect an avian flu breakout."

As Sharon went deeper with his questions about the poultry industry, the agriculture minister was now in the hot seat. After the detailed discus-sion, Sharon looked at the health minister and said, "Okay, let's vote on the plan." And that was it. Balicer couldn't believe it was happening. He had just been following his idea to see where it might lead, as if the idea had a mind of its own. It was like a balloon that kept going up and up, but didn't pop. What began as a training exercise would become a 300 million shekel ($67 million) program. That's a lot of medicine for a small country.

What Balicer did not realize at the time was that in the future he would return to the cabinet room in a pivotal role fighting a real pandemic. He also could not have imagined that in doing so he would again cross paths with the young finance minister.

RNA to the Rescue

"Patch him in," Albert Bourla told his secretary. It was the Israeli prime minister, calling again. He looked at the clock. It was 8:00 p.m. at Pfizer's global headquarters in New York City, so it was 3:00 a.m. in Israel. It was March 2020, at the height of Israel's first lockdown during the COVID-19 pandemic.

As the CEO of one of the first companies racing to develop a COVID-19 vaccine, Bourla had been fielding calls from many countries, including from heads of state. But for Bourla, speaking to the prime minister of Israel was different. He could feel the reverberations of history, the history of his own parents' survival, against all odds, through the carnage of the Holocaust, of the rebirth of the Jewish state. He was now in a position to help Israel—and through Israel, the world—emerge from a pandemic that had already taken over a million lives.

Bourla had grown up in Thessaloniki, a small city in Greece that Alexander the Great named after his sister 2,300 years ago. The Jewish community has been there almost as long. The Apostle Paul wrote that he visited the synagogue there. When the Jews were expelled from Spain in 1492, the Jewish community in Thessaloniki swelled and became the majority of the city. The Bourla family came with this tide and can trace its heritage back five centuries there.

As Bourla was growing up, he heard stories from his parents of how they survived the Holocaust. When the Nazis occupied Greece in 1941, the Bourla family was forced out of their home to live with four other Jewish families in the ghetto. In February 1943, the Germans blocked all the exits of the ghetto, and no one could leave. As it happened, the patriarch of the Bourla family and two of his sons were outside the ghetto. The father told his sons to escape and go into hiding, and that he would go back into the ghetto to be with their mother and two younger siblings. The two brothers watched from afar as their family marched to the train station along with the rest of the Jewish community. Almost fifty thousand Greek Jews, including most of the Bourla family, would perish in Auschwitz. The brothers survived the war in Athens, posing as Christians with fake IDs. One of the brothers was Albert Bourla's father, Mois.

While Mois Bourla's family was poor—his father was a tin maker—Albert also heard stories about another family, one of the richest in town. This family owned silk factories in different cities, with the headquarters and largest factory in Thessaloniki. There were seven children in the family, five boys and two girls. The oldest girl fell in love with a prominent Greek official and got married. This was almost unheard of in the Jewish community at that time. She converted to Christianity, and her father disowned her.

When the Nazis came, this wealthy family was stripped of its factories and its property and forced to move into the ghetto. As it became clearer that the Jews would be deported to an unknown future in Poland, the father of the family reached out to the daughter he had cut off and asked her to hide her teenage sister. That was Sara, Albert Bourla's mother.

Sara not only didn't have any papers, but she was highly recognizable in Thessaloniki, so she had to stay in hiding twenty-four hours a day. But she was a strong-willed teenager and sometimes went out. One of these times, she was recognized, reported, and thrown into prison. It was well known that at noon every day, a truck would pull up and take some of the prisoners to be executed at dawn the next morning. Sara's older sister persuaded her well-connected husband, Kostas Dimandis, to pay off the top Nazi official in the city to gain Sara's release. The official took the money and agreed, but Sara's sister didn't trust the official. Every day, she went to the prison at noon to watch the prisoners being loaded onto the truck. One day, she saw her sister among them.

At great risk to himself, Dimandis called the Nazi official directly and challenged him. "When Greek officers fail to keep their word, they commit suicide," he told the official. "What do German officers do?" The next morning at dawn, Sara and the other prisoners were lined up to be shot and the firing squad was already behind their machine guns. As Albert Bourla tells the story, "A BMW military motorcycle with two soldiers, one sitting in the sidecar, pulled up and handed an officer some papers. The officer removed two women from the line and loaded them back on the truck. As they pulled away they could hear the sounds of the machine guns firing. One of those two women was Sara, my mother."

After the war, Mois Bourla and his brother returned to Thessaloniki, where Mois was introduced to Sara by a matchmaker. In 1961, Albert was born, the first of two children. Unlike many Holocaust survivors, his parents were open about telling their stories from the war. His parents' response to being a small remnant of a destroyed community was to celebrate life. Albert grew up as a proud Greek and a proud Jew. He graduated as a doctor in veterinary medicine from Aristotle University in his hometown and got a job in the animal products division of Pfizer.

In 1996, Bourla left Thessaloniki to begin his career at Pfizer, living in eight cities in five countries. In 2018, he became the company's chief operating officer and, in 2019, the CEO. It was a steady rise from a small city in Greece to the top of Pfizer, a $210 billion company with seventy-eight thousand employees.

On January 10, 2020, the genetic sequence of a novel coronavirus that had appeared in Wuhan, China, was published online. On March 11, the World Health Organization declared COVID-19 a pandemic. About one week later, Pfizer's vaccine development and manufacturing team told Bourla that they could produce a vaccine by the middle of 2021. The average time to develop a vaccine was ten to fifteen years and the fastest vaccine ever developed was for the mumps in 1967: it took four years.

Bourla thanked them for their quick work. But then he surprised everyone in the room. "Not good enough," he said. "We need a vaccine to be ready for this winter, when the next wave of COVID will hit at the same time as the regular flu season." And so over the following months, Pfizer dedicated $2 billion to the development of its COVID-19 vaccine, including extensive human trials involving forty-four thousand volunteers. When the results came in, the vaccine proved 95 percent effective.

But there was still a long way to go. "The most important ingredient in all vaccines is trust," said Barry Bloom, a professor at Harvard's T. H. Chan School of Public Health, who has battled infectious diseases for more than forty years. Quoting another giant in the field, Walter Orenstein, Bloom added a truism that every epidemiologist knows: "Vaccines don't save lives. *Vaccinations* save lives."

In some ways, developing a vaccine is the easier part. It is a technical and scientific problem. Getting people to *take* the vaccine is a human problem, and vaccine hesitancy had grown in many countries as getting the shot came closer to becoming a reality.

Despite the overwhelming success of the clinical trials, Albert Bourla and Pfizer were facing a wall of fear. Due to confusing signals from governments, public health authorities, and the scientific community, trust had eroded in the array of institutions that were saying that the vaccine was safe. In some places, the fight against the pandemic had become political. COVID-19 was scary, but many people seemed to be even more scared of the vaccine.

Pfizer had a limited window of opportunity to prove that vaccinations could end the pandemic and return society to normal life. There was only one way to do it. Seeing is believing. As Bourla put it, "We knew it would be opportune for humanity if we could find a country where we can demonstrate that vaccinations can quickly crush COVID and reopen the economy."

Bourla had a good idea what his poster country should look like. It had to be a place where the government was trusted enough so that the people would be mobilized, and not just passively. The public would have to come out with open arms (literally), despite the uncertainties.

For that to happen, the country would need a government and health system that could make getting vaccinated quick, seamless, and simple. The country had to be digitally savvy, partly because that was key to making the process efficient, but also so that Pfizer could obtain the data it needed to tackle many unanswered questions.

Not just Pfizer, but the world needed to know: How well would the vaccine perform outside the artificial conditions of a clinical study? How long would the vaccine be effective? Did it really have to be stored at such a low temperature? How long could it be used once unfrozen at the vaccination centers? Would vaccinated people still be able to transmit the disease even if they didn't get sick?

One leading candidate for the poster country was the tiny nation of Estonia in northeastern Europe, on the Gulf of Finland not far from the Russian city of St. Petersburg. The smallest of the three Baltic states with just 1.3 million people, Estonia had a reputation for innovation. Skype had been founded in Estonia, and the country had a vibrant start-up scene. Estonia had perhaps the most digitally advanced paperless government. Paying taxes takes three minutes online and setting up a company is not much longer. Even voting in elections can be done from smartphones. Estonia offered virtual citizenship to anyone from around the world. Iceland was another leading candidate, with a number of the same attributes as Estonia. Both countries had largely homogeneous populations.

It's Bibi, Again

"Good evening, Prime Minister," Bourla began the call with Benjamin Netanyahu (Bibi, as he was known). "Isn't it pretty late on your end?"

"Never mind, it's fine," the Israeli leader said in his signature baritone, tinged with fatigue. "How do you think the vaccine will do against the new UK variant?"

Bourla had gotten used to the fact that Netanyahu would be conversant in all the epidemiological lingo, asking about details that only health ministers, or even those a few rungs below, would know about. It was as if Netanyahu were his own staffer. Later, as they were trying to close the deal, the Israeli prime minister would refuse to let the lawyers draw up the details in separate meetings that might last days. To save time, he insisted that he and Bourla join the lawyers for these discussions, to smooth out any sticking points.

But the intense barrage of calls had been in the months before, when Netanyahu sought to convince Bourla that Israel should be the first country to receive Pfizer's vaccine on a national scale. "We want to buy enough vaccines to protect our entire population," he had said on his first call. "We will pay double the price the European Union is paying, up front." Netanyahu knew that he would be criticized for overpaying. But by his lights it was worth it. The size of Israel's economy was about $400 billion. This meant that every day the economy was shut down would cost the country about $1 billion in lost economic activity, he roughly calculated. The vaccine, even at an inflated price, would cost a few hundred million dollars, total. A bargain if it meant he could get Israel's economy opened sooner.

In any case, Netanyahu knew that price wouldn't be the key. Another country could come along and outbid him. But Israel had other cards to play, cards that other countries didn't possess.

"Israel has a combination of advantages that you won't find anywhere," Netanyahu told Bourla in full-pitch mode. "We are the perfect size—small enough to cover quickly, yet large enough to provide an undeniable success story. We are also extremely genetically diverse. Israelis come from Ethiopia, Russia, Europe, throughout the Middle East, North and South America, and Australia. You don't find this kind of diversity in most larger countries, let alone a small country like Israel.

"Our ability to execute a vaccination campaign is unparalleled," he continued. "We have four very efficient health funds covering the entire country, and we know how to organize and come together during a crisis. When we are in crisis mode we all stand together.

"But most of all," Netanyahu said, playing his best card, "we have data. Not just quantity, but quality. Many countries can provide you with data going forward. But I don't think you will find another country that can match the data from millions of vaccinated people with their medical history going back over two decades."

Bourla fielded dozens of calls from Netanyahu and from the prime minister's close advisor Ron Dermer, Israel's ambassador to the United States. "It was kind of strange for me to be involved because I didn't know the first thing about viruses or pandemics," Dermer recalled. But Netanyahu wanted a senior Israeli official who was in the same time zone as Bourla to be plugged into the negotiations to handle any follow-up; no single hour in any twenty-four-hour period would be wasted.

In the end, Bourla was persuaded. "I was impressed with the obsession of your prime minister," Bourla later explained in an Israeli television interview. "He called me thirty times. He would ask about vaccinating children, or about opening the schools, or about pregnant women. Frankly, he convinced me that he would be on top of things."

Bourla was also aware of something even more important: "I knew that Israelis had much experience with times of crisis because they live surrounded by hostile nations, to a large degree. So I felt that they could do it and that there was a leader who was really going to guarantee that it would happen, so we placed our bet on Israel." Pfizer agreed to supply 8 million doses, enough to vaccinate Israel's entire adult population (with two shots each), at a cost of $237 million, in exchange for access to medical data related to COVID-19, pre- and post-vaccination.

Even Netanyahu's most scathing critics acknowledged that he deserved credit for doing something that no other world leader had been able to do. Gideon Levy, a columnist for the Israeli newspaper *Haaretz*, credited Netanyahu with playing "a decisive role in obtaining vaccines" and wrote that the prime minister's opponents "need to put in a kind word—even Satan occasionally does something that's praiseworthy, and he must be told so."

But Netanyahu could not have achieved what he did without the facts on his side. And the facts went beyond Israel's size and diversity to much deeper aspects of Israeli society.

On December 20, 2020, Benjamin Netanyahu became the first Israeli to receive Pfizer's COVID-19 vaccine, on live television. But now came a no-less-daunting challenge. The vaccine had arrived, but would Israelis take it?

The first 20 percent of the population, largely those most at risk, would be relatively easy, the prime minister knew. But what about the next 20 percent, and the next, and the next? Half the population would not be enough. That Israel's population was so young cut both ways. On one hand, it meant that Israel was less vulnerable to the virus overall. On the other hand, it meant that one-quarter of the population (children sixteen and under) were initially ineligible to be vaccinated. There seemed to be no way around it. Israel would have to vaccinate an almost unimaginable 80 percent of the over-sixteen population for broad-based immunity. And fast.

On the day Netanyahu received his vaccine, Israel's daily new case rate was 290 per million—about half that of the United States. By January 5, the day a third nationwide lockdown was announced, Israel's rate had more than doubled to 772 per million, surpassing the United States, and was rising fast. Israel was experiencing its third wave and it was by far the worst. This time, about 80 percent of the infections were the new B.1.1.7 variant, first discovered in the UK. This variant was much more infectious. Israel now faced its biggest challenge since the pandemic began. As Netanyahu put it at the annual Davos conference of world leaders being held remotely, "We're in an arms race, but this time it's between vaccination and mutation." Running the vaccination campaign was "like checking on munitions in a war. You have to get the vaccines and then distribute them in an optimized way that keeps changing," he said.

What Netanyahu didn't say is that the troops in this war were not in uniform, yet Israel could rely on them. The roots of the health organizations that carried out the campaign went back over a century. Israel had been laying the necessary groundwork, based on the intimate ties between the people and their health system, since well before the founding of the state.

Call the Data Crunchers

A few years after his early triumph—or beginner's luck—in convincing the Israeli government to stockpile drugs in case of a pandemic, Ran Balicer decided it was time to leave military service. "As an epidemiologist who loves data and wanted to change the world, it was clear where I needed to go." Not a hospital or the health ministry. "I chose Clalit," Balicer said.

Clalit is the largest health maintenance organization (HMO) in Israel and one of the largest in the world. It covers just over half the population. It was "the hand that rocks the cradle," in Balicer's words. The joke was that if you throw a stone you will hit a Clalit clinic. Go to the most remote place in Israel and there will be a house and a tree and a clinic.

"As someone who loves data, I saw that there was so much untapped potential there," Balicer told us. Now this seems obvious, but back in the early 2000s the field of "data science" didn't exist. The main tool to extract insights from data, a type of artificial intelligence called machine learning, was in its infancy. To Balicer, however, data was at the heart of the future of health.

In his view, the existing paradigm of medicine was broken. It was reactive. Generally, you only went to the doctor when you felt sick. By then, for many conditions, much of the damage had already been done. If that same condition—including the two biggest killers, heart disease and cancer—had been caught earlier, so much suffering and death could have been prevented.

The new frontier was to replace reactive medicine with predictive medicine. "There are two ways to predict the future," he explained. "Either you get a really good crystal ball or you use data." And Clalit had a lot of data.

To pursue his vision of predictive medicine, he founded the Clalit Research Institute. The idea was to take doctors, epidemiologists, and public health specialists and train them to swim in the new world of data science.

How could data predict the future? "Let's say you have complete medical records for a million people going back twenty years," Balicer said. "You pour all that data into the computer and ask it, is there some pattern, some signature that shows up just as a cancer or heart disease is starting to develop? You tell me what disease you want to predict and I have the machinery ready, right here and right now." He tapped his laptop. "And we can create a predictive model on the fly. By looking for a disease's signature in the data, we can predict for people today that five years from now they will have the problem, and take action today to prevent the problem."

When Balicer started with this approach in 2009, it took him two years to produce the first predictive model. When COVID-19 came around, it took his team a few weeks. They had it in hand *before* the virus landed in Israel.

Balicer and his team were no longer an obscure band of data crunchers. They were on the front lines of the war against a deadly virus. And they knew with surprising accuracy how it would play out.

In an article in a prominent newspaper that appeared in March 2020—when only a small number of cases had been discovered in Israel—Balicer included a graph that showed the number of serious COVID-19 cases coming in three waves of growing intensity, the highest one touching the ominous dotted red line at which all of Israel's intensive care units would be overwhelmed. Israel was then at the beginning of the first wave. The rest of the graph predicted what would happen as the country imposed lockdowns and eased them.

The accuracy of the predictions were uncanny. But the models from Balicer's team were not just predicting, they were able to reduce Israel's fatality rate. Using a model they developed that was shared across the country, Clalit was able to rank individual patients into risk categories. Everyone in Category 5—the highest-risk group—would get a phone call warning them of the danger, coaching them on how to protect themselves, and urging the use of remote care rather than visiting a clinic. And it worked. After the model was put into place, serious cases in the top-risk category dropped by almost half and in the elevated category by almost a quarter.

This achievement saved lives. An October 2020 study comparing case fatality rates (CFRs—the percentage of cases that become fatal) in Italy, Spain, South Korea, Israel, Sweden, and Canada found that Israel had the lowest in every age category. The difference was particularly pronounced in the sixty-to-eighty age group: Israel's CFR was less than half that of the next best country, South Korea, and less than one-quarter the rate of the worst performers, Sweden and Italy. In terms of overall "excess mortality," which measures deaths compared to the previous year, Israel's rate was at least 50 percent below that of the United States, the UK, Italy, and Spain. While many factors likely contributed to Israel's lower case fatality rate, Balicer said that the impact of his team's data-driven warning system was "significant."

Without the reservoirs of health data that Israel's HMOs had collected over the past quarter century, no amount of data science could produce the predictive medicine that saved lives in this case and continually throughout Israel's health system.

If Israel did not have this rare data trove—and no less important, a willingness and ability to share and use it—Israel would not have become the test bed for Pfizer's vaccine rollout in the first place. This was where the stories of Albert Bourla, Benjamin Netanyahu, and Ran Balicer came together.

Poster Country

"The basic deal I'm willing to make," Netanyahu had told Bourla, "is vaccines for data. I don't know a single other country in the world that is able to do this." This was true in more ways than one. It was not just that Israel had decades of health data for millions of people that it could compare against the vaccine's real-world performance. It was something even rarer: the willingness of the leadership and citizens to *share* critical performance data with Pfizer, a pharmaceutical company.

In the Real-World Epidemiological Evidence Collaboration Agreement, as it was delicately called, Pfizer committed to put Israel at the front of the line, providing enough vaccines to inoculate the entire adult population as quickly as possible. In exchange, Israel agreed to provide a wide array of aggregated epidemiological data. This arrangement would allow Pfizer and the world to obtain the most highly anticipated data point: actual vaccine effectiveness. Pfizer also needed the specific characteristics of those who contracted the disease despite being fully vaccinated—so-called breakthrough infections. It was critical to know not just how well the vaccine was working but who was most at risk for it *not* working.

Netanyahu was open, even proud of the vaccines-for-data deal. "Israel will be a global model state," he said. "Israel will share with Pfizer and with the entire world the statistical data that will help develop strategies for defeating the coronavirus."

The agreement stipulated that no individual-level health information would be shared, and that the relevant research would be published in a prominent medical journal. Israel would also comply with its health data privacy law, similar to HIPAA in the United States.

Medical data is the most sensitive data there is and, at least in the United States, sharing it with either big companies or the government is controversial. A 2019 survey of 1,010 Americans found that only 16 percent were willing to share their medical data with pharmaceutical companies, and 9 percent with the government. Only 36 percent of Americans were willing to share their medical data with their health insurer.

Not surprisingly, a critical factor in determining a person's comfort level with sharing medical data is trust. In a 2018 poll in the UK and France, 94 percent said that trust was important to them when it came to sharing data. And in Israel, HMOs are among the country's most trusted institutions; they are the repositories of everyone's medical data.

But in this case it was not the HMOs that had made the data-sharing deal with Pfizer, it was the national government, and specifically one person: Benjamin Netanyahu. Politicians, in Israel as in most places, are among the least trusted members of society. In just about any other wealthy democracy, a politician hoping to gain popularity, and eventual reelection, on an "I shared your data to get vaccines" platform would be insane. But in Israel, it was the opposite. Netanyahu was hoping to ride the deal to victory in the next election. How could this be?

Coming Together

Yonatan Adiri served as the chief technology officer for the late president Shimon Peres and then founded a digital health start-up, Healthy.io. To explain the element of trust in the vaccination campaign, he launched into a history lesson.

"Well before the birth of the state, the founders made a fundamental decision: health care had to be universally accessible," he said. "By law, everyone must belong to one of the four nonprofit health funds, and the funds are not allowed to deny coverage."

By the late 1980s, however, the system had decayed. Weighed down with stifling bureaucracy, wait times rose as quality fell. In 1995, this crisis led to a sweeping structural reform. Members were allowed to switch from one health fund to another. The funds couldn't compete on price—health care was mostly free—so they had to compete on quality, cost-efficiency, and convenience.

Then, in 2012, came the revolution that redefined the competition: the system went mobile. As a founder of an app-based health start-up, Adiri started to get animated when describing how far these formerly stodgy health funds have come. "The mobile apps of the Israeli health care system are fantastic. I would say that they could go head-to-head with the top ten apps that you would find in the Google Play Store or the App Store. And these are nonprofit state-sponsored organizations," he gushed.

Each health fund (or HMO) now saw its digital arm as key to its competitive edge. The funds ran TV ads showcasing the services they offered via the app. One ad showed a couple at a restaurant. While the husband pestered the waiter for a minute about the menu, his pregnant wife set up an appointment for a checkup via the app. Another ad showed a mother getting a virtual live checkup with a doctor in the middle of the night without her sick daughter having to leave her bed. The ad showed the mother using a device created by an Israeli start-up and provided by the health fund to check her daughter's symptoms, giving the doctor all the information needed to diagnose and write a digital prescription that could be filled in any pharmacy.

A key aspect here is that the health funds are paid by the number of members, not by the number of tests or procedures ordered. This arrangement means that their incentive is to keep their customers out of the hospital by focusing on primary, preventative, and remote care. That the health fund, for its own reasons, shares your desire to stay healthy and out of the hospital helps build trust in the system.

Though the health funds were not deliberately preparing for a pandemic, their emphasis on decentralized care—spread out to neighborhood clinics and individual homes—turned out to be a great advantage, both for treating COVID-19 cases and then for the vaccination campaign.

"One of the reasons Israeli health care is so effective," Ran Balicer told us, "is that it is very personal and community-oriented." The better people know their doctor and neighborhood clinic, and the easier it is to get them continuously engaged, the earlier problems will be caught and the less people will need to go to the hospital. This community orientation also leads to trust.

"The best way to deal with hesitancy is for people to see that everyone around them is getting vaccinated and to hear from a trusted authority—citing high-quality local data—that it is safe and effective," Balicer said. "That trust cannot be produced at the last minute, it has to be built up over years."

Operation "Give a Shoulder"

Israel's vaccination campaign began on December 20, 2020. By January 15, 2021, over 80 percent of Israelis over the age of sixty had received at least one dose. Thus, in less than one month, Israel had vaccinated the vast majority of those most at risk, plus over one-third of the population aged sixteen to sixty.

The world looked on in awe. As the *Telegraph* put it, "[Israel] is not just ahead of all others but the pace of its rollout is astonishing. It begs the question: how is it being done? And what might other countries learn from it?"

Some people assumed the explanation was that Israel was a small, compact country. But the facts didn't bear this theory out. Surprisingly, many smaller countries were doing worse than larger ones. By March 1, small and efficient Switzerland and Denmark had administered under ten vaccine doses per one hundred people. The United States and the United Kingdom, meanwhile, were way ahead of these nations, having administered about three times more—thirty-two and twenty-seven doses per one hundred people, respectively. But Israel was at another level. At eighty-seven doses per one hundred, Israel had succeeded at vaccinating over twice as many of its citizens as the U.S. and the UK, and almost ten times as many as countries like Switzerland and Denmark.

Another part of this mystery was how the Israeli campaign managed to reach so many younger adults. By March 16, three months after the vaccination campaign began, nine out of ten Israelis over forty years old were vaccinated. But what about under forty years old? Many people below age forty didn't feel personally threatened by the virus. In addition, by that time nearly all the at-risk population had been vaccinated, so protecting them seemed less urgent.

Here the vaccination campaign started to get creative. The city of Tel

Aviv began offering free pizza, hummus, and kanafeh—a popular Middle Eastern pastry—to whoever came through two pop-up vaccination centers. A week later the city parked a mobile vaccination center outside a popular bar. This time, the deal was a shot for a shot—free drinks, no appointment necessary. One town enlisted DJs to attract a younger crowd.

Another critical element was gaining the endorsement of the leading Haredi rabbis. This job fell to Ran Balicer, who joined a weekly meeting of Haredi doctors to answer their questions. "I've never sweated so much in a briefing; they were very well informed," Balicer said. By the end, they were convinced, and a short time later some of the top rabbis issued an official ruling that according to Jewish law everyone should get vaccinated. From that point on, vaccination rates in Haredi communities—which had lagged well behind most of the country—rose to about the national average.

Israelis became wrapped up in warding off a common foe. "It's really being treated like a war . . . and Israel is experienced in battles," said Allon Moses, director of the infectious diseases department at Jerusalem's Hadassah Hospital. It's very similar to battle: you have an enemy, you have the right ammunition . . . and you just have to deliver," he told the *Telegraph*. As Ran Balicer explained, "We know how to switch gears in an emergency. And so when the whistle is blown, our teams know how to create a large-scale plan."

In other countries, vaccination campaigns became tied up in knots by complex rules determining who would get vaccinated first. In Israel, speed took precedence over prioritizing. Vaccinations were open to health care workers, those with a high-risk condition, and anyone over sixty. But it was fine if you showed up and said you were taking care of your elderly parents. They would take your word for it and wave you in.

Since everyone was getting vaccinated so quickly, there was little stigma about "jumping the line." (Anyway, Israelis are not good at standing in line to begin with.) It was also important not to waste any vaccine that, once thawed from a deep freeze, needed to be used or thrown away. If they ran out of "customers" at the end of the day, the health workers would offer shots to anyone coming by, regardless of age.

Benjamin Netanyahu has, over his long career, been one of the most divisive leaders in Israeli politics. In the five elections under four years, there was one dividing line that stood out above all the others: for or against Bibi.

Half the country tended to trust Netanyahu; the other half distrusted, if not despised, him. In such a situation, it might be expected that Netanyahu's ability to gain across-the-board support for a vaccination campaign would be a nonstarter. Especially since there were other objective reasons for Israelis to hesitate.

The first possible reason for distrust was that the Pfizer jab was based on a new, mRNA-based technology that had never been used in a vaccine. The second was that the vaccine had been developed and tested in a matter of weeks rather than years. Then there was a third factor, which, unlike the other two, was a hurdle of trust that was unique to the Israeli case: being the world's "guinea pig."

While other countries could, and did, look to Israel to see if the vaccine was as safe and effective as claimed, Israelis had no such assurance.

In a way, being an early adopter is a form of trust. Like Clalit, Israel's second largest health fund, Maccabi, had been keeping electronic medical records for decades. Varda Shalev was the founder and CEO of Maccabitech, the fund's Big Data innovation center. "Start-ups sometimes come to me from other countries and say, we want to buy your data. I tell them that's not how we work—we are not a shopping mall," Shalev told us. "We see the work with a start-up as a partnership. We are part of a community."

Shalev says that she was always looking for "win-win-win," meaning the patient, the start-up, and Maccabi all benefit. The spirit of cooperation is infectious, she said: "Long before COVID, we would ask our customers, when you are doing blood, urine, or other tests, will you let us take a little more for our Biobank and use this for research purposes? Well over 50 percent say yes. No questions about who will profit, no questions about privacy, no request to be compensated . . . nothing. People here just want to help."

This mindset endured through COVID-19, during which you had a Big Pharma company making a deal with a polarizing leader to offer an untried vaccine technology that had been rushed to market in record time. Why did Israelis so willingly embrace the idea of being first? Why did they line up to be vaccinated at an incredible rate? Why did they listen to a leader they might have just been in the streets protesting against?

That they did says a lot about Israeli society. The pandemic created a natural experiment across countless countries and cultures. Which would be torn apart and which would come together? In this test, Israeli society demonstrated a core strength: a deep current of solidarity that allows Israelis to toggle between acting as individuals and as a collective, creating a unique balance of both.

Chapter Nine

NO PLACE LIKE HOME

*When I was growing up, most of the tourists visiting Israel
came to see the Holy Land. Today they come to see the
Start-up Nation. Israel used to be a place people came to visit
the past. Now it's also a place to see the future.*

—Micah Goodman

"How scared are chief executives about cyber attacks?" That was the opening of a Bloomberg News article covering the annual World Economic
Forum in 2015. "Scared enough that dozens of top brass showed up for
a Davos breakfast with Nadav Zafrir, former commander of the Israel
Defense Forces' technology and intelligence unit, 8200, and founder of
the IDF's Cyber Command. . . . Zafrir looks like the movie version of a
counterterrorist."

The article went on to name-check the Davos A-listers—the CEO
of Citigroup; the president and CEO of Loews; the cofounder of Carlyle
Group; and top Silicon Valley venture investors—who were captivated
by Zafrir as he was interviewed in a fireside chat by Thomas Friedman of
the *New York Times*. This Davos breakfast was hosted by Start-Up Nation
Central, a Tel Aviv–based nonprofit organization that connects Israel's
tech ecosystem with companies, governments, and NGOs around the
world looking to Israeli innovators to solve their most pressing challenges.
According to Start-Up Nation Central's research, in the five years leading
up to 2023, the Israeli cybersecurity sector raised about 10 percent of all

capital in the sector globally. This was more than the entire European cyber sector raised during the same period.

Zafrir had made it to the pinnacle of three fast-growing sectors: fintech, cybersecurity, and venture capital. Investors in Zafrir's Team8 included Singapore's sovereign wealth fund, Barclays, Walmart, Moody's, Airbus, AT&T, Eric Schmidt's venture capital fund, and Bessemer.

While cyber and cloud security might seem only of concern to the types of CEOs and investors who show up at a Davos breakfast, it would be more accurate to look at it as part of the basic infrastructure that permeates our daily lives—like the water supply, electric grid, and the internet. It's the infrastructure that enables all the others.

Health care systems are particularly vulnerable. A malicious piece of ransomware called WannaCry crippled the UK's National Health Service in May 2017. Up to seventy thousand devices—including MRI scanners, blood storage refrigerators, and surgical room equipment—were affected. All told, the self-propagating WannaCry attack, which demanded $300 per computer to obtain a decryption key, affected about 200,000 computers in 150 countries.

In September 2020, as the pandemic was raging, a ransomware attack hit US Universal Health Services—a company that operates in thirty-eight states. One of their doctors sent out an SOS: "All but one of our cath labs are down and our sister hospital has no cath labs. They are transferring patients to us. No anesthesia services. It took out the outpatient offices as well. I'm here trying to figure out what's going on with my patients."

Dozens of Fortune 500 companies were now clients of Team8 startups. With all this traction, Zafrir and his wife, Maya, decided to uproot their family (three young kids) and bring them to New York City to be closer to his customers. It was sometimes difficult to be in Tel Aviv, six thousand miles from the financial capital of the world and even farther from Silicon Valley.

Soon after Zafrir's family settled in, life in the U.S. became very comfortable: "My daughter was a high school freshman. She was doing great. The college application counselors told us she was destined for the Ivy League. My son, a couple years behind her, would be on a similar track." Four years later, Zafrir turned his life upside down again. This time, it was to get his kids closer to a different kind of action. "I want my children to serve in the army," he told us. So he uprooted his family to return to Israel.

In eleventh grade, Israeli teenagers around the country receive a terse notice from the IDF with a date for them to show up at an induction center to take various tests. Shortly after, they can go online to see their "*manila*" (as in manila folder), listing different units for which they are eligible, some of which require further tryouts. They can rank their preferred options, which may or may not influence their eventual assignments.

Zafrir had a reality check: "I knew that if we didn't move back soon, my kids would get more and more comfortable with their lives, which was a mix of cushy living and a rat race. . . . While they might ultimately wind up with a degree from Harvard, they will have never truly served something larger than themselves."

So the pull of Israeli life is what brought Nadav Zafrir back to Israel. This was not a trivial business decision, since many of the company's customers and investors were based in the U.S.

It is hard to imagine a tech CEO from anywhere else deciding to relocate so their children could serve in the military. It spoke to many aspects of what makes Israeli society different: the instinctive commitment to a larger cause, including contributing to the country; the essential need to be part of a group; the recognition that there is something healthy about Israeli society that should not be missed.

In the past, many of Israel's top entrepreneurs were pulled by opposing magnets: the pull to live in the market they were addressing (usually the

U.S.) and the pull to not miss out on the strengths of Israeli society. Israeli venture capitalist Chemi Peres has thought a lot about the three years he spent living in Silicon Valley during a previous tech boom. "The quality of life—personal life and business life—was wonderful. And, yet, every night during those three years, I would stay awake thinking something didn't feel right. I knew it was not home, not my community, not my country."

The pandemic era accelerated the realignment of these magnets. The Israeli magnet became stronger, while the pull to live in foreign markets became weaker. It's a trend that is also visible among Israelis working as senior executives in some of the world's largest corporations.

The case of Zafrir and his family is a good example of why Israelis would want to give their children the unique experiences they had growing up and starting out in life. This is part of the increased pull of the Israeli magnet. The other part is on the business side. The need for Israelis, even those who have risen within big foreign tech companies, to move to the mother ship city is lessening.

The Land of Multinationals

Michal Braverman-Blumenstyk grew up in Yad Eliyahu, a working class neighborhood in Tel Aviv. Her mother was a teacher and her father owned a laundromat. "Belonging to the pioneering generation, my father had this notion of what it means to be Israeli—someone strong intellectually and physically. He raced me, played chess with me, and pushed me to take risks," she recalled. She would get into fights with boys three years older than her. Her father wasn't worried. "He'd say, 'Never mind, next time you'll win.'"

Braverman-Blumenstyk spent her military service in an air force electronic warfare unit, during which time she met her future husband. After their military service, they both decided to study in the United States, he in pediatric dentistry and she in computer science. She was on the PhD track at Columbia University, but after taking leave for a year to work in the private sector, she was hooked. "All of a sudden, once I started developing products and interacting with users, I thought, 'Wow, this is immediate satisfaction,'" she said.

So, to the consternation of Columbia and her parents, Braverman-Blumenstyk dropped out of her PhD program and, some years later, headed back to Israel to work in a series of start-ups. She ended up at Cyota, a cybersecurity company that pioneered the use of artificial intelligence for security and was eventually bought by RSA, the industry-leading data security transmission company in the U.S. One of Cyota's founders, Naftali Bennett, would later serve as Israel's prime minister.

After the acquisition, Braverman-Blumenstyk became the head of RSA Israel. RSA ultimately entered a joint venture with Microsoft, after which Microsoft's soon-to-be CEO, Satya Nadella, asked Braverman-Blumenstyk to relocate to the company's headquarters in Redmond, Washington, and launch Microsoft's flagship cybersecurity center there. She not only refused to relocate but made a strong case that Microsoft's global cyber center should be in Israel:

> I told Satya, in cyber the fact that I'm in Israel is a huge advantage. Where else in the world do you have, in an area of ten square kilometers, a slew of multinational cyber centers, start-ups, and AI scientists who all know each other? Even though we might be competitors, we exchange ideas. All this interaction creates a unique sandbox, where innovation just rolls.

Nadella relented, and Braverman-Blumenstyk remained in Israel, taking on a global role as the chief technology officer of Microsoft's cloud and AI security division. In early 2020 she also became the head of Microsoft Israel. Braverman-Blumenstyk made the case to stay in Israel based on the company's global interest. Attracting and keeping top talent was critical for Microsoft and, as a working mother, she believed that Israel was a better place to raise families. "Israeli women," she explained, "are less obligated to choose between having children and launching a career." At Columbia, she already stood out as one of three women in the computer science department, but then she did something unheard of. Just like in Israel, if she found herself in a pinch, she would bring her baby to class.

"Weaving children into work is the norm in Israel," she told us. So when Microsoft Israel built its new headquarters, Braverman-Blumenstyk insisted on an Israeli twist—"family rooms" with workstations and a large play area in the same open space. In Israel, workplaces are not treated as child-free zones.

Braverman-Blumenstyk is most animated when discussing her work in diversifying Israel's growing tech labor force. She has been a champion for bringing more Haredim and Arabs into the tech sector. She thinks that the Israeli tech workforce can be doubled, from one in ten workers today to one fifth of Israel's labor force.

Her experience at the helm of Microsoft in Israel has also put her at the forefront of a fast-moving trend. When we wrote *Start-Up Nation* in 2009, there were fewer than 150 multinational companies with operations in Israel. As of 2023, the number has grown to more than four hundred, according to Start-Up Nation Finder, representing thirty-five countries spanning North America, South America, Europe, Africa, and Asia.

The companies include tech giants like Microsoft, Amazon, Google, Apple, IBM, Infosys, Intuit, Salesforce, Meta, and Intel and life sciences and pharmaceutical companies such as Pfizer, Moderna, Medtronic, and Merck. The tech and health multinationals are logical fits for setting up innovation R&D operations in Israel. But more recently, other companies on this same trajectory have included automakers Mercedes-Benz and GM, heavy-equipment manufacturer John Deere, and global consumer companies such as Coca-Cola, PepsiCo, Walmart, and Procter & Gamble.

These global behemoths are building operations in Israel not to access its local market (it's tiny) or to serve as a logistical hub to reach other regional markets (they can do that more seamlessly from nearby countries such as the United Arab Emirates). They are setting up in Israel to solve problems through unconventional technology-based innovation.

The new opportunity for rising Israeli tech stars like Braverman-Blumenstyk, who want to develop into top corporate executives in multinationals, is to do it without giving up their rooted, communal life in Israel. By insisting on living in Israel, they, too, are now part of the magnet that attracts other multinationals to set up shop there. Suddenly, the "small pond" of the country's tech ecosystem has become a lot bigger.

We have also increasingly observed this dynamic with start-ups that are acquired by global companies. For the first couple decades of Israel's start-up boom, when these Israeli companies were acquired, they would relocate, often to the Bay Area or New York City. But then there was the Waze effect.

"Should I Stay or Should I Go?"

Waze was the navigation start-up designed to help drivers avoid traffic jams and take the quickest possible route to their destination. But the founders of Waze pursued a different path from most Israeli start-ups, which tended to develop technologies that became buried deep inside big companies like Qualcomm, Intel, IBM, and Microsoft. In general, selling directly to consumers was not an Israeli specialty. Their strength was in the initial innovation, not in design, sales, and distribution in faraway markets that Israeli entrepreneurs didn't fully understand.

Waze began its life in 2006 as a nonprofit called FreeMap. It was the quintessential people-powered app, effectively extending Wikipedia's crowdsourcing revolution to navigation. Before Wikipedia, encyclopedias were painstakingly compiled by companies that would sell them to consumers. Before Waze, mapping companies did the same. The founders of Waze—Ehud Shabtai, who had the original idea, was later joined by Uri Levine and brothers Amir and Gili Shinar—had a crazy idea: What if maps could be crowdsourced by the drivers themselves?

As drivers used the app, streets would appear on the map where they had driven. The idea seemed to make no sense because of the chicken-and-egg problem: It needed drivers to use the app for the map to develop, but why would drivers use the app if there was no map? Waze's luck—or brilliance—was that it was able to tap into the passion of "early adopters," those individuals who don't mind if a product is not perfect, or even functional, if they can be part of building it.

The social element was no less important. As you used the app, you could see your fellow Waze users—called "Wazers"—moving around the map with you. Today, with thousands of users around you, this is no big deal. But in the beginning, it was a revelation. One of the aspects that hooked CEO Noam Bardin on the company was when his wife said that seeing other Wazers gave her the feeling that she was "not alone."

Bit by bit, the maps accumulated, first in Israel and slowly in other countries. In places like Costa Rica and Malaysia, Wazers helped produce the first navigable maps for parts of the country. The more drivers used it, the more useful the map became. Eventually, there were enough users to show traffic jams and allow the app to steer drivers around them.

In July 2012, Waze announced that it had 20 million users, half of whom had joined in the previous six months. Wazers had used the app to drive more than 3.2 billion miles. Waze got an unexpected boost in September of that year when Apple Maps was released, because that app included a range of bizarre mistakes, such as phantom airports and missing or misplaced cities. Apple CEO Tim Cook issued a public apology for the "frustrations" the app caused, pointing users to alternatives, such as "Bing, MapQuest, and Waze." This mention boosted Waze's downloads by 40 percent. It was such a pivotal moment that every year the company would celebrate "Tim Cook Day" to commemorate the event.

Facebook, Apple, and Google lined up like suitors to buy Waze, which wasn't out in the market trying to sell. The company hadn't even hired an investment banker at the time. In the end, Google won the bidding with what at the time seemed like an enormous sum for an Israeli start-up—over $1 billion. As a headline in TechCrunch, a popular Silicon Valley news site covering the start-up world, put it, "WTF Is Waze and Why Did Google Just Pay a Billion+ for It?" It was especially puzzling because Google Maps was already leading the world of online maps by far. Why buy another map app?

The difference was social. None of the existing tech giants—Google, Microsoft, and Apple—had a social component. By contrast, as the *New York Times* put it, "With Waze, the mob is the map, and like a mob, it can be churning with energy." About one-third of Waze users were sharing information about slowdowns, speed traps, and road closures. And their participation allowed Waze to update routes in real time.

Waze "created a culture where you can really help others," said Bret McVey, a graphic designer in Omaha, Nebraska, who had contributed about 280,000 changes to Waze's maps in one year. The most dedicated map editors gained direct access to Waze employees around the clock to make urgent updates, such as for road closures. And millions of regular users reported road conditions in real time. No other app had this level of participation, immediacy, and user impact.

Waze had set a new bar for ambitious Israeli entrepreneurs. According to *Business Insider*, "In an instant, the whole 'Startup Nation' decided to quit aiming for fast exits and build billion-dollar companies instead."

Seven years after the 2013 exit, during a global pandemic, Waze co-founder Uri Levine claimed that "Google's acquisition of Waze gave birth to fifty other Israeli unicorns." ("Unicorn" is start-up slang for privately held companies valued over $1 billion.) In the popular imagination,

Waze was the first Israeli start-up to make the leap above the $1 billion valuation bar. Actually, there had been others before Waze, but they were companies with technologies deeply embedded in large companies, not something that millions of people used every day. Levine was arguing that Waze had inspired other start-ups to aim higher.

It is true that Waze demonstrated to Israeli entrepreneurs that they could build larger stand-alone companies—rather than start-ups to be quickly flipped—and this was an important development in the maturation of Israel's tech economy. But even more important, yet less understood at the time, Waze's executives insisted on keeping the company in Israel. "Facebook balked, and Google committed," the newspaper *Haaretz* reported. In an interview with *Business Insider*, Levine said, "What made Google pretty attractive for us was that No. 1, the company stayed in Israel."

After the Waze experience, an increasing number of Israeli entrepreneurs began to draw a red line: they would only agree to sell, even when life-changing wealth hung in the balance, if the foreign acquirer would allow the Israeli executives to continue to live in Israel, raise their families in Israel, have their children serve in the army, and give their employees the option to stay and build Israel. Remaining in Israel became nonnegotiable.

Counting unicorns has become passé since the global market slowdown in 2023. Still, it is a helpful measure to compare start-up systems across countries and over time. As of 2023, Israel had eighty unicorns, which put Israel fourth in the world, behind only the U.S., China, and India. Israel has about five percent share of the world's unicorns, which is forty-four times its relative share of the global population.

Valuations can also be a measure of where entrepreneurs are setting their sights. Alan Feld, dubbed "Israel's tech barometer" by the business newspaper *Globes*, is the founder and managing partner of Vintage Investment Partners. Vintage manages over $3.6 billion as of 2023, and its annual conference is a premier event convening Israel's top venture fund managers and CEOs. Feld pointed out that, while Israeli entrepreneurs used to target unicorn status, at the height of the venture capital boom year of 2021 some were reaching decacorn—$10 billion—valuation levels. The boom didn't last, but the change in attitude may be more lasting, even if dormant by necessity during market doldrums. "It's not true of all entrepreneurs, of course, but enough of a critical mass of entrepreneurs has decided they want to build their companies into larger, long standing companies, which I think is extremely exciting."

A more consistent measure of a company's size and maturity is its actual revenues. In 2013, there was only one tech company in Israel producing over $1 billion in annual revenue. A decade later, there were nearly a dozen at that level and many more earning over $100 million annually. From 2018 through 2023, some of the world's largest investors that mainly invest in private companies—such as Insight Partners, Blackstone, and General Atlantic—opened Israeli offices.

Lifestyle and societal factors have contributed to Israel being home to a higher concentration of innovation centers for multinational companies than any country in the world. But Israel is now birthing its own multinationals at the precise moment that the AI revolution is entering a new chapter—what venture capital investor Chemi Peres calls "the fourth decade of Israeli high tech."

The 1990s, according to Peres, were mainly about developing technologies to sell to multinationals. The 2000s were defined by turning Israeli technologies into actual stand-alone businesses. The 2010s were the "unicorn decade," Peres said. "That decade was about growing fast and in an unsustainable way to achieve scale and unicorn status." Which brings us to the 2020s: "We are connected to the world, we have data, AI, and automation. We are now entering the fourth decade, where companies are ready now to become major global players. Israeli companies are now working on a ticket to the Fortune 500 club." That is, multinational companies in the leading technology sectors, headquartered in Israel.

The Making of the Fourth Decade

The Japanese engineer couldn't contain himself. His hand shot up and, interrupting the speaker, he asked, "Excuse me, Professor, are you implying that it is possible to detect a vehicle with one camera?" The assumption at the time was, just as people used two eyes to give them depth perception, a car would need two cameras. The professor had come all the way from Israel to give a technical lecture to a select group of Toyota engineers about what, back in November 1998, sounded like science fiction: computer vision.

The young professor responded: "Sure, I think it's possible. Can't you drive a car with just one eye?" and continued with his talk. Professor Amnon Shashua had no idea that this question from the audience would lead him to found the largest company in Israel and to a pivotal role in the technological revolution of our age: artificial intelligence. Back in 1998, he was focused on making automobile computer vision compact, efficient, and inexpensive so it could become standard in all cars and save lives.

Shashua was born in Ramat Gan in 1960. As a child, he built gadgets—communication devices, amplifiers, a tape recorder, a walkie-talkie. "It was all about electronics," he told us. He went to a technical high school near home that had just introduced a new subject: computer science. "I was fascinated. Until then I had thought that the only way to do things was with hardware. But here they showed how you could solve problems with software. I was hooked."

He started learning programming languages in school, and during the summers he worked at a bank. The bank had a computer that used punch cards—without a screen. His supervisor told him to feed the machine cards in batches of ten. Shashua asked, "Okay, but why? What is it doing?" The supervisor responded, "I don't know, this is what you need to do."

While completing this mindless task, Shashua figured out the algorithm. "I went to my boss and explained it to him. I was thirteen years old. And he said, "Okay, you're not in the right place." The bank moved Shashua to another department. Shashua's new boss asked him to program the computer to adjust loan payments for inflation. "It was very exciting. I made money. I had responsibility, I solved problems using my mind and not using my hands." And all this was eight years before the first personal computer came out.

In 1978, at age eighteen, Shashua was drafted. He considered trying out for an intelligence unit. "But my life path was clear to me, I would do a PhD and become a professor of computer science." So he chose to do something different. He went into the armored corps, where he rose to be a tank company commander. "It was a fascinating period. You learn to work under stress, have responsibility, solve problems, and work with people." He fought in the 1982 Lebanon War.

After the army, he wanted to go straight to Tel Aviv University to study computer science, but his non-science grades weren't good enough to get in. He went to the head of the department to lay out all his practical experience, but was told that rules are rules, no exceptions. "So this is where my army experience came in," Shashua said. "I asked the department head, 'Who is your boss?' He was kind of taken aback. He responded, 'Okay, it's the head of the school.'" The head of the school was impressed with Shashua's tenacity and decided to give him a chance. "The army trains you to always keep pushing through bureaucratic resistance. That's what I did."

After graduation, as he was thinking about the next step in his studies, he came across an article by Professor Shimon Ullman about the human eye. "All of a sudden, I'm reading about a biological computer. The field was part artificial intelligence, part perception, part computer vision." He applied to the Weizmann Institute of Science, where he worked with Ullman for two years. In 1987, Shashua wrote his first academic paper with Ullman. It was about how the eye's computer decided what was important. "It received a lot of attention. That was my ticket to MIT."

Shashua finished his doctorate in three years and then a postdoc under Tomaso Poggio, one of MIT's star faculty. Poggio arranged a faculty position for Shashua at MIT. But there was a problem. "I had promised my wife, Anat, that we would return to Israel after five years. When the time came, I wanted to stay and teach at MIT. She said, 'For all I care, you can go wait tables, but we're returning to Israel.'" The pull of Israeli life drew them home.

Back in Israel, Shashua started a postdoc at Hebrew University in Jerusalem and later joined the faculty, where he still holds a professorship today. He also started a company. Shashua recruited some of his students and friends and founded CogniTens, a company built on the 3D optical scanning technology that he had developed in Poggio's lab at MIT. Shashua made plenty of business connections during his first start-up experience, but the most significant started as a social one.

Anat Shashua had a close childhood friend, Idit, and from time to time Anat and Idit would bring their husbands to all get together. "I didn't really know Idit's husband, Ziv, but he was a business guy and I had a lot of questions as an academic building a start-up. He got more and more interested." Ziv Aviram had run a number of established companies. One day in 1998, Shashua called Aviram when he returned from Japan. "We need to have coffee."

After the lecture at Toyota, where an engineer interrupted him with that fateful question, Shashua had been swarmed by engineers wanting to know more about his idea for detecting a car with one camera. They explained that a competing company was working on doing this with two cameras, which was much more expensive and complicated. They offered Shashua $200,000 to build a working prototype.

Shashua and Aviram dove into the world of road safety. It was a huge unsolved problem. "I told Ziv, the industry has it wrong. They are looking at radars and two-camera systems. If we can do it better and cheaper with one camera, the regulators will require companies to buy it because it saves lives. Every car will come with it. And we will have a huge advantage because we'll be working on a solution that nobody believes would work. So we will be in a completely blue ocean. We have two hundred thousand dollars. Let's start a company." Aviram said he would sleep on it. The next day he agreed.

The year 1999 was both a great and a terrible time to start a company. The "internet bubble" was in full swing, but all those investment funds were backing internet companies. Anything automotive was old-school. Aviram came up with a creative way to raise money—not from venture funds but through brokers for individual small investors. Within a week the company, now called Mobileye, had another million dollars.

It took eight years for their first product to be on the road. In 2007, GM, BMW, and Volvo launched Mobileye's EyeQ chip—the brains behind the camera—in their cars. From there the growth was exponential. It took another five years for the one-millionth chip to be shipped, and in 2015—just three years later—the ten-millionth chip. In the meantime, in 2014 Mobileye went public on the New York Stock Exchange. It was the biggest Israeli IPO to date, raising $1 billion at a $5.3 billion market cap.

By 2016, major carmakers were beginning to think about the next step: a driverless car. BMW knew they couldn't build this technology on their own, so they formed a partnership with Intel and Mobileye. Intel was also thinking about how they could become a player in the autonomous vehicle future. Both companies needed Mobileye, which by this time had vast experience and real-world data from millions of cars.

In 2017, the close working relationship between Intel and Mobileye resulted in what Shashua called a "reverse merger." Intel bought Mobileye for $15.3 billion, by far the largest sum ever paid for an Israeli company. Shashua made two conditions for the sale: that the company stay in Jerusalem and that Intel's autonomous-driving division would come under Mobileye, not the other way around. Also that year, Ziv Aviram retired, leaving Shashua as President and CEO.

As part of Intel, Mobileye grew even faster. Mobileye expanded from about eight hundred employees to over three thousand. In 2021, Mobileye announced that its chips were in 100 million cars, preventing untold numbers of accidents and saving lives. Mobileye had captured 80 percent of the advanced-collision-avoidance market. And on October 22, 2022, Mobileye made history again by going public for a second time on the NASDAQ stock exchange.

As of July 2023, Mobileye was valued at over $32 billion, about the value of the next two largest Israeli companies combined. Mobileye's revenue alone was just short of $2 billion in 2022. Of its 3,500 employees globally, about 90 percent are based at its headquarters in Jerusalem. When Waze became the first consumer unicorn, it was impossible to imagine that just a decade later a company headquartered in Jerusalem would be worth thirty-two times as much.

Your Move, Humanity

It was 1985, in Hamburg. The world's new chess champion, twenty-two-year-old Garry Kasparov, stood in the center, surrounded by thirty-two computers. He went around the circle again and again, playing each one in turn. It took five hours, but he beat them all. If the computers could think, and talk, they might have said on behalf of their kind, "We'll be back."

In 1996, Kasparov squared off against a three-thousand-pound computer made by IBM. It was called Deep Blue. The computer won the first game, marking the first time a computer had beaten the world chess champion. But a game is not a match. Kasparov trounced the computer in the next game. The next two games were draws, followed by two wins by Kasparov. Humanity triumphed.

But just a year later, the two faced off again. Deep Blue entered the ring with twice the power. It had, literally, studied Kasparov's every move.

The world's eyes were on the game. A banner above the table read "Kasparov vs. Deep Blue: The Rematch."

Kasparov started out strong in the first game. He was on his way to a win, when the computer did something strange. It made a ridiculous and fatal move. Its IBM operators resigned on behalf of the seemingly idiotic machine a few moves later. But in the next game the computer made a brilliant move that caused Kasparov to bury his head in his hands. The champion resigned ten moves later. He never beat the computer again. Speaking on behalf of humanity, one American news anchor commented on air, "We humans are trying to figure out our next move." A young Amnon Shashua was following all these developments from afar.

Many human abilities progress slowly, while AI keeps steaming ahead. Having conquered chess, AI moved on. In 2016, a program called AlphaGo, built by the British company DeepMind, took on the game of Go, beating Lee Sedol, a player at the highest level of the game. Go, a game of strategy comparable to chess, was invented in China more than 2,500 years ago. This was another milestone for AI because this ancient board game could not be conquered by the "brute force" method of trying all possible moves. In chess, after two moves there are four hundred possible next moves. In Go, that number is 130,000. Just over a year later, the company built AlphaGo Zero, which was trained not by human games but by playing itself. Within three days, AlphaGo Zero beat AlphaGo one hundred games to zero.

As impressive as these game-playing feats were, for Shashua the game that mattered was elsewhere. "People have been talking about artificial intelligence for many years, but it was never clear how it could be turned into a business," not just beating humans at games. The significance of autonomous vehicles, and the reason why there was a global race to build them, is that they were among the first applications of artificial intelligence that could reshape a very large industry in the real world. And, according to industry analysts, Mobileye was a global leader in developing this technology. While cars are not yet fully autonomous, chances are that you have a Mobileye chip in your car that could save the lives of you and your family.

But as a leader in applied AI, Shashua did not stop with applying this technology to cars. Along with Mobileye, Shashua has cofounded four other AI companies in four different industries. Already in 2010, Shashua and Aviram founded OrCam, which developed a clip-on camera that can help visually impaired people navigate day-to-day life. Eight percent of the population is "legally blind," meaning that they are not fully blind but their vision is so limited that it cannot be corrected by glasses. They can see that a bus stop or a sign is there, but they cannot read it. They can't see the denomination of a bill, or read a newspaper or a book.

OrCam's small device, which clicks on and off any pair of glasses, can read out all these things so the user can hear them. It can even recognize faces and tell the user who they are with. The company's website shows videos of people moved to tears when they use the device for the first time and realize that they can do simple tasks that will transform their lives, such as recognizing the items in a grocery store.

Helping the visually impaired is just the beginning. According to Aviram, who is OrCam's CEO, the company could become as large as Mobileye, as the potential is "infinite."

Next, Shashua applied AI to banking. He cofounded Israel's first digital bank, called One Zero, the first new Israeli bank of any kind authorized in decades. With no branches or tellers, the bank promises to use AI to give better, more personalized (and more human) financial advice to everyone, not just the wealthy.

After that, Shashua founded Mentee, a company designing a humanoid robot to assist with chores around the house. All this sounds like science fiction, but much less so since AI entered a new era.

Chatting Up a Storm

On November 22, 2022, the company OpenAI released a chatbot called ChatGPT. Located on a simple website, within weeks it became a global phenomenon. The internet was already flooded with chatbots. What was special about this one that made it feel like the biggest thing since Steve Jobs held up the first iPhone fifteen years before?

ChatGPT was powered by a new kind of AI that had been developing among computer scientists for a few years, but had never been accessible in an intuitive way to the general public before. Previously, AIs had been trained the way Deep Blue learned how to play chess, by being shown millions of human chess games.

ChatGPT was different. It was built by dumping growing portions of the entire internet into a pot, like a giant information soup. These soups were called "large language models" (LLMs) because they contained billions, possibly trillions, of words. The LLM behind the ChatGPT was called GPT-3.

LLMs form a new species called "generative AI," which can produce art, music, prose, poetry, fashion, books, PowerPoints, explainer videos, entire websites, apps, and so on, however clunky. Most powerfully, but less appreciated by the public, LLMs know how to write computer code. This ability allows them to reason and solve problems, since many problems can be expressed in the form of code.

Because they are fed on gigantic quantities of information and require computer heft, LLMs cost tens of millions of dollars just to run and billions to develop. They would seem to be the province of large companies and countries. While OpenAI began as a small start-up, it later received a $10 billion investment from Microsoft, bringing it under the roof of a tech giant. Previously, AI was built on what was called "big data." LLMs dwarfed "big data" as *War and Peace* does a business card. How could a small start-up in a small country possibly play in this arena?

This brings us to Shashua's fifth and perhaps most ambitious company: AI21 Labs. Founded in 2017 with an investment of a few tens of millions, not billions, of dollars, the start-up built an LLM that—according to some industry experts—rivaled GPT-3. Called Jurassic-1, it was built on hundreds of billions of parameters, definitely qualifying it for the "large" aspect of LLMs. While not released as a public chatbot like ChatGPT, Jurassic-1 went on the market directly competing with OpenAI and a small handful of other companies offering their LLMs to companies seeking to build AI into their products. AI21 Labs' next iteration, unsurprisingly named Jurassic-2 (or J2), did an 18 percent better job at generating summaries than OpenAI's product, according to human evaluators.

Amnon Shashua's suite of companies—Mobileye, OrCam, oneZero, Mentee, and AI21 Labs—all of which revolve around AI, are part of a wider Israeli strength in this sector. We asked Shashua how he thought Israel's start-up ecosystem fit into the global AI landscape. Would Israel be a significant competitor in this field? "What is Israel's strength in computer science?" he said, answering a question with a question. "AI is software." If you look at the competitors to OpenAI, you can count them on one hand. And AI21 is one of them.

"It is not a coincidence that AI21 is in Israel," Shashua went on. "Advanced software is really a sweet spot of the Israeli skill set." As of early 2023, there were sixty-six generative AI start-ups in Israel and over two thousand more employing various forms of AI, according to Start-Up Nation Central's Finder (an interactive database that tracks every tech company in Israel). And Shashua thought that if the government put in a relatively small amount of funding to subsidize the expensive training process for AI models, other companies like AI21 Labs would pop up.

The challenge, according to Avi Hasson, "was that our government was not making the investments to make the leap." Hasson had a unique vantage point. He was an alumnus of Unit 8200 in the IDF, a former partner at Gemini Israel Ventures, and a board member of SpaceIL and Sheba Medical Center (globally ranked as one of the world's most innovative hospitals). He served as head of Israel's Innovation Authority (which replaced the government's Office of the Chief Scientist) and is currently CEO of Start-Up Nation Central.

According to Hasson, "While cyber has been a big part of Israel's tech story, the reality is that there are even more Israeli start-ups addressing challenges in climate, health care, food security, and agriculture. But underlying many of these companies is AI, which is becoming a utility, and that's where I was excited and concerned for Israel."

Hasson's concern was the lack of the local infrastructure—the server farms that provide the computing power required to build LLMs—in Israel. But that was before a surprise announcement by Nvidia, the chipmaker that plays an outsized role in AI-related computing. On May 29, 2023, Nvidia announced that it would build its flagship supercomputer in Israel. It would be called, appropriately, Israel-1.

While the announcement may have been a surprise, Nvidia's choice was a natural one for the company. In 2019, Nvidia bought Mellanox, a large Israeli chipmaker, for over $7 billion. Mellanox's headquarters became Nvidia's largest development center outside the U.S. And one of Mellanox's Israeli founders, Michael Kagan, became global CTO of Nvidia.

Kagan is another example of Israel's "stickiness." When Nvidia bought his company, Kagan didn't for a moment, it seems, consider moving to Santa Clara from his home in Zichron Yaakov, one of Israel's first towns, founded in 1882 on Mount Carmel, overlooking the Mediterranean Sea.

"Do you know how far it is from the house here (in Israel) to Santa

Clara? It's about ten milliseconds," Kagan told the Israeli tech website Geektime. His day begins around noon and goes until about 10:00 p.m., when it is noon in California. The post-pandemic reality "gives me the flexibility to be in China, Israel, and America on the same day," Kagan said. He has traveled to the U.S. only three times since becoming one of Nvidia's most senior executives.

But it's not just that Kagan prefers to live in Israel and is able to work remotely. As in the case of Michal Braverman-Blumenstyk and Microsoft, it makes sense for Kagan to be where what arguably is the beating heart of Nvidia—its biggest supercomputer and the demonstration platform for the business that helped make it a trillion-dollar company. Nvidia dominates the market for the computing infrastructure that powers the new, computer-heavy brand of AI based on LLMs.

When completed, the Israel-1 supercomputer will be the sixth largest in the world, the Israeli business newspaper *Globes* reported shortly after Nvidia CEO Jensen Huang's visit to Israel. Hasson believes this is a vector change for the already large AI start-up ecosystem. Even though the LLMs these companies need are in theory accessible from anywhere, Hasson says that having that infrastructure developed and located in Israel matters. "It's a totally different level of intimacy, knowledge of the stack, and the ability to test and pilot on a world-class AI platform if you have it in your home court."

The Flywheel

Why was it so important to Waze to stay in Israel that they turned down an offer of a billion dollars? Why did Michal Braverman-Blumenstyk refuse Satya Nadella's offer to start Microsoft's new cyber division in Redmond and insist that she could build it better in Israel? Why did Amnon Shashua insist that Mobileye stay in Israel when it was sold to Intel? Why did Nadav Zafrir uproot his family from living the dream in America and come back to Israel?

Many countries work hard to create economic dynamism to attract more investors and talented people. Generally, they do so by beefing up government subsidies and creating a business-friendly tax and regulatory environment. They try to move up the global "ease of doing business" rankings. They hope that this economic momentum will help lead to a healthy and thriving society.

Israel does not stand out as a place that is easy to do business in, such as Singapore or Dubai. More in practice than by design, Israel has flipped the typical model: social health and dynamism create economic dynamism. Israel's messy but infectious solidarity, energy, and confidence in the future are increasingly rare. Being a better place to raise families and to innovate has created a flywheel effect. The more attractive Israeli society is, the more the economy grows, and this in turn feeds the feeling that it is a good place to live.

But the events of 2023 show that the flywheel is not invulnerable. In the wake of the Netanyahu government's campaign to strip the Supreme Court of some of its powers, thousands of reservists threatened to stop volunteering for military service and the number of Israelis seeking foreign passports increased.

"Israel is a country that is both Jewish and democratic," a reservist told the *New York Times*. "If . . . that agreement is broken, I can't serve anymore." A woman who was applying for foreign citizenship said, "Israel is more than a country to me; it's true love. But I'm heartbroken. It's like when you find out your true love has gone insane, and the relationship doesn't work anymore."

Israel cannot afford to drive away what Yossi Klein Halevi calls its "sacrificial elite." These are the people who are not only the backbone of the innovation economy but of the national defense. In the next two chapters, we will pull back the lens of history to see the full picture of the past and future of Jewish and Israeli internal conflicts.

Chapter Ten

THE WARS OF THE JEWS

We survived Pharaoh, we'll get through this too.

—Meir Ariel, singer-songwriter, "We Survived Pharaoh"

There has never been anything to be taken for granted about the very existence of democracy in Israel. It emerged . . . in an environment about as favorable to liberal democracy as the Dead Sea is to fishing. Nevertheless, Israel over time became more—rather than less, as is often claimed—of a liberal democracy.

—Alexander Yakobson, Israeli historian

It had been a while since Roni Numa's phone had rung at midnight. At fifty-three, Numa had been retired from the IDF for two years, his final post having been as the head of Central Command, which oversees the brigades in the West Bank and Jerusalem. He still held the rank of major general. When he was on active duty, no hour of the day or night was safe from phone calls. It was almost never good news. There always was something to be done.

When the phone rang, he reflexively readied himself to go into crisis mode. If someone was calling him at this hour, it wasn't a small matter. He had seen just about everything in his career, which included commanding a number of elite commando units, including Duvdevan. But this call was from a different direction.

"My name is Avraham Rubinstein. I'm the mayor of Bnei Brak," the caller said. Numa's mind skipped over wondering how the mayor got his cell number. In Israel, anyone can get to anyone.

He had never gotten a call from a mayor. Certainly not this mayor, from this town, which was just a few minutes away from his home but might as well have been on another continent. Bnei Brak is a city of 210,000 people shoehorned between a big highway and the city of Tel Aviv. Its western edge is about a fifteen-minute bike ride through Tel Aviv to the beach. But you won't see many of Bnei Brak's residents on that beach because it is the largest Haredi city in the world.

The garb of Haredim, also known as "ultra-Orthodox" Jews, is familiar in many countries. Black hat, white shirt, black jacket for the men; modest dress and covered hair, or wigs, for the women. Their dress looks like it's from another era and place because it is: late eighteenth-century Poland and Ukraine. Haredi life is designed to be separate in every way from their surroundings, whether in Israel or anywhere else.

Haredi neighborhoods tend to be crowded and bustling. By the time they are forty years old, 63 percent of Haredim have had three to six children, and 28 percent have had *seven or more*. Incomes are half the national average, as many of the men study full-time and the women are left both to work outside the home and to take care of the family.

When Mayor Rubinstein called Numa on March 30, 2020, Israel was in its first and strictest lockdown. The mayor himself was in isolation because his wife had COVID-19. His personal experience with the virus tempered the instinctive resistance of Haredi communities to dictates from the secular Israeli government. The mayor understood that this was a real crisis. He needed outside help.

Numa took the short drive from his home in Ramat Gan to Rubinstein's home. "I was somewhat embarrassed as I thought to myself that I had never set foot in Bnei Brak before," Numa told us.

Rubinstein didn't even know what to ask for. The infection rate in Bnei Brak was about double the national average. The national lockdown required people to stay within one hundred meters (about the length of a city block) of their homes, unless they worked for an essential business or had to buy food or medicine. This restriction was untenable in apartments packed with children, where it was often impossible for a sick person to isolate in a separate room.

Numa also had no idea what to do to help the mayor and his city. On *this* battlefield, the enemy was an invisible virus, not a foe he had been trained to fight. Was it even the military's job to divert resources from defending the country to dealing with a civilian challenge?

This last question was not one that Numa asked himself. Other countries do sometimes call in the military to help deal with natural disasters. But the initiative comes from above. In Israel, it was Numa who worked up the chain. When a top advisor to the prime minister worried that the government might look incompetent if the military were brought in, Numa enlisted a well-connected minister from a Haredi party to lobby the advisor to call in the military.

As alien as his new environment was, there was something about it that he recognized, and it wasn't good. "There are some units where you come in and really feel that there is a crisis. Especially after a failure." Nothing was functioning. "You ask questions and they don't know the answers. And when they do have the information, they don't know what to do with it."

When news got out that Numa was in Bnei Brak, some of the officers he had once commanded somehow appeared. "I didn't reach out to them," he recalled. "I just saw them there. And they knew what to do without me saying anything." They established a command-and-control center and built a community communications division. "Even my driver came," he marveled.

Militaries excel at building operational structures, but carrying out the mission depends on good intelligence. The IDF officers had to create a granular map with information that didn't exist. In a city of 210,000 people, they needed to know where every sick person was, who was in isolation, and who was alone and needed food.

Numa told the mayor's advisors that he needed a point of contact in every apartment building. They looked at Numa blankly, as if he were living in a fantasy world. They said it could take weeks to find someone for each of Bnei Brak's 4,500 apartment buildings. Then one of Numa's military buddies piped up. "Say, how do you guys get your people out to vote at such high rates?" The advisors looked a bit sheepishly at each other. Everyone knew how it worked: every Haredi party had a network of campaign workers, each of whom had a list of people they were personally responsible for walking to the polls to vote. It was an effective system. Haredi voter participation is typically about 80 percent, compared to some 60 percent in more secular areas like Tel Aviv.

"They didn't want to share the lists at first, but we were able to combine them into an instant intelligence network," Numa said. And none too soon, as the needs of the residents trapped in their apartments were overwhelming. The municipality hotline went from receiving a thousand calls a day to about twenty-five thousand. But the back-office challenge wasn't even the hardest part.

With the Passover holiday approaching, Numa realized that he was about to face his first potential super-spreader event. The Passover Seder is held on the first night of the holiday, which that year fell on April 8. Everyone understood that the lockdown would prevent them from gathering in the usual way. The Seder itself was not the problem. The problem was the morning before.

One part of the reenactment continues the whole week of the holiday—eating matzah, the flat, dry squares of unleavened bread. This food symbolizes the Jews having to leave Egypt in such haste that they didn't have time for the bread to rise. Not only is it prohibited to eat regular bread; it must be purged from the home. On the morning before the Seder, observant Jews take the last bits of bread and burn them outdoors, marking the transition from eating bread to eating only matzah. On that morning, the whole community can be seen outdoors. Children would be everywhere as families gathered around small bonfires in scarce open areas, burning the last bits of bread from their homes.

Community leaders in Bnei Brak told Numa that there was no way they could cancel this ritual, which was required for the holiday to commence. Numa responded that he would not allow such a massive violation of the lockdown. It was a standoff.

Numa offered an alternative. "What if we collected the chametz [Hebrew for bread that on Passover is not kosher] from every home and had the municipal rabbi burn it all together?" he asked. The community leaders thought he was crazy. "How are you going to take the chametz from forty-seven thousand apartments in just ninety minutes?" they asked. Numa persisted—*but if we could, would it be acceptable?* They told Numa that in theory yes, but he had to convince the leading rabbis in the city to go along with it.

Numa's staff came up with a plan. The rabbis did not believe for a second that it would work, but they told Numa he could try. If it didn't work, they made it clear, they would do it their way.

"Luckily, I had the best battalion of paratroops under my command," Numa recalled. "They finished the job in one hour."

Looking beyond the Passover holiday, the paratroops' main job for the coming weeks was to deliver food to thousands of people who could not or would not leave their homes, or who were in quarantine. Soldiers went through the narrow stairwells in cramped, shabby apartment buildings, knocking on doors. "You don't know who is going to open the door," he said. "Could be a man or a woman, an old person or a kid. Some only spoke Yiddish. But everyone was very excited. They came out on the stairs, they were singing songs and blessing the soldiers." For the first time, Numa felt that he was truly connecting with a community in Israel that was so different. "We were being embraced like brothers and sisters. I have seen a lot in my career, but I must say, this is going to be one of the scenes that I won't forget for the rest of my life," he told us.

Many towns duplicated the model that Numa built, particularly those with the most cases, which invariably had large Haredi and Israeli Arab populations. These two groups generally live separately from the secular and national religious Israeli population that has been the focus of this book, and their separation cannot be overlooked in judging Israel's ability to resist the cultural trends that have challenged other Western societies. In looking at how the Haredi and Arab communities have adapted or resisted the customs in secular Israeli society, we can see some challenges to the larger trend of success that we have outlined in the earlier chapters.

One of the first experiences that separate the Haredim and the Arabs from other Israelis is that they are largely exempted from military service. This is one of the reasons these segments of Israeli society often seem foreign to the large majority of Jewish Israelis who have served in the IDF. "Who would have thought that on the Arab side of Jerusalem, they would ask for help from the military forces of Israel?" Numa asked, reflecting on similar experiences during the pandemic as he had encountered in Bnei Brak.

Yet the honeymoon didn't last, even during the battle against the virus. A few months later, Numa went to explain the need for a second lockdown in the "red" cities—those where the case rate was rising most rapidly. This time, he faced a lot of hostility from the Haredi leaders in Bnei Brak. "They were suddenly skeptical of the information that I was showing them," Numa said. "They were under intense pressure. The lockdown would not only shut down offices, but schools. The education system is the lifeblood of this community. They can't live without it."

The already endemic resentment of the Haredim, seen as neither contributing to the economy nor serving in the military and instead living at the expense of the hardworking Israeli taxpayer, was brought to new levels by the open defiance of the COVID-19 rules by many. Some Haredi groups gathered in super-spreader events such as funerals, weddings, synagogue services, and study halls. The result was predictable: much higher sickness and death rates than in the wider population. In their defense, the Haredim argued that some of their neighborhoods are dense, they live in small apartments, and have many children, all factors that contribute to higher incidences of COVID-19.

Three years later, the Haredim were a major factor in one of the largest political and societal crises in Israel's history. Following Israel's fifth election in less than four years, Benjamin Netanyahu formed a coalition and returned to power after just one year in the opposition. His coalition was the most right-wing in Israel's history, composed of Netanyahu's own Likud party, three Haredi parties, a party representing the right wing of the national religious community and, at the furthest extreme, the Otzma Yehudit (Jewish Strength) party.

Within days of the new government's installation, the new justice minister proposed an overhaul of the judicial system that would effectively remove the Supreme Court's power of judicial review. This move sparked one of the greatest upheavals in modern Israeli history. As opposed to other crises, this one was not about questions of war and peace, but of the balance of power within the state. However unique the crisis was, to understand it, we have to take a step back not only in Israeli history but to the history of ancient Israel.

Baseless Hatred

"The Jewish people had some form of self-rule over ancient Israel for about twelve centuries. During that time Jews fought each other in twelve civil wars, on average one every four generations," Amotz Asa-El told us. Asa-El is a veteran journalist and the author of *The Jewish March of Folly*, a book tracing Jewish political leadership back to ancient times. He chooses his words carefully and punctuates them with the intensity of someone who has made an important discovery and is on a mission to make the world understand it.

We met with Asa-El to help us make sense of the hundreds of thousands of Israelis turning out in the streets each week to protest the new Israeli government in 2023. Would the cohesive Israeli society we were writing about hold under such heated disagreement, or splinter? What could history tell us?

The most famous and catastrophic of the twelve civil wars was fought as the Roman army stood at the gates of Jerusalem in the year 70 CE. Inside the walls, the Jews were killing each other. As four Roman legions were heading to Jerusalem, Jewish factions in Jerusalem burned each other's food, so that when the Romans did arrive the Jews trapped within the city walls had already started to die of starvation. Flavius Josephus, a former Jewish general who went over to the Roman side, wrote an eyewitness account of these tragic events, called *The Jewish War*. "The real tragedy was that the different Jewish factions fighting each other over who would lead the war against the Romans and bring the final redemption were responsible for the destruction of so many Jewish lives, both before and during the Roman siege of Jerusalem," said Jonathan Price, professor of classics and ancient history at Tel Aviv University. To this day, Jews have two fasts three weeks apart to mourn the sacking of Jerusalem and the destruction of the Temple, one on the day the Romans breached Jerusalem's walls, the second on the day the Temple was destroyed.

Ten centuries earlier, the Jewish kingdom that had been led by Kings Saul, David, and Solomon broke into two when Solomon died. The Northern Kingdom comprised ten tribes and the Southern Kingdom comprised the tribes of Judah and Benjamin. The war between these kingdoms went on for centuries, culminating in the dissolution of the Northern Kingdom, known throughout history as the famous "lost tribes." The

Jews owe their name to the surviving remnant, the tribes of Judah and Benjamin. In Hebrew, Jew is *yehudi*, which means someone from Yehuda, the tribe of Judah.

The history of the Jews in ancient Israel is replete with savage civil wars, including during rebellions against the Greeks and the Romans. So was the 2023 political crisis a modern version of its historic pre-state past? Or does it resemble the heated—sometimes violent—political debates that Israel has experienced almost every decade since the founding of the modern state in 1948?

Over two millennia of exile, the Jews were known for having strong communities, while, at the same time, always arguing. There is the old Jewish joke about a religious Jew who became a castaway on a deserted island. His rescuers were surprised to find that he had built three buildings for himself. "Why three?" they asked. "Well, this one is my house, this is my synagogue, and this is the synagogue I would never set foot in."

It might be assumed that the movement to re-create a Jewish state would have wall-to-wall Jewish support, given that Jews had been praying for centuries to return to Jerusalem. At the very last moment of a Jewish wedding ceremony, at the height of happiness and just before the celebrations begin, the groom says these words just before breaking a glass, symbolizing the fallen Temple and everything that remains broken in the world: "If I forget thee, Jerusalem, let my right hand wither."

But the road to modern Israel was filled with bitter disputes. The Zionist movement, founded by Theodor Herzl at the first Zionist Congress in 1897, barely survived because so few Jews supported the idea. Zionism was opposed from both sides: by many religious Jews who believed that only God could return the Jewish people to its land, and by many secular Jews who feared that the nationalist movement would jeopardize their already precarious position in their home countries. And even the Zionists were divided into various factions with different visions and tactics.

Even during Israel's War of Independence, as the nascent state was in a desperate fight against five invading Arab armies, Jews opened fire on other Jews. On June 20, 1948, the *Altalena*, a ship carrying arms to the Irgun, a Jewish militia that had been fighting to drive the British out of the country, attempted to land on the beach of Tel Aviv. Prime Minister David Ben-Gurion had just declared that all the pre-state militias must be folded into the Haganah to form the new Israel Defense Forces. Negotiations between Ben-Gurion and Irgun leader Menachem Begin over the fate of the weapons on the ship fell apart.

Claiming that Begin would use the weapons to set up a "state within a state," Ben-Gurion called an emergency cabinet meeting that issued a fateful decision: "Arrest Begin . . . and sink the ship." His orders were followed: Haganah soldiers bombarded the ship with cannon and machine-gun fire. All told, sixteen Irgun soldiers and three Haganah soldiers died in the bombardment and in battles on the beaches.

In 1952, when the state was still young and struggling to absorb hundreds of thousands of Jewish refugees from Europe and the Arab world, Ben-Gurion's government negotiated an agreement with West Germany to accept reparations for the Holocaust. Menachem Begin, the leader of the Herut (Freedom) party, opposed the move, claiming that it was a form of pardon for Nazi crimes. Addressing a crowd of some 15,000 people (at a time when Israel's population was only 1,630,000), he gave an incendiary speech in which he attacked the government and called for its violent overthrow. Proportionately, this would be akin to 3 million people protesting in the United States.

The demonstrators began marching toward the Knesset, which was then located in downtown Jerusalem. Policemen, who had set up roadblocks, were unable to control the angry crowd, some of whom managed to reach the doorstep of the parliament and began throwing stones into the plenum hall. The protests were eventually quelled, but not before rioters injured several lawmakers.

In 1982, Israel was back at war, again. In response to incessant attacks on Israel's north, Prime Minister Menachem Begin ordered an invasion of Lebanon to push the PLO (Palestine Liberation Organization) terrorists out of range of Israel's northern border. This war was the first to split the Israeli public. As Yossi Klein Halevi wrote:

> War had always united Israelis; now war was dividing them. Once inconceivable, huge anti-government demonstrations took place even as the Israel Defense Forces were fighting at the front. Reservists completing their month of service would return their equipment and head directly to the daily protests outside the prime minister's residence in Jerusalem. If an external threat could no longer unite us, what would hold this fractious people together?

The protests held in Tel Aviv against the war and calling for Prime Minister Menachem Begin's and Defense Minister Ariel Sharon's resignations were by far the largest in Israel's history, before or since. About 350,000 people went into the streets, in a country of just 4 million people.

A few months later, a right-wing activist lobbed a grenade into a left-wing protest, killing thirty-three-year-old Emil Grunzweig and wounding nine others. Grunzweig was a teacher, and had served as a paratrooper in the Six-Day War, the Yom Kippur War, and the Lebanon War. His murder shocked the country and became a symbol of what happens when a political debate devolves into violence.

It is hard to imagine a greater societal, if not existential, crisis in a country like Israel than enormous popular protests against a war being fought just across its northern border, about a two-hour drive away. And yet Israel's ability to unite in the face of a crisis survived.

In 1993, it wasn't a war that split the nation but a peace agreement—the Oslo Accords, named after the city where confidants of Foreign Minister Shimon Peres (with a skeptical nod from Prime Minister Yitzhak

Rabin) and PLO chief Yasser Arafat negotiated it in secret. At that time, it was a crime for an Israeli to meet with the PLO, the main terrorist organization shooting missiles and planting bombs to kill Israeli civilians. That the government had been negotiating with Arafat shocked Israelis. The agreement was ultimately signed in a celebratory spirit on the White House lawn, culminating in an iconic photograph of a beaming President Bill Clinton with arms outstretched behind Rabin and Arafat as they made their historic handshake.

The sense that peace had arrived was short lived. Within months, Palestinian terrorist groups that opposed the Oslo Accords—Hamas and Islamic Jihad—carried out suicide bombings in Israeli cities. Tension was rising in Israel with growing rallies for and against the Oslo Accords. On November 4, 1995, as Rabin was leaving the stage after the largest pro-Oslo rally in Tel Aviv, he was shot twice in the back by Yigal Amir, a right-wing Jewish extremist.

Weeks before, three extremist rabbis had issued a ruling that *din rodef* (law of the pursuer) applied to the prime minister. According to *din rodef*, Jewish law says that if a murderer is chasing someone it is permissible to kill the pursuer to save lives. The claim that *din rodef* applied to Rabin was absurd and inciteful. Moreover, it was just one example of the atmosphere of violence building on the extreme right.

The entire country, not just the left, mourned the prime minister and for a country that might never be the same. But the left did not blame only Yigal Amir, it blamed the entire right camp that supported Netanyahu—then leader of the Knesset opposition—and opposed the Oslo Accords. The widowed Leah Rabin refused to shake Netanyahu's hand at her husband's funeral. The left camp also blamed religious people because they tended to be on the right. Most shameful of all—particularly for religious people—Amir came from a religious family, studied in religious schools, and wore a kippah, the head covering of religious people.

Rabin's assassination was another unthinkable, wrenchingly polarizing moment. One political camp blamed the other for the most heinous crime in Israel's history, while the other camp felt tarred with a crime it abhorred. It was hard to imagine how the bonds within society could ever be rebuilt.

Another time when it seemed that tensions between Israelis might become violent was when Prime Minister Ariel Sharon pushed through his "disengagement" plan in 2005. Sharon, who during his whole career was a champion of the settlement movement in the West Bank and Gaza, ordered a unilateral withdrawal of Israeli forces in Gaza and the dismantling of all the Jewish settlements there, plus four more settlements in the Shomron area of the West Bank.

The sense of betrayal within the settler movement cannot be exaggerated. It was not just that Sharon had been one of the strongest proponents of the movement. It was that they were there with the acquiescence, approval, or even encouragement of multiple Israeli governments of both the left and the right, and were considered, even by many opponents, to be some of the bravest and most patriotic Israeli citizens. When the day came for the evacuation, after months of tension and buildup, thousands of settlers had to be dragged from their homes, sometimes by soldiers who were crying along with the people they were evacuating. The settlers' greenhouses had to be abandoned and the remains and gravestones in their cemeteries dug up. Though many Israelis disagreed with and even resented the settlers, especially for the need to send their own sons and daughters to defend these settlements over the years, watching the evacuation on live television was a wrenching human drama.

These are just some of the deeper disputes that have roiled Israeli politics, sparking large protests, some of which ended in violence. Unlike most democratic countries, Israel has also demonstrated an ability to unify. Three times, Israel has formed "unity governments," in which the two main rivals for the role of ruling party join together in forming a government with a large Knesset majority. It is hard to picture an American cabinet with a balanced number of Democrats and Republicans, or in the UK with Labourites and Tories, but this has happened in Israel.

In 2022, the Bennett government wasn't technically a unity government because it did not include the main party of the right, the Likud. But it was the most ideologically diverse—from Bennett's Yamina party ("Right" in English) to Mansour Abbas's Ra'am, the first Arab party to serve in a governing coalition. Left-wing, center-left, and center-right parties joined the government as well.

The first unity government was formed during one of the most existential crises in Israel's history. In May and June 1967, Egypt and Syria made it clear that they were about to launch a war that would destroy Israel once and for all. Arab leaders spoke of "driving the Jews into the sea." Egyptian leader Gamal Abdel Nasser ordered the United Nations to evacuate its peacekeeping force from the Sinai. World leaders, and the Jews in the Diaspora, began to believe that Israel was about to be wiped off the map.

The prime minister at the time, Levi Eshkol, was considered a lightweight compared to the indomitable David Ben-Gurion, who preceded him, adding to the sense of panic in Israel. On June 1, 1967, responding to Eshkol's call, opposition leader and Ben-Gurion nemesis Menachem Begin joined the government and Moshe Dayan became the defense minister. It was this government that, five days later, launched a preemptive surprise attack on Egypt and Syria (Jordan joined the war later), resulting in the defeat of these three armies in just six days and Israel's capture of the Sinai, Gaza Strip, Golan Heights, and West Bank, leading to the reunification of divided Jerusalem.

The next unity government formed in September 1984 in response to a near deadlocked election and the collapse of Israel's economy in a spiral of hyperinflation, about 400 percent a year at its peak. This government, formed by ideological and political rivals Shimon Peres and Yitzhak Shamir, passed drastic budget cuts and other measures that reduced inflation to normal levels.

Constitution in the Streets

The fight over judicial reform in 2023 is the most intriguing, disturbing, unexpected, and improbable yet. It began, as mentioned, with the reelection of Benjamin Netanyahu in 2022, at the head of the most right-wing coalition in Israel's history. In a surprise move, the first item on the government's agenda was to restructure the foundations of the judicial system.

The government's original proposal, all recognized, would have effectively stripped the Supreme Court of its power to overturn laws that it deems in violation of Israel's Basic Laws. Though Israel has no constitution, in 1995 the Supreme Court decided to treat a small collection of Basic Laws as if they were a constitution. These Basic Laws themselves passed with only a fraction of the full Knesset voting. Parliamentarians were not even aware at the time that these Basic Laws would one day be reinterpreted into quasi-constitutional documents. So, the Basic Laws were considered a weak substitute for a constitution, as they were passed piecemeal over the years, sometimes with just a plurality rather than an absolute majority, and could easily be (and often were) amended in the same way.

Yet the new Netanyahu-led government's determination to neuter the Court's power of judicial review was still considered egregious by a large number of Israelis. Opponents of the judicial overhaul pointed out that, like other governments that rest on parliamentary majorities, Israel only had two legs of the triangle of "checks and balances" that exists in other democratic countries, such as the United States and France.

In many democracies the executive and legislative branches counterbalance each other. In parliamentary systems like Israel's, the governing coalition by definition has a majority in the legislature (otherwise the government would fall). This means that the legislature acts as more of an arm of the government than a check against it, leaving the courts as the only check against the combined power of the executive and legislative branches. The situation is compounded by the fact that Israel's parliament is unicameral, not bicameral like the U.S. Congress (House and Senate) or the National Assembly and Senate in France. There also are no state or provincial governments, only a national government.

It is not just the Knesset that has taken advantage of Israel's amorphous judicial order. Arguably, the Court itself has done so even more. Indeed, the political right's judicial revolution can be seen as a backlash against the Court's accruing to itself wide powers and being, ideologically and ethnically, unrepresentative of the general public. This perception is not limited to proponents of the overhaul. The majority of the public concedes that the judicial system needs reform, but that this should be done by consensus, not through a narrowly supported legislative blitz.

As the government rammed its proposal through the requisite hoops in the Knesset, street protests against the plan grew in size and intensity. In numbers that had not been seen since the 1982 protests during the Lebanon War, Israelis came out mainly in Tel Aviv, but also elsewhere in the country. The largest protests were estimated to include over 200,000 demonstrators in Tel Aviv and around 150,000 in other cities. This would be the equivalent of about 13 million protesters (4 percent of the population) in the United States turning out week after week for months.

The normally politically indifferent and studiously neutral high-tech sector not only joined the protests but became a prominent force behind them. The sea of techies waving Israeli flags at the protests dispelled a stereotype about this part of Israeli society. As Israeli journalist Yaakov Katz told us, "Many of these protesters had been written off by their fellow citizens as having abandoned Zionism and embraced post-Zionist thinking. They were the so-called Tel Avivians who were said to be more interested in traveling overseas and going to various European embassies to take out a second passport than fighting for the country." Yet, the high-tech sector could not have been more energized. One slogan that captured this mood and became prominent in the protests read "SAVE OUR STARTUP NATION."

The crisis even managed to bring together Israel's largest business and labor confederations. As one top business leader put it, "This is the first time in Israel's history that the business sector, together with the Histadrut [Israel's main labor union] and local government, are joining forces to save the country from terrible chaos."

The protests also included the weightiest sanction of all: the refusal of some reservists to show up for *miluim*, their reserve duty. In Israeli culture, refusing to serve is the doomsday weapon, the most serious form of protest a citizen can take. To be clear, the service that the reservists were threatening to boycott was volunteer service—not their mandatory service. Ten former air force generals—among the most elite military leaders in Israeli society—stopped short of backing refusal to serve, but wrote to Netanyahu warning that the crisis posed "a grave danger to Israel's security." Two hundred reservist pilots went further. They refused to participate in one of their weekly training flights. This was a symbolic step that would not impact military readiness or the pilots' participation in ongoing operations, but it still was almost unthinkable that a conflict with the government would get to this point.

One way to make sense of this is through the greatest visual symbol of the protests against the Netanyahu government's judicial overhaul: the Israeli flag. This may have seemed strange for a protest substantially driven by leftist opposition to a rightist government. In other countries, the flag is often a symbol of the more nationalist conservative side of the political spectrum. In the United States, if you saw two crowds of demonstrators facing off, most would assume that the one with lots of American flags was from the right.

Unlike other mass protests in Israel's history, which were almost all related to questions of war and peace, the judicial overhaul protest went to core questions about the balance of power in the country and also to minority rights. What did it mean to be a "Jewish and democratic" state, as stated in Israel's Declaration of Independence? Both sides claimed that they were defending democracy. The protesters said that taking away the court's power would lead Israel down a path to dictatorship, with no protections for minorities. The governing coalition said it was taking power from the Court to give it to the people's elected representatives.

It was as if Israel was, out of nowhere, holding its constitutional convention not in an august legislative chamber in Philadelphia but on the streets and in back-room negotiations seventy-five years late. And what the flags made clear was that the protesters felt they were fighting for their country, a country they cared about saving.

At this fraught moment in Israel's history, the country seemed like it had never been more divided and at the same time, oddly, united. One of Israel's most famous authors, David Grossman, struck a chord when he spoke to a sea of protesters waving Israeli flags a few days before the entire country was about to pause for the Passover Seder:

> We did not realize how deeply we belong to this state. Belonging, caring, solidarity: words that have taken on existential dimensions and solidity as this night falls upon us. We ourselves did not imagine how much love was hidden inside us for the way of life we have managed to create here in Israel.

It has been said that Israel does not have the option of losing a single war. The same could be said about Israeli society: Israel cannot afford to fight a single civil war, let alone lose one. Because Israel has external adversaries who would take advantage of any weakness, Israel does not have the luxury of being disunified. Everyone knows it. This does not mean that Israelis are always unified; far from it.

What it means is that Israeli society is like a very strong rubber band. However stretched it becomes, there are strong forces pulling it back together. There is a powerful desire for and belief in the necessity of unity. There is a strong underlying sense of, as Grossman put it, belonging, caring, and solidarity that spreads across ideological, ethnic, religious, and socioeconomic lines.

The bitter crises that have pockmarked Israel's history demonstrate both forces, perhaps most dramatically in the most recent crisis, which was characterized by painful division and inspiring unity. How these forces play out in the future depends in part on the currents running through Israel's two largest minorities: the Haredim and Israeli Arabs.

Chapter Eleven

THE OTHER ISRAEL

The true issue underlying the protests sweeping through Israel is demography rather than democracy. . . . The solution depends on Haredim espousing an attitude of broad responsibility and the rest of Israel inviting them to participate as equal partners.

—Yehoshua Pfeffer, editor, *Tzarich Iyun*

The hit Broadway musical *Fiddler on the Roof* told the story of Tevye the Milkman and three of his daughters. Set around 1905 in the Pale of Settlement, the Russian enclave where Jews were allowed to live, *Fiddler* portrayed the unraveling of Jewish shtetl life in the face of the onslaught of the modern world.

In the play, Tevye struggles with the erosion of centuries of Jewish tradition through his daughters' increasingly heretical choices. First, Tzeitel spurns the institution of arranged marriage and marries for love. Next, Hodel goes further by marrying an anti-religious Jewish communist and fleeing with him to Siberia. Finally, Chava breaks what then was the ultimate taboo by marrying a Christian.

Tevye's upraised hand was no match for the crashing waves of modernity. His was the last generation when what is now called "Orthodox" was just what Jews unquestioningly were. What was left of Tevye's world was wiped out by the Holocaust, when the Nazis murdered two-thirds of European Jewry. In Poland, there were 3 million Jews in 1933. By 1950, there were only 45,000.

When modern Israel was born in 1948, there were only a few thousand local Haredim—the Hebrew word for these tight-knit, most strictly observant and insular Jewish communities in Israel—out of a local Jewish population of six hundred thousand. The Haredim were not Zionists—they believe that only God can bring the Jewish people back to their land. Zionism was for them anathema because it was a reflection of secular nationalism, not Jewish law. In 1937, Agudath Israel, an organization started by Haredi leaders, declared that it "rejects outright any attempt at despoiling the Land of Israel of its sanctity and considers the proposal to establish a secular Jewish state in Palestine as a hazard to the lofty role of the Jewish People as a holy nation."

To secure their support for declaring a Jewish state, David Ben-Gurion, Israel's founding prime minister, negotiated what came to be known as the "status quo." This was when many of the Jewish features of the state, such as the ban on public transportation on the Sabbath, were established. Most significantly, the Haredim were exempted from compulsory military service so long as they were full-time yeshiva students.

Ben-Gurion thought the Haredim were a dying remnant of the shtetl life in Europe. They symbolized everything that the new state's socialist pioneers didn't want to be: weak, backward, insular, and oppressed. In the new state of Israel, Jews would re-create themselves as tanned fighters and farmers. They would drain the swamps and make the desert green.

Religion was deliberately absent from this heroic vision. Ben-Gurion himself had no mezuzah on the doorpost of his own home and his marriage was not solemnized according to Jewish law. Today, it would be hard to find a Jewish home, even among secular Israelis, without a mezuzah (a small decorative case attached to a doorway and containing a parchment scroll on which is written part of the Shema, a central Jewish prayer).

The pioneers were passionately engaged in creating a "new Jew," who would, as they saw it, be free from the oppressions of both Judaism and hostile rulers. The rejection of religion was not just a by-product of state-building; it was at the center of Israel's founding ethos, and persisted so long as Ben-Gurion's Labor Party had control of the levers of the state. Secularism was the religion of Israel's founding generation and was central to their identity.

But the Haredim did not fade away. They succeeded where Tevye failed. Against all odds, they reversed the tide. They re-created a world where family and Jewish learning were paramount, where marriages were arranged, where Jewish law reigned under the guidance of the giants of learning, their rabbinic leadership.

In *Fiddler*, Tevye sings wistfully about what his life could be if he had a "small fortune." Near the end of this song, he arrives at the peak of his fantasy: "If I were rich, I'd have the time . . . / To sit in the synagogue and pray . . . / And I'd discuss the holy book with learned men, several hours every day."

In Israel, the Haredim flourished. They were not only free from the oppression and insecurity of exile, but the state helped finance Tevye's dream: a "society of learners" in which a majority of men could devote themselves to yeshiva study full-time or for hours every day.

Overcome or Overwhelm?

The realization of Tevye's dream, according to some, is nothing less than the greatest threat to Israel's future. Dan Ben-David is a prominent Israeli economist and the founder of the Shoresh Institution for Socioeconomic Research, one of the country's most-cited think tanks. It is not the extremely high fertility rate of the Haredim—6.7 children per woman in 2021—that concerns Ben-David per se. It is that about half of Haredi men don't work at all, and many of the rest work in very low-paying jobs.

Ben-David decries Israel's education system generally, pointing out that the standardized test scores of non-Haredi Israelis in math and English are below the OECD average. But the situation in the Haredi and Arab sectors is much worse.

While the scores in the Arab sector are abysmal, almost none of the Haredi schools study secular subjects such as math and English, and don't take the standardized tests. Together, the Haredi and Arab sectors made up 44 percent of the 0–14 population in 2015. According to the projections cited by Ben-David, by 2065, if present trends continue, the two most poorly educated sectors will together comprise a full 64 percent of Israel's 0–14 population. The economic contribution of these sectors is further reduced by the low workforce participation of Haredi men and Arab women.

Eugene Kandel, a former chairman of the Israeli government's National Economic Council, warns that the economy's high-tech growth engine could flounder as its workers leave to escape the rising taxes needed to support a growing low-productivity population.

Ben-David writes that it is the responsibility of non-Haredi Jews to "save Israel's future." "We need to wake up while we can still do something about it. There is no reason why a still-large majority should continue to finance a minority insisting on a lifestyle jeopardizing its own future as well as ours."

Other economists and demographers believe that this picture is based on faulty assumptions. "The government projections are based on a static picture," said Alex Weinreb, a demographer with the Taub Center for Social Policy Studies, a nonpartisan research institute. "The reality of Israeli society is very dynamic."

The widely cited government projections assume that there is no net change due to people joining or leaving the Haredi fold. Based on data from the Haredi school system comparing enrollment in first grade and ninth grade and other data, a study by Weinreb and his colleague Nachum Blass estimated that there is a net movement of about 15 percent of Haredim leaving that community through their early adulthood, that is, after accounting for those who become Haredi. And this underestimates the change because a good number of traditional religious, but not Haredi, families send their children to the Haredi school system at early ages and pull them out later. What is more, those who leave the Haredi community don't disappear. They increase the size of the non-Haredi sector, resulting in a substantial swing in the demographic balance.

Weinreb refuses to say what he thinks the Haredi population will be in 2065 because projections out that far are impossible in a case where so many factors are in play. His projection in the twenty-to-twenty-five-year time frame (to between 2043 and 2048) is that the Haredim will grow from 13 percent to around 15 to 17 percent of the population—a considerably more modest shift than in the official projections. He also estimates that during this same period the Haredi fertility rate could plummet by more than two children: 6.7 today to 4.4 in roughly two decades. According to Weinreb, "the Haredi population will grow, but much less than the methodologically flawed official projections. There are real challenges, but it is irresponsible for people in their Tel Aviv bubble to claim that the barbarians are at the gate and Western civilization is hanging by its fingernails."

Yehoshua Pfeffer speaks carefully, in a slight British accent. He has a beard and, in his WhatsApp profile picture, wears a black hat, suit, and a patterned bordeaux tie. A Torah scroll rests on his shoulder. He's in motion, his hand caught gesturing. Where a secular person might display his or her aspirational self on a mountaintop or in the midst of their image of the good life, for a Haredi, that celebratory moment is carrying the holy book itself, the book that is God's gift and the guiding force of life. Fortyish, he and his wife have eight children, the oldest of whom just got married.

Pfeffer is a rabbi and head of the Haredi Israel division at the Tikvah Fund. He served as chief halachic (Jewish Law) assistant to Israel's Chief

Rabbi. Today he is also the founding editor of *Tzarich Iyun* ("Requires Investigation"), an online journal for Haredi thought. In it, Pfeffer takes courageous stands, such as arguing for the moral imperative of military service. For now, the positions of Pfeffer and many of his contributors are not mainstream in the Haredi community, at least not publicly. But they are a revealing window into the powerful currents coursing through Haredi society.

Pfeffer's criticisms are paired with pride and admiration for Haredi society. The Haredim are among the poorest Israelis. In most parts of the world, poverty goes with poor health, low life expectancy, violent crime, and drug abuse. But among the Haredim, Pfeffer points out, "life expectancy is higher than the Israeli average, while violent crime and drug abuse are almost nonexistent." Similarly, poverty usually reduces happiness. But the Haredim register the highest levels of life satisfaction. How could it be that one of Israel's poorest communities brings up the Israeli averages for longevity and happiness?

To Pfeffer, it's no mystery. "Many of the factors behind the success of Israeli society are epitomized in the Haredi community. We have a rich sense of belonging that comes from strong families and deep community associations. These human connections create a kind of inbuilt optimism and, I think, the highest level of happiness in Israel."

But as it relates to the high rate of poverty in the Haredi community and low contribution to the country's labor force and economy, Pfeffer agrees that the current situation is unsustainable and will become more so as the community grows. But he is not a doomsayer, nor does he agree that the solution must be imposed from the outside. There are already powerful grassroots forces that are "Israelifying" the Haredim.

Moshe and Menachem Friedman stood out. Wearing the signature black pants, white shirts, black jackets, and black hats of Haredim, the two brothers bravely showed up at DLD, a tech conference held at the old train station in Tel Aviv. Start-up entrepreneurs and investors milled about in T-shirts and jeans. It was a sweltering hot day and all the start-up exhibition booths were outside and the keynote presentations were in un-air-conditioned tents.

Yossi Vardi, the impresario of the global empire of DLD conferences, stood at the entrance to the main tent. Vardi, as the main investor in the iconic company ICQ, was a legend in Israeli high-tech. ICQ catapulted the nascent Israeli start-up ecosystem onto the global tech radar when AOL bought the revenue-less start-up for $407 million in 1998. Vardi became the top angel investor in Israeli internet start-ups after the internet bubble burst in 2000, when it was almost impossible to raise funding for anything with ".com" in its name.

Vardi stopped the Friedman brothers at the entrance. *Excuse me, who are you looking for?* Vardi asked. Moshe said, *We're entrepreneurs. We have a start-up, and we want to participate in this conference.* Vardi challenged them: *I'm seventy years old and I've never seen a Haredi start-up entrepreneur. I'm sure the rabbis wouldn't permit it.*

Vardi didn't disguise his hostility. But Moshe persisted. *Everyone complains that the Haredim don't work. So here we are, and instead of saying, "Welcome, please join us," you make us feel like we don't belong,* Moshe said. Vardi admitted that they had a point. He suddenly became very friendly, Moshe recalled.

But when Vardi heard about the Friedmans' start-up—an idea for video-editing software—he was characteristically blunt. "Your start-up is nothing, you're wasting your time," Vardi said. "But the idea of Haredim building tech start-ups—that's a real start-up."

On Vardi's advice, Moshe Friedman closed his start-up and founded KamaTech, a nonprofit organization to promote Haredim in high tech. Friedman named it after the Talmud tractate Baba Kama, which means "First Gate" in Aramaic. KamaTech would be the gateway for the first Haredi pioneers stepping into the alien world of high-tech entrepreneurship.

In 2012, Friedman met Chemi Peres, the founder of Pitango, one of Israel's largest and most established venture funds. Peres had established a program to help Israeli Arabs build companies in high tech. Friedman asked Peres if he would start a similar program for Haredim. Like Vardi, Peres was initially skeptical. Peres and Friedman decided to launch a start-up competition to test the idea.

Finding Haredim to participate was not easy. No one in the Haredi media would agree to advertise a start-up competition. Friedman posted about it on social media, but few Haredim were on social media at the time. "Praise God, word of mouth is strong in the Haredi community," Friedman said. He started hearing of Haredim working on an idea at the back of a synagogue or in someone's apartment. After much sleuthing, Friedman managed to find twenty start-up entrepreneurs or teams and convince them to enter the competition. He selected ten to present at the conference.

On December 25, 2013, KamaTech held the first ever Haredi start-up competition. Chemi Peres was there and Yossi Vardi was the master of ceremonies. As the auditorium filled up, the Haredi and non-Haredi attendees sat apart. Vardi looked sternly at the audience. "We didn't return to the Land of Israel after two thousand years of exile so that Haredim and secular Israelis will sit separately. I want everyone to stand up, and every non-religious person needs to sit next to a Haredi person. Then we can continue."

One of the resulting odd couples was Avreimi Wingut, a young Haredi who came to the event because he was curious, and Yizhar Shai, a seasoned venture capitalist who later became a government minister. Within the hour, Wingut and Shai became friends, and Shai offered to mentor him if he founded a start-up. Wingut started exploring ideas with Shai, but a few months later he approached Friedman at another event and said he wanted to work with Friedman at KamaTech. "Avreimi is a Hasid from Jerusalem and I'm a Litvishe from Bnei Brak," Friedman explained, referring to two of the three major streams of Haredi Judaism in Israel (the third is the Sepharadim). "We would never have met in normal life, but we became great friends and he joined KamaTech as a cofounder."

Soon after, Friedman managed to convince Amnon Shashua, whom we met in chapter 9, to speak at a KamaTech event. Shashua, surprised and impressed by the energy in the room, urged Friedman to create an accelerator to help fund and mentor the best Haredi start-ups. Just a year after only 20 teams applied for the first start-up competition, 224 Haredi start-ups sought to join the KamaTech accelerator.

According to Friedman, about a decade ago, Haredim were only 0.5 percent of the high-tech workforce. By 2023, that number increased sixfold, to 3 percent. Furthermore, out of the ten thousand or so aspiring tech workers graduating out of universities, colleges, training programs, and high-tech units in the military, about one-tenth are Haredim. As for Amnon Shashua, his company Mobileye now employs over fifty Haredim and expects to hire more.

It is getting harder for the Haredim to isolate themselves from the outside world. "The internet is much harder to filter out than television was," Pfeffer observes. And, in this sense, the COVID-19 pandemic was an accelerant as more and more members of the community turned to the internet for the latest information on the health crisis. When the Haredi leadership waged war against television, it wasn't so hard because you could see if an apartment had an antenna sticking out. "Anyone with an antenna would be ostracized. They might be kicked out of their shul [synagogue], and their children would have trouble finding *shidduchim*," he explained.

A *shidduch* is when a young woman or man is matched by their parents, usually with the help of a matchmaker (*shadchan*) with the person they will marry. In *Fiddler on the Roof*, in the song "Matchmaker, Matchmaker," Chava and Hodel sing about their impatience for the matchmaker to "bring me my groom." After Tzeitel, the oldest, reminds them that they come with "no dowry, no money, no family background," the sisters change their tune: "I'm in no rush / Maybe I've learned / Playing with matches / A girl can get burned."

To modern ears, all this sounds like a quaint recollection of a bygone world. But one mark of the success of the Haredim in maintaining their way of life is that the institution of arranged marriages continues as if over a century had not passed since Tevye's day. Today, the "*shidduchim* market" is one of the most powerful enforcement mechanisms for norms in Haredi society. As one Haredi leader put it, "Every parent wants their child to have the best marriage prospects possible. Anything that affects a child's *shidduch* potential, for better or worse, affects how the entire society is organized." What makes a man or a woman more desirable in this market? The answer says a lot about what is happening on the ground, regardless of the wishes of the rabbinic leadership.

The stereotype of the Haredi world is that it epitomizes traditional gender roles. Women take care of the home to free up the men for more prestigious pursuits, whether it is being the principal breadwinner or, in the Haredi world, studying in yeshiva full-time. The reality is the opposite: in many homes, the women go off to the office to support the family, while the men—who have more flexible schedules—take the kids to school, bring them home, and cook for them. In effect, Haredi men are way ahead of secular men in shouldering their share of the childcare burden.

As Haredi computer programmer Shira Carmel writes in "The Kollel-Man Masculinity Crisis," many of the men are "pushing strollers in the morning and early afternoon, a trail of kids in tow." Because of women's integration into the outside world of the workplace, "the situation on the ground is that, with the exception of strictly religious spheres, politics is practically the last bastion where male exclusivity is preserved. Everywhere else, women dominate."

The *shidduch* market has been reinforcing this strange turn of events. As one prominent rabbi put it, "Some matches are made based on the woman's high salary that can . . . enable the husband to sit and study, resulting in his being entirely enslaved to the home." The opposite is the case with Haredi men. The more they work rather than study, the lower their status. Women who earn the most and men who study the most are the most highly valued matches.

The number of Haredi women in the workforce has risen rapidly over the last two decades to close to 80 percent, which is about equal to the employment rate of non-Haredi Jewish women. But, as mentioned, only about half of Haredi men work, and nearly all Haredi men do not serve in the military. At the same time, the Haredi population is increasing rapidly, increasing the cost to non-Haredi Israelis of subsidizing the Haredim through welfare and other payments.

The massive protests against the government's judicial reform in 2023 might seem to be about a constitutional debate, but in reality they were a volcanic eruption of resentments that had been building for decades. While the main chant of the protesters was "Democracy!" another common theme was "It's over." The "it" was understood without saying: the sense of unfairness of non-Haredi Jews that they were shouldering the economic and military burden of the nation and the Haredim were not.

"It's not just an argument about constitutional law," Micah Goodman said. "It's a clash of emotions. One tribe is terrified that Israel is becoming a place they won't want to live in," he explained, referring to the protesters' fear of the growing power of the Haredi and far-right-wing political parties. "And the other tribe feels like for the past seventy-five years, Israel wasn't the country we should have lived in, it should have been different," meaning their feeling that liberal elites had, regardless of party control, held hegemony over the state since its founding. The deeper clash, Goodman argued, was over "past versus future, frustration versus anxiety."

In the Belly of the Whale

The Haredim are not the only significant minority in Israel. There is another that is almost twice their number: Israeli Arabs. As of 2022, just over one in five Israelis were Arab, most of them Muslims. The status of this large community, while improving, is far from ideal and still could deteriorate.

Israeli Arabs are Israeli citizens in every way (except for Arab residents of East Jerusalem, unless they apply for citizenship). They have the right to vote in elections (with a high participation rate); they can run for public office (serving as mayors and city council members across the country, and with a major presence in Israel's national parliament); some serve as justices on the Supreme Court; others are in senior positions in business, medicine, creative arts, journalism, and academia. They have access to the same health care as Israeli Jews. They are not drafted into the Israeli military, but may volunteer, and a small number do so.

The history of how Israel came to have a large Arab minority goes back to before the founding of the state. According to Israeli author Daniel Gordis, "Who's an Israeli Arab and who's a Palestinian on the West Bank or in Gaza, or in Southern Lebanon or Syria or Jordan or wherever, is really an accident of history." Haifa had large Jewish and Arab populations in 1948, and still does today—it's Israel's third-largest city. During the 1948 war, "the local Arabs were worried that the rumors that Jews were winning might be true, and many of them decided, 'Let's get out of here. We'll come back when the war is over,'" Gordis said.

"Imagine there are other families from the same neighborhood as the ones that drove to Jordan in 1948, except that their cars wouldn't start. Or they just decided to stay put. And they survived the war. And now they're in this new state." The Arabs who were living in Haifa (or elsewhere in Israel) before the war and remained were suddenly citizens of Israel. "Their children and grandchildren can now go to Hebrew University, Tel Aviv University, wherever, they get world-class health care, they have equal representation in Israel's democracy, and so on."

While Israeli Arabs have equal political rights and a growing middle class, this demographic also has high poverty rates. According to the Jerusalem Institute for Policy Research, six out of ten of Jerusalem's Arab population live in poverty, more than twice the rate of their Jewish counterparts. At an age when young Israelis are serving in the military and starting their careers, about one-third of Arab men and half of Arab women are unemployed.

Israel has four separate school systems: Haredi, religious (non-Haredi, modern Orthodox), secular, and Arab. Each has its own curriculum to fit the demands of each community. Most Haredi schools, particularly for boys, teach only religious subjects above the lower grades. Both the (modern Orthodox) religious and secular school systems combine religious and secular studies, but, naturally, there is a lot more religious content in the religious school system. The result is that each community gets what it wants, at the expense of integration across the communities.

The quality of most Arab schools is much lower than in Jewish schools (though the small Christian Arab minority has some of the top schools in the country). Many qualified Arab engineers have trouble breaking into Israel's booming tech scene. This, too, is changing, as Arab engineering students now make up large numbers of the classes of the science and technology programs at Israel's top research universities. A large majority of Israeli Arabs want to be more integrated in Israeli society, but they don't belong to the tight networks formed among non-Haredi Jews through the military. In addition, there is the biggest hot-button issue for Israeli Arabs: crime.

In 2021, almost three-quarters of all murders in the country were in the Arab community, which is only one-fifth of the population. In one Arab town, shootings in the streets by masked men from rival gangs out of car windows became so common that residents built a stone wall dividing the town into two.

Police have solved only 20 percent of the murders in Arab areas, compared with more than half in the Jewish community. A senior police official admitted to *Haaretz*, "We have lost control over the street in Arab communities." Kamal Ryan, who heads an Islamic anti-violence organization, told the *New Yorker* that sixty thousand Arab men work for the mob as drug dealers, loan sharks, and protection-money collectors.

Local officials are also victims of extortion and violence. In 2020, fifteen Arab council heads were targeted by gunfire or Molotov cocktails. Crime affects every part of society; young couples turned away by banks are forced to seek mortgages on the black market. And the housing itself may be illegal because the Israeli government has issued few construction permits in Arab areas, despite the growing population.

In May 2021, for the first time in decades, Israeli Arabs rioted in cities with both Jewish and Arab populations, such as Jerusalem, Haifa, Jaffa, and Lod. At the same time, Hamas fired rockets into Israel, leading to a major Israeli military operation into Gaza. The fighting within Israel was considered a major deterioration in Jewish-Arab relations. Though day-to-day relations between Jews and Arabs seemed to go back to normal, the possibility of a recurrence, in the wake of some future spark, remains.

Despite these worrisome factors, there are also efforts and desires on both the Jewish and Arab sides for greater integration. In 2020, a full 65 percent of Israeli Arabs said they were proud to be Israelis. This level was a record high since the question was first surveyed in 2003, and more than double the low mark of 31 percent in 2007. A 2020 poll conducted by the Israel Democracy Institute (IDI) found that eight out of ten Arab citizens want to be an integral part of Israeli society.

Nasreen Haddad Haj-Yahya is the director of the Arab Society in Israel program at IDI. She has a doctorate in history from Tel Aviv University and speaks fluent Hebrew with a slight Arabic accent. "There's one area where Jews and Arabs are in agreement: that Israeli Arabs are discriminated against and the state must make every effort to reduce social and economic gaps."

There is a paradox, Haj-Yahya pointed out. As societies, there is a seemingly unbridgeable chasm of distrust between Jews and Arabs. But on the personal level, it is a different story. "Ninety percent of Jews and Arabs who work together say that their interpersonal relations are great," Haj-Yahya said. This is the experience of the hundreds of Israeli Arab volunteer medics at United Hatzalah, the largest volunteer emergency medical service in Israel. Its 6,500 volunteers use Hatzalah's unique GPS routing technology to scoot around the country on ambulance motorcycles and achieve some of the fastest emergency response times in the world. As one Israeli Arab Hatzalah medic explained to us, "Most East Jerusalem Arabs work in West Jerusalem during the day, and wind up responding to emergencies in ultra-Orthodox Jewish homes in West Jerusalem. They are saving Jewish lives. And if there's an emergency in an East Jerusalem Muslim home, it's usually one of the ultra-Orthodox medics working in the Old City who will be saving an Arab's life. We work together. We are comfortable with each other. We don't even think about it."

From time to time, Israel has formed "unity" governments, that is, a coalition composed of the main parties of both the left and right blocs. The coalition formed by Naftali Bennett and Yair Lapid in 2021 stretched from one end of the political spectrum to the other. Bennett, the leader of Yamina ("Right" in Hebrew), a party with only six seats, became prime minister. Though Bennett had run on the right bloc, his coalition, negotiated by Yair Lapid, the leader of a center-left party, included parties on the far left. Perhaps most significantly, the coalition included a historic first: an Arab party, called the United Arab List, led by Mansour Abbas.

In Israel, the party is better known by its Hebrew acronym, Ra'am (literally, "thunder").

Until then, the Arab parties had focused on fighting against Israel's legitimacy as a state, and were seen as sympathizing with terrorist groups, such as Hamas, that were attacking Israel. This agenda made the Israeli Arab political parties so toxic that no Jewish Israeli party was willing to include them in a coalition, even had they been willing to join one.

Abbas's Ra'am broke with this tradition. It set aside the Palestinian-Israeli conflict and focused on bettering the lot of the Arab minority in Israel. Abbas went further in openly accepting Israel than any Arab leader before him. "Israel was born as a Jewish state, and so it will remain," Abbas said at a media conference in Hebrew, but he has also made the same point in Arabic. "The question is not about the state's identity—but what the status of Arab citizens will be in it," he went on.

By bringing his party into the ruling coalition, Abbas made history, but he wasn't just a junior member of it. He came in as the kingmaker. Ra'am had only four seats in the Knesset, but his were the only four that could go either way, and therefore determined which of the major blocs—Netanyahu or anti-Netanyahu—could form a government.

How, at age forty-seven, Abbas became one of the most prominent figures in Israeli politics is an unlikely story, full of contradictions. As Michael Milshtein, a professor of Palestinian studies at Tel Aviv University, wrote in the *Haaretz* newspaper, "The message of change that many in both Jewish and Arab society longed for has arrived, but the identity of its bearer is different from what many had expected."

Abbas's rise started in a mosque in his hometown of Maghar, a small town in the Galilee, one of the few places where Muslims, Christians, and Druze live together. Already at age seventeen Abbas was giving impassioned sermons at one of the town's mosques. The young orator caught the attention of Sheikh Abdullah Nimar Darwish, a towering figure in Israeli Arab political and religious life. Abbas became a disciple of Darwish in heart and soul. To understand Abbas, it is necessary to understand Darwish.

Born in 1948 in Kfar Kassem, another Arab town, Darwish founded the Islamic Movement in 1971. In 1979, he established Usrat al-Jihad ("The Family of Jihad"), which aimed to replace Israel with an Islamic state. The organization attempted to burn down an Israeli textile factory and set fire to forests, leading the Israeli government to brand it a terrorist organization. In 1981, Darwish was convicted of being a member of a terrorist organization and served four years in prison.

When Darwish was released, he became an advocate for nonviolent pursuit of the movement's goals. He condemned attacks by Israeli Arabs on Israeli soldiers and civilians, and he supported the 1993 Oslo Accords signed by Yitzhak Rabin, Bill Clinton, and Yasser Arafat. This caused a split in the Islamic Movement. The "Southern Branch," led by Darwish, stood for nonviolence and participation in the Israeli electoral process. The "Northern Branch," led by former Darwish protégé Sheikh Raed Salah, opposed the Oslo Accords and Arab participation in Israeli elections.

Darwish's position toward the State of Israel was clear. The Israeli Arab predicament was that they were "in the belly of the whale." They didn't choose to live in a Jewish state, but that was the situation. The job of their political leadership was to fight not Israel's existence but for their rights as full Israeli citizens. For decades they had received the short end of the Israeli budgetary, regulatory, services, and infrastructure stick.

In 2007, Darwish became the first Muslim leader to speak at the Global Forum for Combating Antisemitism. In his speech, he criticized Iranian president Mahmoud Ahmadinejad for denying the Holocaust, saying: "Tell all who deny the Holocaust to ask the Germans what they did or did not do."

Going back to his student days, Abbas identified himself as a devoted religious and political disciple of Darwish. At Hebrew University in Jerusalem, Abbas studied dentistry—a respectable occupation in the eyes of his parents. But his real passions were religion and politics. While the Arab student activists at the time were immersed in Arab nationalism and verbally battling the Israeli-Palestinian conflict, Abbas went in another direction.

Along with some other religiously observant students, and other students frustrated with what they saw as fruitless ideological battles, Abbas founded his own political group. Called Tahaluf (the Covenant), they fought to solve concrete problems, such as conditions in the dorms. "He didn't present himself as a candidate of the Islamic Movement, but as the students' candidate," according to Nihad Bukai, who was an activist with a competing political party at the time. "Abbas said, 'We're fed up with ideology, let's deal with what's important for the Arab students, we'll concentrate on getting benefits.' And it worked."

Following this same formula years later, Abbas became the leader of Ra'am and split it from a coalition of Arab parties. He promised to deal with the most urgent challenges, such as the rampant Arab-on-Arab shootings in Arab towns. To maximize his leverage to realize his practical agenda, Abbas was willing not only to join a governing coalition, but to do so with Benjamin Netanyahu's Likud. Reportedly, they had almost reached an agreement, but Netanyahu's right-wing allies vetoed the deal.

Essentially, Abbas was employing the long-established strategy of the Haredi parties, which historically were willing to ally with either side. As happens in other countries, such small swing parties gain negotiating power well beyond their electoral strength in the parliament.

We went to Ra'am's party headquarters in the northern town of Kafr Kanna (the ancient village of Cana, according to Christian tradition, where Jesus turned water into wine) to meet with Abbas. When we arrived at the address, there wasn't anything that looked like an office, let alone a party headquarters. Just a small street with apartment buildings opposite a mosque. We called and someone came out onto a balcony and waved us over. An advisor to Abbas and a translator welcomed us, and motioned for us to sit in one of half a dozen overstuffed leather couches arranged in a large square in the style of the living rooms in Arab homes.

About half an hour later Abbas walked in. Stout with a round face, he seems to have a permanently peaceful smile. It is the smile of someone who seems surprised at the heights he has reached and, still with some humility, is enjoying the view. He spoke to us in Arabic, with a translator.

While focused on practical steps, Abbas was also aware of the underlying source of most of the problems he was addressing: distrust. "The main barrier that still exists is a psychological one. There are still existential questions, nationalistic questions, so you have that fear and that dominates the relations between both sides. It's not about physically being together. It's about opening up to each other at this point."

Abbas is seen as a traitor to the Palestinian cause by some Arabs, who label him a Zionist. He was physically attacked at a campaign event in Umm al-Fahm, a radical stronghold, and has since stuck to speaking to friendlier audiences. At the same time, some Jewish Israelis think that Abbas is being conciliatory just for tactical reasons, and that he is as opposed to Israel as his radical colleagues.

It remains to be seen whether Abbas's courageous stands will mark a lasting shift toward integration in Israeli politics and in Jewish-Arab relations more broadly. It is possible that riots and extremism will intensify, setting back the forces of integration. That possibility would be tragic not just because of the direct damage to the lives of Jews and Arabs, but because of the lost opportunity.

The area where Israeli Arabs have had the most opportunity for advancement is in medicine. The first wave of Arabs in the field became pharmacists. Today, if you go into any hospital in Israel it is likely that you will encounter an Arab doctor or nurse during your treatment. During the COVID-19 pandemic, Arab medical workers were seen to be on the "front lines," defending the country against a deadly enemy.

Much of the success of Israeli society that we have described in this book is built on the sense of belonging, solidarity, and shared sacrifice inherent in the Israeli experience. But when we write of "Israelis" in this context, there is often an unspoken asterisk next to it denoting "except for Haredim and Arabs." But what if these large and important communities were no longer exceptions but much more integral parts of Israeli society? What if "they" were no longer a "they" but a "we"?

Yehoshua Pfeffer sees a future where Haredim regard themselves, and are accepted, as full Israelis, while retaining the strengths of their communities and way of life. There is a plausible future in which the Haredim are an asset to the economy rather than a drain on it, and who serve their country in a meaningful way rather than shirk their responsibility to share national burdens.

Nasreen Haddad Haj-Yahya envisions a world where Arabs are integrated not just into the medical professions, government, and popular culture but also high-tech. In this future, the massive gaps in education, income, and infrastructure in the Arab sector would be closed, boosting the Israeli economy as a whole.

The Happiness of Dispute

Yedidia Stern is, quietly, one of the more influential jurists and thought leaders in Israel. After receiving a doctorate from Harvard, he became a professor of law at Bar-Ilan University. For many years, he was a senior fellow at the Israel Democracy Institute, a leading social policy think tank. In 2020, he was tapped to lead the Jewish People Policy Institute, an organization whose mission is to develop policies to advance the Jewish people as a whole. During the 2023 constitutional crisis, Stern was part of attempts to negotiate a compromise.

He wears a knitted kippah, placing him in the middle of the Israeli spectrum religiously. Even his mustache somehow renders him a bridge between the clean-shaven seculars and the long beards of the Haredim.

Social solidarity is crucial to the preservation of Israeli society. But there is a paradox. How is it that Israel has a feeling of social solidarity and a maze of deep divisions at the same time? Is Israel unifying or spinning apart?

Stern believes that the divisions are serious and, depending on the direction they go, still could tear the country apart. He pointed to a well-known speech that Israel's then president, Reuven Rivlin, delivered in 2015, in which he pointed to what he called the country's four different "tribes": secular Jews, religious Jews, Haredim, and Arabs. Stern said, approvingly, that Rivlin had put his finger on the problem: each tribe feels that the visions of the other three "are a real threat to their dream of how Israel should be and what's good for their kids."

But even in light of Rivlin's description of a divided society, Stern remained optimistic. "Israel is in a much better place than most of the relevant countries in Europe, America, and elsewhere," he said, adding, "The question is whether it is sustainable."

He went on: "When you look at the major disputes in society over the last generation, you will see that nobody is satisfied. . . . If any one of these major groups is too happy, that's a terrible thing. Because it would mean that one—or all—of the others had been defeated." So is it best for everyone to be unhappy? This sounded like a Jewish joke. But Stern was serious.

Widespread dissatisfaction didn't sound like a great situation. It seemed to contradict Israel's stellar ranking in the UN's World Happiness report. But Stern doubled down: "Dispute is the solution for our national life. We need it—because we have irreconcilable goals."

Much of the culture war is over the balance between the "Jewish" and "democratic" sides of the state. For the secular public, Israel is "too Jewish." Stores and public transportation are shut down on the Sabbath.

Rabbinical courts control marriage and divorce laws. Much of the secular public considers all this to be religious coercion.

At the same time, many religious Jews, and essentially all the Haredim, believe that the state is not Jewish enough. The Haredim feel that they are a small island in a sea of secularism. The government, Knesset, courts, schools, media, and the public sphere are all dominated by secular laws and culture. Immodesty, to say the least, abounds. Tel Aviv, to them, feels about as heathen as Berlin, Amsterdam, Ibiza, or South Beach, with values to match.

Not surprisingly, Israeli Arabs feel that the Jewishness of the state is all-enveloping. How are they supposed to relate to the Israeli flag, and to a national anthem that expresses only Jewish yearnings, not theirs? It is one thing to be a minority, another to feel excluded from the national narrative and purpose. For most Arabs, it seems like there is nothing about Israel that isn't Jewish. None of this seems like a recipe for coexistence, let alone solidarity. But for Stern, all of this is what makes Israel work. As the techies would say, dispute is a feature, not a bug.

"The dispute mentality is very Jewish. It's in our blood. It's one of the advantages that Israeli society has compared to others that are not as used to living with disputes—that are used to being stable and homogeneous," Stern continued. "David Ben-Gurion was able to silence the rest of the visions for a while. But obviously that hegemony is not there anymore, and thank God it's not there."

The flip side to Stern's contention that everyone is somewhat unhappy is that each group is happy enough. To be more precise, each tribe is happy in practical terms and unhappy in ideological terms. He rattles off the ways: "Each one is getting most of what they want. The Haredi way of life is flourishing. Secular Israel is growing. The religious Zionists are all over the place—one was prime minister and one will soon be head of the Supreme Court. A small Arab party has become one of the most important in the Knesset. Over one-fifth of the incoming class of the Technion—Israel's MIT—is Arab."

Yet, Israel as it currently exists is not the dream of any of the tribes. It is not a purely secular, religious, Haredi, or Arab state. No tribe can get all it wants, but they can get much of what they need. One reason for this, and this is the third lens through which to view the paradox of Israeli unity and division, is that behind all the heat and light around political debates, Israelis are largely in agreement on a wide range of issues.

Naftali Bennett, who led Israel's most ideologically diverse coalition to date, liked to say that 70 percent of Israelis agree on 70 percent of issues. How could that be? It is not true in other places suffering from political polarization, such as the United States and the United Kingdom. One reason might be called an accident of history.

Through most of Israel's history, starting slowly after the 1967 war and intensifying in the wake of the 1993 Oslo Accords, Israelis divided over one issue: how to achieve peace and security. The left believed that the territories captured in 1967 could be traded for peace (as did happen in 1979 with Egypt); the right believed either that the Arabs would not agree, or that giving up territory would lead to more war, or even to Israel's destruction. The stakes were high. Life and death, peace and war. Each side believed the other would lead to the end of the Zionist dream. Yitzhak Rabin was assassinated over this issue. Indeed, it looked like this was the *only* issue on Israel's political agenda. As Henry Kissinger famously quipped, "Israel has no foreign policy, only domestic politics."

One might think that Israelis are still split down the middle over foreign policy. On paper, this issue divides the two major blocs represented by the two or three major parties. But the last few elections haven't been fought over this, even on paper. The fulcrum of politics was not one issue but one man, Israel's longest-serving prime minister, Benjamin Netanyahu. Indeed, opposition to him was all that united the smorgasbord of parties in Bennett's coalition.

In his book *Catch-67*, Micah Goodman lays out how the left and right ideologies around peace and security collapsed. In the meantime, a new direction opened up that has little to do with the future of the territories. The official opening of ties between Israel and the United Arab Emirates, Bahrain, Sudan, and Morocco—called the Abraham Accords—has wide support in Israel.

The collapse of the conflict as a political issue has left a vacuum. While in most countries the economy is by a good stretch the main issue, in Israel most people could not tell you the difference between the parties on the economy. Everyone agrees: housing prices and the cost of living should be lower. Who will do what to make this happen? There is little confidence among voters that any party has a solution.

According to Goodman, the razor-thin margin between the pro- and anti-Netanyahu blocs hides the high level of agreement on the issues across a wide swath of centrist parties. Whether such a coalition materializes is another matter. But even the possibility of such governments separates Israeli-style polarization and what is happening in other countries.

Amotz Asa-El pointed us to a reason for this difference. "Israelis know each other well, intimately. Even those who are entirely different from us. Even the Israeli who was born and raised eating pork knows the ultra-Orthodox Israeli in whose home he never was and never will be."

This is not true in the United States or the United Kingdom, Asa-El continued. It is possible for someone living on the coasts of the U.S. not to know or even come across a single voter from the other party. In the UK, many voting against Brexit were surprised by the outcome, since they didn't know anyone who voted for it.

"Somewhere in an Israeli's family, somebody might have become ultra-Orthodox. And in the ultra-Orthodox families, there are secular people—sometimes their own children. There is a social dynamic out there, there's interaction. . . . It's not an idyll," Asa-El said. "But they know each other a lot better than in other Western societies where people don't know anyone from the opposing camp."

Political arguments in Israel are between people who both love their country and have, at the most basic level, a shared purpose. This widespread feeling of common destiny is powerful, but not invincible. Israelis are aware that it can be shattered. Multiple times the country felt like it was on the brink of civil war, or at least an unhealable fracture. But each time the sense of solidarity survived. Whether this will continue is the ultimate question and challenge for Israeli society. Greater integration of Israel's two largest minorities is essential to sustaining Israel's societal success.

The good news is that there are strong integrative winds blowing in both communities, each for its own reasons. But there is also resistance. Much depends on the internal battle—for and against becoming "more Israeli"—within these communities. The policies and attitudes of the Israeli mainstream will also greatly influence outcomes. Israel has gone to great lengths to welcome and encourage Jewish immigration from around the world. With similar popular support, combined with sensitivity to each group's desire to preserve their identity, the next great wave of "immigration" into Israeli society could be from the third of Israelis already living there.

Chapter Twelve

SECOND CHANCES

Since we get our soldiers for free, we are committed to bringing in as many as we can, providing them with tools for life, and giving them a second chance and sometimes a third chance to reach their human potential.

—Aviv Kohavi, IDF Chief of Staff (Ret.)

Glenn Cohen was crestfallen. A year before he had moved to Israel from New York to become an Israeli citizen and join the IDF. He was set on becoming a pilot, but arrived too late for the tryouts for the air force. So he tried out for the paratroopers and got in. But he didn't give up on his dream of being a pilot. Over his first three months in the paratroopers he kept requesting to be transferred to the air force. Then, during training, he tore a ligament in his ankle. A military doctor lowered his physical profile from 97 (the maximum possible) to 64, below the necessary level for a combat soldier.

Cohen got his wish to be sent to the air force, but as a photocopying clerk. "I was doomed to depression," he told us. "I was going to run a copy machine for the next two and half years."

Then there was a bureaucratic miracle. The air force didn't realize that his physical profile had been lowered. Cohen was invited to try out for flight school. But at the flight school, a doctor discovered his injured ankle. Again, he was told that he couldn't be a combat soldier. He was sent to another doctor, who would officially decide his fate. "The final doctor was a British immigrant. He liked my story and my motivation.

He said, 'I'm willing to let you in even though you have a 64 profile.' That's unheard of," Cohen marveled.

The next problem he discovered was his height. Cohen was six foot four and the limit for pilots was six two. They sent him back to the base to see if he could fit in the smallest fighter jet with his helmet on. Cohen got in and the instructor started closing the canopy. "I saw it was too tight. They told me, 'Sit straight.' Of course, I slouched. The canopy closed, literally on my helmet. I gave him the thumbs-up. 'No problem.'"

But then Cohen ran into yet another problem. Pilots need a security clearance and you can't get one unless you have been in the country for five years. What to do? Once again Cohen was sent through the process anyway, and once again, after many hours of grilling, he was granted an exception to the rule.

"My friends in the pilots' course called me the most outstanding soldier in the IDF because I didn't meet any of the criteria and I managed to get into the course anyway," Cohen recalled. He graduated from the grueling course and served for seven years as a helicopter pilot and then was recruited by the Mossad, where he served for twenty-five years, ending up as the Mossad's chief psychologist. After leaving the Mossad, he was frequently brought back to give resilience training programs for special units in the IDF, Mossad, Shabak (similar to the FBI in the U.S.), and the police.

"Looking back, the way I was given so many second chances to become a pilot was an example of how the military can sometimes see beyond how you look on paper and look at the deeper qualities that determine success," Cohen said. "As someone who broke all the rules, it's ironic that I was put in charge of making them."

Glenn Cohen's path to becoming a pilot was not typical, but it does illustrate an important part of the IDF's ethos. While often falling far short, the IDF ideal is to maximize each soldier's chance to reach their human potential. The IDF does this not just because it needs all the talent it can get, but also because it has a societal role. For the military, radical inclusivity is not just a favor to society, but integral to its core mission. Over the years, the IDF has figured out how to reach all the way from street kids once in trouble with the authorities to young adults on the spectrum to the most gifted and ambitious. Crucially, the IDF tries to optimize the placement of the majority who are neither dropouts or superstars, but who make up the mainstream. Compared to the elite education funnel that acts as a societal sorting system in other countries, the IDF is a truly merit-based system that is neither gamed by wealth and power nor socially engineered to advance designated underrepresented demographics.

We reached Maya Shadmi in Mexico, on the last leg of her belated post-army trip with her fiancé. "There was a year where we only saw each other for a total of about one week," she said. He was in Sayeret Matkal, Israel's top commando unit, while she was a company commander at Havat Hashomer, a base that takes in soldiers with the toughest personal backgrounds in the IDF. "It was a special time in our lives when we each could give one hundred percent of ourselves to something important," she said.

Both Shadmi's parents were born on kibbutzim. Her father served as an air force pilot, her mother is a psychologist. Shadmi was born on Ramon Air Force Base, named for Ilan Ramon, the Israeli astronaut who died in the *Columbia* disaster. Before she was seven, the family had lived on two other air force bases and near IDF headquarters in Tel Aviv, where her father had also served.

Then her family settled in Shimsheet, a communal village in forested hills overlooking the Jezreel Valley in the Galilee. The valley is the nation's largest agricultural plain, earning it the nickname "Israel's breadbasket." In and around it is a patchwork of Muslim Arab, Christian Arab, Druze, and Jewish small towns and cities bearing names that go back to biblical times, including Nazareth, Megiddo, and Mount Tabor.

In the small communities sprinkled around the Jezreel Valley, the spirit of service was part of growing up. Especially in Shimsheet. Shadmi knew the youth movement counselor, the national service volunteer, the kids going into the elite military units, and older kids headed to officers' school.

Shadmi remembered her own journey along that track. As a young kid, she joined Bnei Hamoshavim, the youth movement (similar to the scouts we described in chapter 2) for all the villages in the area. As a teenager, she became a counselor in the movement. After graduation, "it seemed that everyone went to *shnat sherut* [service year] before the army and then would try to get into the best military units. That's all we talked about toward the end of school," Shadmi said. During their senior year in high school "all the boys were going to the same grueling multiday tryouts for the various commando units. Only about half of those who are selected to try out succeed in finishing them, and only about half of those who finish are accepted into a commando unit. It was very stressful for everybody."

Like her friends, Shadmi interviewed to become a *shinshinit*, the nickname for those doing *shnat sherut* between graduation and their military service. "I wasn't good at making first impressions back then, so I wasn't accepted initially. But I kept pushing and they let me in." That was her first second chance. As a *shinshinit*, Shadmi was sent south to the Negev, near the air force base where she was born. She worked with kids from another branch of the youth movement where she had been a camper and counselor. She was responsible for working with children with eating disorders, others who had challenging upbringings. It was Shadmi's first time living away from home, with five other volunteers in the program whom she didn't know. While it wasn't a military experience, it helped prepare her for some of the main shocks that hit young people in the military.

When it came to interviewing for her first position in the IDF,

Shadmi had the same kind of problem as when she interviewed for her service year. "I got very low scores on the screening tests for command positions. But I pushed to get as many interviews as possible to hopefully make an impression that would balance out my scores." In the end, she managed to get a special set of interviews that gave her the space to describe her experiences working in the Negev. Shadmi was accepted into the basic training commander course. Third chance.

She served in Nitsanim, a main training base. "You see massive numbers of people. You feel like you're inside a large factory that turns kids into soldiers. In three weeks, you see they are transformed."

Working at Nitsanim, Shadmi learned what it meant to be part of an enormous system. She learned how to navigate—and challenge—the hierarchy and what it means to be given a mission. "You need to know how to behave inside and outside the base, and understand that you are now the soldier that you looked up to with awe as you were growing up." And it was Shadmi's job, though she was only nineteen years old, to drill a new mentality into the eighteen-year-olds under her command.

Shadmi was in charge of basic training for noncombat soldiers in the navy and air force. But she wanted even more responsibility. She pressed and was offered to serve in Michve Alon, a unique base run by the IDF's Education Corps (formerly commanded by Tzvika Fayirizen; see chapter 6). This base was for soldiers judged by the IDF needing extra preparation to cope with the stresses of basic training and army discipline. It was another chance of many to pivot within a short army career in a way that would change her life trajectory.

Her first job in Michve Alon was to run a three-month pre-army course for soldiers whose parents were Ethiopian immigrants. They faced an especially hard time because, in addition to the problem that many immigrants have that their parents did not serve in the military and couldn't prepare them for the experience, the Ethiopian community as a whole has had greater challenges than most in integrating into Israeli society. Next,

Shadmi was put in charge of soldiers with various mental health problems that disqualified them from normal basic training. "The IDF decided they could do their army service, but they needed a different form of basic training," she explained. "They needed a *maatefet* [support system]." The Hebrew word comes from the word for "envelope," which gives it a more empathetic, less bureaucratic, sound than the English equivalent.

At Michve Alon, she realized that working with soldiers who needed extra help was what she was looking for. That's when she decided that she wanted to stay longer in the army, "because I found my place." After going through officers' school, she was sent to a base known for taking in the toughest teenagers to prepare them for army service: Havat Hashomer (Guard's Farm).

Havat Hashomer has a storied past. It was established as an agricultural training center and guard post for the region before the founding of the state. One of the workers there was David Ben-Gurion. Its current incarnation dates from 1981, when one of the IDF's legendary chiefs of staff, Rafael "Raful" Eitan, launched a new program there to prepare at-risk youth for military service. The program's graduates were nicknamed "*Na'rei Raful*" (Raful's Youth).

Shadmi arrived as a platoon commander, still not much older than her soldiers. All of them were deemed to be unfit to be drafted. If they hadn't joined this program, they would have been told that they didn't qualify for service and sent home. In Israel, not being accepted for army service can be a stain for life, which is why the base commander told them that they were being offered a rare and precious chance to change their destiny and "become equals in Israeli society."

Many of them had criminal records or had run from violent homes or both. A criminal record wasn't automatically disqualifying for military service, but these soldiers had committed multiple crimes.

Every commander at Havat Hashomer has stories of the struggles of these youth to overcome their backgrounds, serve successfully in the military, and start new lives. Shadmi told us about one of her soldiers who, as a child, decided he had to get out of a toxic home environment. "His parents cut him off. He lived on the streets from age ten. He hadn't been in school since about the seventh grade. He wasn't violent himself, but he would steal and get into fights, and had some bad run-ins with the police.

"He became a combat soldier, in tanks," Shadmi recalled with pride. After leaving the military, he got a college scholarship and later "a good job earning real money." Shadmi didn't credit herself or even the program for these transformations. She was awed by "their passion and ambition to be part of Israeli society. Some of them even became commanders and officers."

Shadmi finished her army service as a platoon commander, left the military, and began, like a typical Israeli, her post-army life. She was surprised to receive a call from the base commander of Havat Hashomer, asking her to return to the military as a company commander.

As company commander, Shadmi was put in charge of about 180 soldiers, officers, and staff. She was twenty-three years old. In the IDF she was not considered young for the job. Recall that Shadmi had been rejected twice based on her initial interviews, for the service year position and for officers' school. In other countries, this might be the equivalent of failing at a university or job interview. Havat Hashomer may be an extreme example of giving young people a clean slate. But this chance to start over is also being given to the broad middle of Israeli society that did not grow up as part of the elite, or were not star students.

"If you looked at the academic grades of our best battalion commanders or brigade commanders and how they performed in high school, many of them were average," IDF Chief of Staff Aviv Kohavi told us. But when they come to the military, "they discover qualities in themselves that they would never have known that they had—like creativity, courage, teamwork abilities, and leadership." Education systems are not built to recognize or reward nonacademic qualities. Kohavi's point was not just that these young people learn different skills, but that a much broader swath of people have a chance to succeed. "Essentially, the military is a greenhouse where many types of plants can grow," he said.

Nadav Zafrir (whom we met in chapter 9) went from a career leading the IDF's top intelligence units to founding a company that is a global leader in cybersecurity, and is now branching out into the financial technology and digital health sectors. "In some ways, what's happening in Israel is more impressive than Silicon Valley, except that you don't have to go to Stanford," he told us. "Because here it's much more inclusive."

We had not realized the sheer numbers of young people who leave the military with command experience. At any given time, Kohavi told us, there are about thirty thousand commanders of all kinds. Thousands of nineteen-year-olds, just a year after they were drafted, are commanding ten soldiers. Company commanders, who have about ten commanders and one hundred soldiers under them, are typically under twenty-five years old.

"Right now, there are thousands of commanders who are taught by us to assume the heavy responsibility for the mission and for the soldiers under them. Think about the management expertise they gain. The IDF is a school of leadership," Kohavi went on.

The IDF estimates that there are 640,000 men and women in the country today aged twenty-five to sixty-five who have had experience leading soldiers (Israel's total population is 9.7 million). But it is not just about command experience.

"When a soldier enlists to the IDF, he or she begins a personal journey. The many transitions between courses and units develop adaptation skills," Kohavi said. "Moreover, the IDF is a mission machine. They become doers and problem solvers. Many of these missions are under stressful conditions, physical or mental. To complete these missions, they need personal responsibility, self-discipline, and perhaps most of all, the ability to work in a team. These are quintessential skills for life in a career and as a member of a community and even broader society."

There are other affluent democracies that have compulsory service, such as South Korea, Singapore, Taiwan, Finland, and Switzerland. But while the first four of these countries do have real national security concerns, majorities of their youth generally do not expect to be in live combat themselves or deal with minute-to-minute security threats as part of a formative period in their young adult lives. Service is shorter (from eighteen weeks in Switzerland to two years in South Korea, compared to a minimum of two years and eight months for men and two years for women in Israel). Finally, as we have seen, the Israeli military gives its junior soldiers and officers considerably more responsibility than is typical in most militaries.

Swapping in a lengthy and challenging military service for university studies does not just affect those years—roughly ages eighteen to twenty-two. It profoundly changes the experience of growing up in Israel, the formative decade of young adulthood, and the values of the society that guide people throughout the rest of their lives.

Why Doesn't Israel Have a Rat Race?

The old world was an aristocracy. If you were born a peasant farmer there was next to nothing that you, your children, or your children's children could do about it. Your place in the hierarchy was called your "station" or "lot" in life. The language is telling. Stations are fixed and lots are determined by pure luck.

The new world, starting with the United States, would be something different: a meritocracy. Expressing the ethos of America's founding, Thomas Jefferson called for "an aristocracy of virtue and talent, which nature has wisely . . . scattered with equal hand through all its conditions."

Jefferson's ideal has become deeply ingrained throughout the modern world. The "pursuit of happiness" rested on the principle that everyone should be able to rise as far as their talents and hard work will take them.

In the UK, Tony Blair described his political party as "committed to meritocracy," adding, "We believe that people should be able to rise by their talents, not by their birth or the advantages of privilege." U.S. presidents, including Ronald Reagan and Barack Obama, invoked the same credo: that anyone could make it with enough talent and hard work.

The stakes in a meritocracy are high. In America, the consequences of not having a university degree are profound. A high school degree was once sufficient to earn a respectable living and to provide one's children with the opportunity for a better life, but that is no longer the case. In 1990, the U.S. median wage for college graduates was over one-third higher than for those with only a high school degree. By 2021, the gap had almost doubled—college graduates had two-thirds higher median incomes than high school graduates.

Young adults without a college degree are almost four times as likely to live in poverty as college graduates. And a substantial majority of Americans—62 percent—still do not have a college degree. Well-educated white men on average live thirteen years longer than their less-educated counterparts. In the United States, if you are a middle-aged man without a college degree you are three times more likely to die from suicide, alcohol abuse, or a drug overdose—the "deaths of despair" mentioned earlier.

In his book *The Tyranny of Merit*, the Harvard philosopher Michael Sandel calls this bright line between those with and without a college degree the "diploma divide of death." This is echoed by the journalist Paul Tough in his book *The Years That Matter Most: How College Makes or Breaks Us*: "It sometimes felt as though the country was splitting into two separate and unequal nations, with a college diploma the boundary that divided them."

The psychologist Peter Gray describes the typical situation while growing up in other wealthy countries, particularly among elites:

Our whole schooling system, by design, is a constant competition for children. Everyone's on the same track, running supposedly to the same goal, and those who fall behind or wander down some other track are deemed "failures." By extension, many people grow up feeling that all of life is a competition, like school, where some are winners and others are failures. I've even heard parents argue, seriously, that the main value of school is it teaches children to compete.

Real community service, according to Sandel, has been supplanted by "internships and good deeds in distant lands designed to impress college admissions committees—all supervised by anxious hyper-parents."

The diploma divide is not as stark in Sweden or Denmark as it is in the United States. But it is prominent in the UK, France, and Australia. And the pressure and stakes in South Korea are even higher. From their early years, young Koreans spend almost every waking moment studying for the Suneung, a single test that is considered so life-determining that air traffic is diverted in order not to disturb the students on the day the test is given in Seoul.

Education systems have become "sorting machines." *Where did you go to school?* is a question people ask to place each other in their mental status hierarchy. It has become the job of education systems—particularly those who guard the gates of higher education—to determine who has merit and who doesn't.

The Merit of Service

Israel also has a meritocracy, but with an important difference. Merit is judged by service. In most meritocracies, the criterion to reach the pinnacle of merit is individual academic excellence. In Israel, the most meritorious are those who seek and are chosen for the most challenging service.

What it takes to be chosen is also very different than in other societies. No matter how impressive your individual talents, you cannot be of much use to the top units if you can't work with others. Individuals don't carry out missions; teams do. In addition, the mission is not for the benefit of individual soldiers or even just the unit. Soldiers must be willing to sacrifice everything for something larger than themselves.

What happens when a society selects for those willing and able to do the toughest service rather than those who have the perfect academic record? The more you look, the greater the differences become.

When we spoke to Nadav Zafrir, he was in the process of moving his family back to Israel after spending a few years in the United States building his business. A major reason for returning to Israel was so his children could go into the Israeli army rather than to an American university. "I looked at my kids and I said, 'This is what I want for them,'" Zafrir told us. "Not because I'm a Spartan, but because I honestly think it's a better education."

The IDF values many traits and talents, such as high motivation, problem-solving skills, determination, the ability to self-criticize, and a capacity to work in teams. What is clear, as General Kohavi suggested, is that many of the IDF's star performers would have been quickly weeded out by meritocracies that require perfect academic performance.

A meritocracy based on service draws from a much larger talent pool. But is this just switching one elite for another? What about those who don't make it to the top in either system?

The prestige of universities is measured in part by how many applicants they keep out. The IDF's job is different. It can't just think about the top. It has a strong incentive to maximize the human potential of every draftee. Often it understands that potential better than the teenagers understand themselves. "Everybody is screened with a superior prediction model that's been optimized over decades," Zafrir said.

This process is hardly perfect. There are plenty of stories of people who could have had a more "meaningful service" than they did. The boring jobs need filling, too. But there are also many stories of young people who were given challenges and responsibilities that they could never have imagined.

In other countries, meritocracies select for *individual* achievement. This is having cumulative effects. Over time, it has become harder to get into top schools, higher education costs have soared, and a glut of college grads has led to more competition for jobs that require a degree. At the same time, individualism has been increasing, which has led to smaller families and greater emphasis on work as a source of meaning. The growing pressure for career success has its price.

The dictionary defines a "rat race" as "the unpleasant situation in business or in life in which people are always struggling to compete against each other for success." Not everyone is in a rat race, of course. It is possible to escape, and many do choose to pursue a life that is less pressured and more conducive to happiness. The question is, why would there be much less of a rat race in Israel?

The best way to see how much less pressure there is in Israel to immediately start careers is to observe how young Israelis spend their time, both before and after their military service.

The Next Kibbutz

Limor Weissbart speaks quickly. Not because she is in a hurry, but because she is on a mission. Weissbart is part of the senior leadership of the Ein Prat Academy for Leadership, better known as a *mechina*. There are now many types of *mechinot* (plural) in Israel, but most share a basic formula: about forty eighteen-year-olds living together for a year of study, hiking, and volunteering. Put like this, the *mechina* may sound like an indulgence, like an extended summer camp. In reality, the *mechina* may become one of the most important Israeli social inventions since the kibbutz.

There are now about one hundred *mechinot* in Israel, all run independently. Some have a greater focus on religious studies, others are mostly secular. They are in cities and in the periphery. Some emphasize a particular theme, such as environmentalism. The focus of the three Ein Prat *mechinot* is producing leaders whose main goal is to contribute to society in whatever realm they end up in—such as government, business, social organizations, or science.

We live in highly individualistic societies, Weissbart explained, where the goal for people is to focus on themselves. For the *mechinot*, self-improvement is a means. The message the *mechina* works to convey is, as Weissbart puts it, "It's not just about me. I belong to my family, my community, my profession, my people. I am part of something." Pure individualism isn't good for individuals or society, she explained. "I think a major cause of depression is simply loneliness. When I was in the U.S. just now, it was the biggest thing I felt. People are in the same place, but they are very lonely. On the one hand, they are free to do almost anything they want. And yet they don't feel, 'I'm part of something bigger than myself.'"

Weissbart said if one word can capture the ethos of the *mechinot* it is *hineni*. The word's literal meaning is "I am here," but this does not begin to capture its resonance in the Jewish psyche. *Hineni* is the one-word response Abraham, Joseph, Moses, and Samuel made when God spoke to them. In the words of Rabbi Nina Beth Cardin, "'Hineni' . . . ' is a spontaneous, unequivocal commitment promising: 'I am here,' where and as you found me, fully attentive, focused, all in." In *mechina* terms, *hineni* is a declaration that "it's not about me."

Another problem, Weissbart said, is that most of the young people they receive haven't faced adversity. They haven't had to cope on their own.

There are many hikes, increasing in difficulty. In one case, the group has been hiking all night and they reach their destination. Just then, their counselors point to the top of a peak far away and say, "'All right, now we're walking to there.' Sometimes there is crying, arguing, and so on, but in the end we walk there," Weissbart said. "They learn that they can do things they thought they couldn't do."

The study program is based on classics in philosophy, Jewish history, and the great debates among Zionist thinkers and Israeli leaders. It is designed to build Jewish and Israeli identity and to introduce big ideas about human nature and the ideal society. There is volunteering every week. One *mechina* (not part of Ein Prat) is located near Rahat, the largest Bedouin town in Israel. The Bedouin are Israeli Arabs who used to be nomadic and now mostly live in towns. They are among the poorest communities in Israel. Some of the teenagers in the *mechina* would volunteer at a youth community center in Rahat.

Another important component of the *mechina* experience is traveling for a week at a time to learn about some community or part of the country. One week was devoted to learning about the Druze, a community whose secretive tradition combines concepts from Islam, Hinduism, and Greek philosophy. They live in a few towns in northern Israel, and in Syria, Lebanon, and Jordan. Nearly all Druze, unlike Israeli Arabs, serve in the IDF or the police. *Mechinot* commonly spend other weeks learning about the Haredim, Israeli Arabs, and touring Jerusalem.

For Erez Eshel, the founder of Ein Prat, becoming an educational leader was not part of his life plan.

At age thirteen, he started volunteering with the ambulances of Magen David Adom (Israel's Red Cross). By age eighteen, he had delivered five babies and performed numerous resuscitations. He planned to finish his three years of military service and go to medical school. Eight years later he was still in the military, serving as a company commander in the special forces of the paratroops and was on his way to a full military career. Then, on November 4, 1995, Prime Minister Yitzhak Rabin was assassinated.

"The assassination was an earthquake for any Jew, any Israeli, any Zionist. It didn't matter whether you were left-wing, right-wing, religious, or secular. I realized that I must leave the army, because the real mission for the country was a social mission," Eshel said. In 1996, Eshel founded Nachshon, his first *mechina*.

Eshel pointed to the moment when Moses, who was raised in Pharaoh's home, became part of the Jewish people. Moses sees an Egyptian beating a Jewish slave. And the Bible says, "*vayigdal Moshe vayetse el echav, vayar b'sivlotam* [and Moses grew and went out to his brothers and saw their suffering]." What does "Moses grew" mean? To grow in Hebrew is the same word as to become great. This was the moment when Moses realized that he can matter in the world, that he can create change, Eshel said. And "went out and saw their suffering" means he stepped out of his selfishness and suddenly saw the injustice around him. The idea of coming out of yourself, seeing the other, and taking responsibility, that is what the *mechina* is about, Eshel said.

The Odyssey Years

Counting their army service and the time before and after, Israelis can easily have five or six years between high school graduation and attending university. Despite this delay, Israelis have among the highest tertiary education rates in the OECD.

While the norm in many countries, particularly among elites, is to go directly from high school to college to a career, the early twenties can be described as a time of exploration, in Israel and elsewhere. The *New York Times* columnist David Brooks gave this period a name: the "odyssey" years. As he explained:

There used to be four common life phases: childhood, adolescence, adulthood and old age. Now there are at least six: childhood, adolescence, odyssey, adulthood, active retirement and old age. Of the new ones, the least understood is odyssey, the decade of wandering that frequently occurs between adolescence and adulthood.

This new stage in life opened up because people in their twenties have been delaying adulthood, as defined by things like becoming financially independent, getting married, and starting a family. In short, becoming responsible for oneself and for others. According to Brooks, in 1960, roughly 70 percent of thirty-year-olds had achieved these things. By 2000, less than 40 percent of thirty-year-olds had done the same.

But even if young people are pushing off adulthood, they are not taking a break. The odyssey years are in tension with the sense that there is no time to postpone for six months, let alone two years, embarking on the scramble up the ladder of credentials and career. A poll of 228 British university students found that eight out of ten felt significant pressure to find a permanent job within six months of graduation. Less than one-third of those cited pressure from their parents, while four-fifths said they were motivated by personal aspirations for career success, pressure that begins as early as high school.

In Israel, this kind of pressure would be rare in high school, the military, or even in the first few years after the military. The seemingly obligatory post-army trip is a metaphor for the Israeli path through life. Israelis tend to figure out their trip as they go along. Most don't hop around like other tourists, but instead stay weeks or months in the same place. They can show up alone and easily find Israelis to travel with. They travel as cheaply as possible so that they can travel longer before their savings run out.

Israelis specialize in traveling to remote places. In the mountains of

Nepal, the streets of small towns in northern India, around the salt flats of Bolivia, there are so many young Israelis coming through that the local hole-in-the-wall stores and bare-bones hostels have signs in Hebrew.

The ideal trajectory in most wealthy countries is like being shot from a bow—fast and straight. The Israeli model is more like going on an unplanned hike—climb slowly and follow the path where it takes you. The journey, as the saying goes, is more important than the destination.

Young Israelis have their own twist on the odyssey years—they tend to get married during these years, but they don't seem to feel the intense pressure to start their careers that is so common, especially among elites, in other wealthy countries.

In other countries, many young people spend much of their first eighteen years of life trying to get into the best universities. The tremendous and stressful effort made before, during, and after the time spent in university becomes part of one seamless career trajectory. Israelis, by contrast, generally don't spend their school years trying to get into the most prestigious military units, because school performance is seen to be largely disconnected from their placement and success in the military.

Glenn Cohen, whom we met earlier, spent decades developing the selection criteria and methodologies for the IDF and the Mossad. Cohen said that for some units, such as pilots and some intelligence units, academic performance is relevant. But for 90 percent of the units, including elite units, academic achievement is not a significant factor. "Learning ability is more relevant for us than intelligence as measured by high school grades. They are not the same. We look very carefully at learning ability," Cohen explained. In addition, in the military, how you perform on your own is largely irrelevant if you can't work with others.

Having high "EQ"—emotional intelligence—is not a priority for university admission departments. High EQ, by contrast, is critical for elite military units and command positions. "A team mindset, high EQ, learning ability, and ability to not just think about their own interests—that's what this society values," Cohen observed. Israeli life is less individualistic. "I guess that's why our young people don't get caught up in a rat race."

Chapter Thirteen

THE GENIUS OF ISRAEL

*A person cannot be happy if he sees only himself, and judges all in relation
to his personal benefit. If he wants to live for his own benefit,
he must also live for the benefit of others.*

—Seneca

Rabbi Jonathan Sacks, the late Chief Rabbi of the UK, once related a conversation with the British historian Paul Johnson. Johnson, a Catholic who wrote one of the definitive histories of the Jewish people going back thousands of years, approached his subject as a complete outsider. He had also written histories of the American people and Christianity. What struck him most about Judaism as he was writing his book *A History of the Jews*? Sacks asked.

"There have been, in the course of history, societies that emphasized the individual—like the secular West today," Johnson told Sacks. "And there have been others that placed weight on the collective." Judaism, Johnson continued, "managed the delicate balance between both—giving equal weight to individual rights and collective responsibility." This was "very rare and difficult, and constituted one of the Jewish people's greatest achievements."

Johnson elaborated on this idea in his book. "No system of justice in history has made more persistent and on the whole successful efforts to reconcile individual and social roles—another reason why the Jews were able to keep their cohesion in the face of intolerable pressures," he wrote.

We take the ideal of such a balance for granted today, but it was a radical invention in the ancient world, and no small feat to put in practice over centuries and under extreme circumstances.

The Dutch social psychologist Geert Hofstede created a widely used methodology for categorizing countries along an individualism-collectivism spectrum. In Hofstede's model, Israel scores 54 on Individualism on a scale of 0 to 100, about halfway between the U.S., a highly individualistic society, and more collectivist ones.

Is the millennia-long Jewish balancing act between the individual and the community reflected in modern Israeli society?

After going through layers of security checks, we returned to the spacious office of Lieutenant General Aviv Kohavi, then chief of staff of the IDF, in a sleek medium-height tower with a panoramic view of Tel Aviv and a distinctive feature: a large helicopter landing pad that made it look like a flying saucer had landed on top of it. This is Israel's much more modest Pentagon, incongruously surrounded by corporate towers and shopping centers and rimmed by the main highway bisecting the city.

The office was sparse, without the usual plethora of mementos and photos of a leader shaking hands with other prominent people. He is trim, with drooping eyes framed by thick eyebrows that give him an intellectual look. He has a degree in philosophy from the Hebrew University of Jerusalem and master's degrees from Harvard and Johns Hopkins.

Like every chief of staff before him, Kohavi was a household name in Israel. To lead the IDF is to be one of the most respected people in the country. Israelis feel that their safety, and the safety of their children serving under him, is in his hands on a day-to-day basis. Israelis take the loss of any soldier's life personally. When two officers in a commando unit were killed in a friendly-fire accident shortly after our interview, it was Kohavi's job to express the nation's grief and commit to redoubling efforts to prevent such tragedies in the future.

Kohavi started as a private in the IDF. The son of a small shop owner and a physical education teacher, he grew up in a working-class suburb of Haifa, a city in the north of Israel. When he was drafted, he volunteered for the paratroopers—not an elite commando unit, but harder to get into than the mainstay infantry brigades. When in his combat uniform, he still wears the red-tinged boots and beret of the paratrooper brigade he came to command.

Major General Giora Eiland, then head of military operations, re-members a meeting of the general staff in 2000 to discuss the difficult situation in southern Lebanon, where Israel still held a buffer zone to pro-tect its northern border. All the brigade commanders were there, packed into a small room. At the end of the meeting, Kohavi, then a thirty-six-year-old brigade commander—in charge of thousands of soldiers—asked Eiland if they could speak in private.

"He said to me, 'You generals have the same opinions and make the same arguments. You even use the same images. The groupthink coming from you guys scares me.' That really struck me. Not every young colonel would both notice this and raise it with a general two levels above him," Eiland told the newspaper *Yedioth Ahronoth*.

In Israel, the military is not a "them," it's an "us." The army isn't sepa-rate from the people, it *is* the people—a concept known as the "people's army." It may be the only military in the world that sees its social role as such an integral part of its mission, alongside its central mission of defending the country. The military goes to great lengths to grant people normally excluded, such as individuals with autism or who have served in prison for committing a crime—and have done the hard work to reform—the right to serve. Many struggle to arrive at that moment when they first come home wearing their uniform, which is in a sense a rite of passage for an Israeli citizen.

For David Ben-Gurion, a critical function of the military was to be a "melting pot" for Jewish Israelis who came from dozens of countries and cultures—today more than seventy nationalities—into one people. Kohavi disagrees with Ben-Gurion's famous formulation. "We're not talking about a melting pot, we're talking about unity. There is a big difference. I don't want to melt anybody together," Kohavi said. "You can be a man, a woman, religious, traditional, secular, gay, a new immigrant from Africa or Europe or a multigeneration Israeli, whatever—and you can keep your beliefs, your identity."

Having a place where young people can not only meet each other but live and work closely together means that whatever differences there are—political, socioeconomic, cultural, ethnic—there is some underlying commonality that limits how far people can turn on one another. What kind of common ground do other countries have to hold them together? It's not clear. What does seem clear is that polarization within countries has been increasing over time.

"Look, there's a big problem of polarization in the world today," Kohavi told us. "In any other country, leaders have to look for some way to bring people together. Here we have it for free, for two years, three years, and sometimes thirty years," alluding to his own military career and also to the experience of Israelis who have reserve duty through much of their adult lives.

If solidarity is the antidote to polarization, it must be built around something. Being part of humanity is not enough, and even being part of the same country, culture, or religion seems to provide less protection than it once did against spinning apart. Many Israelis across ethnic, political, and socioeconomic lines have something even stronger than a common experience: a sense of belonging.

"What happens in the belly of the ship? In the hull of the tank, or in the warehouse on a base?" Kohavi mused. He went on to argue that it is not just about forming lasting friendships. "The intensity of military service helps create a strong feeling of belonging," he said. "Any soldier who has contributed to his or her country feels that this country belongs to them more than ever. And the importance of belonging doesn't stop there. It also has a profound impact on the individual level."

The power of belonging is not just about keeping a society together. It is also a critical component of our personal well-being. According to a Mayo Clinic study, "We cannot separate the importance of a sense of belonging from our physical and mental health. Depression, anxiety and suicide are common mental health conditions associated with lacking a sense of belonging."

The evolutionary psychologist Robin Dunbar, the author of *Friends: Understanding the Power of Our Most Important Relationships*, put it much more starkly: "You can eat as much as you like, drink as much alcohol as you want, slob about as much as you fancy, fail to do your exercises and live in as polluted an atmosphere as you can find, and you will barely notice the difference. But having no friends or not being involved in community activities will dramatically affect how long you live."

Dunbar goes on to explain that "even just the perception of being socially isolated can be enough to disrupt your physiology, with adverse consequences for your immune system as well as your psychological well-being that, if unchecked, lead to a downward spiral and early death."

Why Are Israelis Happier (and Have Less Despair)?

In 1938, Arlie Bock, a brusque Iowa physician who ran Harvard University's health services, and a department store mogul named W. T. Grant had an idea for a study. What if you took a sample of hundreds of Harvard students and studied them continuously for decades to see who would become more successful? Back then, psychology tended to focus almost exclusively on understanding dysfunction. Bock and Grant wanted to know what were the ingredients of happiness and flourishing. In Bock's words, they were looking for people who could "paddle their own canoe" in the hopes of discovering "that combination of sentiments and physiological factors which in toto is commonly interpreted as successful living."

The study became one of the most celebrated in social science. Officially, it came to be called the Harvard Study of Adult Development. More commonly it was known by the name of its sponsor—the Grant Study.

The study began with 268 Harvard men. (Harvard was all-male at the time.) The vision was to go wide and deep: to study everything from their relationships with their wives, children, schoolmates, and colleagues, and deep into their physiology and psychology. They measured whatever they could—from the squiggles on electroencephalographs down to the size of the "lip seam."

The study was intended to last a long time, fifteen or twenty years. What made it so extraordinary is that it just kept going. Surviving multiple funding crises and four directors, the Grant Study continues to this day, more than eighty years since its inception. Along the way, the Glueck Study—another Harvard study that had started at about the same time with 468 poor inner-city Boston men—was merged under the same roof. Belatedly, the subjects' wives were added. While most of the original participants have died, the study continues with their two-thousand-plus children, all baby boomers in their fifties and sixties.

On November 14, 2015, the fourth director of the study, Robert Waldinger, stood on the round red carpet that is the signature of the TED Conference. A Harvard psychologist and Zen priest with a closely cropped goatee, Waldinger has a pixie-like quality that belies his seventy-plus years. He smiles a lot as he explores something that takes so long to discover and that so many people ask themselves: *What will make me happy?*

The answer is not what people think it is, judging from surveys of millennials who are at the beginning of their careers. According to Waldinger, more than 80 percent of respondents said that a major life goal for them was to get rich. About half said that another major life goal was to become famous.

Waldinger slows down and speaks deliberately as he approaches the big reveal. "The clearest message that we get from this seventy-five-year study is this"—he pauses dramatically—"good relationships keep us happier and healthier. Period."

"The people who end up not just the happiest but the healthiest are the people who have more social connections and warmer social connections," Waldinger said in a 2022 interview. "Connections of all kinds— not just intimate partners, but friends and work colleagues and casual relationships. All of that adds up to a happier and healthier life as you get older."

Waldinger concedes that this conclusion may sound anticlimactic, "as old as the hills." But is it really? If it were so obvious, Waldinger asked, why would we not make building relationships with family, friends, and community a much higher priority? And if this is true, what does it mean if in the wealthiest societies such ties seem to be increasingly fraying or even falling apart?

In their 2020 book *The Upswing*, Robert Putnam and Shaylyn Romney Garrett documented something uncanny. Using the Google Books Ngram Viewer, they looked at the relative frequency of the words "we" and "I" in millions of books published from 1900 to 2010. The resulting graph looked like a mountain. The ratio of "we" to "I" mentions rose steeply from 1900, peaking in 1965. Then it dropped precipitously to 2010, with no sign of stopping.

Were these results a linguistic curiosity? It seemed not. When Putnam and Garrett graphed membership in communal organizations, it matched the "we/I" mountain almost exactly. The authors also pointed to data showing that, since the mid-1960s, people have fewer close friends and higher rates of anxiety, depression, social isolation, and loneliness—particularly among younger generations. Putnam and Garrett argue that these trends have made it harder for people to find meaningful human connections and a sense of purpose and belonging in their lives.

None of this is unique to the United States. There is a basic trend toward greater individualism around the world. And while there is increasing concern about deteriorating mental health and a lack of social solidarity, it would be hard to identify a country that has found a way to withstand the trends that are shredding modern societies, let alone reverse them.

To be clear, Israel is not immune to the social trends besetting the rest of the world. But Israel does seem to have a healthier social immune system that produces marked differences in happiness, optimism, sense of belonging, purpose, and belief in the future. Even Israelis' complaints about the erosion of solidarity are evidence that there is solidarity to erode, and that belief in the ideal is very much alive. When Israelis criticize themselves for falling short of this ideal, they are measuring themselves against a high *absolute* standard. They may be unaware of how well they are doing *relative* to other wealthy, modern nations.

So what are the components of Israel's social immune system? Like any immune system, it has multiple layers of defense. It starts with the Jewish layer that Paul Johnson pointed out: the ability to balance the individual with the group. But Israelis added their own layers on top of Jewish practice, history, and peoplehood. They have an additional layer of connection. Let's call it "Israelihood."

In this book, we have seen four Israeli innovations, all of which are designed to boost the social immune system. The first and most famous was the kibbutz. Even though the kibbutz in its pure form proved unsustainable, before it collapsed it produced much of Israel's leadership and inspired many as a social ideal. Israel's most famous writer, the late Amos Oz, lived on Kibbutz Hulda for over thirty years. Decades after he left Hulda, after the kibbutz movement had dismantled much of its radically collectivist model of living, Oz was asked whether there are any kibbutz genes still in Israeli society. He said, "There is a certain directness, a certain lack of hierarchies, a latent anarchism in Israeli society which I regard as the heritage of the kibbutz, and I think it's a good heritage. I like it."

Sebastian Junger is a war correspondent who has written widely about the societal lessons that emerge from the extremes of the human condition. Junger pointed us to findings that Israeli navy commandos who grew up on a kibbutz were psychologically much more able to withstand the high stresses of their missions than those who did not. To Junger, this indicated that "the more communal your upbringing, the more robust your psychological defenses are. I feel that everybody in the country knows each other at some level. And in some ways, compared to the rest of the Western world, Israel is kind of like one big kibbutz, right?" Junger observed. "So it may be that the entire country is benefiting from a sort of kibbutz effect."

Second, while Israel did not invent youth movements, it shaped them into powerful conveyors of the means and values—such as *gibush*—at the core of the social immune system. Third is the military, with the double duty of defending the country and bringing it together.

These first three innovations are older than the state. The fourth, while only a few decades old and still small, has the greatest room for growth, and—while very Israeli—the highest potential for adaptation to other countries and cultures. That innovation is the *mechina*. Today, there are only about one hundred *mechinot*, producing about seven thousand graduates a year. But in just the last five years, demand for spots has exploded. It used to be that nearly everyone who wanted could find a spot. Now only about one in five get in, and new *mechinot* are opening all the time. Ultimately, the *mechina* could be something that is available to any high school graduate, or could even be integrated into the last year of high school.

This is significant because the *mechina* is a radical social innovation, like the kibbutz. It aspires to counteract individualism itself. It doesn't say the individual is unimportant. On the contrary, personal development is crucial—*not just for the self, but to serve society.* The *mechina* is a place where you connect to your peers, purpose, people, and country in a way that no other institution can do outside of a military framework. It is a shot to the social immune system.

Sebastian Junger delves into the well-documented but still surprising phenomenon that people can feel nostalgia for some of the worst of times. After World War II, many Londoners claimed to miss the communal underground living they had experienced during the Blitz. They missed it even though more than forty thousand civilians lost their lives.

Junger explains why it is so hard for soldiers to reintegrate into civilian life. "Most higher primates, including humans, are intensely social, and there are few examples of individuals surviving outside of a group," he observes. "A modern soldier returning from combat goes from the kind of close-knit situation that humans evolved for into a society where most people work outside the home, children are educated by strangers, families are isolated from wider communities, and personal gain almost completely eclipses collective good."

Essentially, Junger is talking about the flip side of the same coin that Waldinger described. Relationships are what makes people happy.

Without human connection, people and societies become sick. As Sharon Abramowitz, an anthropologist Junger interviews, put it, "We are an anti-human society. Our fundamental desire, as human beings, is to be close to others, and our society does not allow for that."

Israelis instinctively understand that a key reason their country is so high in the UN's happiness rankings is their feeling that they are not alone. Israelis triple down on relationships: large and tight families, multiple strong friendship networks, and a sense of national belonging and connection through shared sacrifice.

Gibush, the act of bringing people together, animates all walks of life, from the schoolroom to the workplace. Having a part in defending the country against a common threat gives a feeling of being needed and creates resilience. The country has youthful energy that fuels optimism. Israelis are connected to Jewish and Israeli history, know how to live in the moment, and feel that the country has a future. A spirit of service translates unity into action and builds a sense of purpose.

President Isaac "Bougie" Herzog has thought a lot about what makes Israeli society work. As president, which in the Israeli system is the post designed to be above politics, his job is to represent all parts of society, including the Haredi community and Israeli Arabs. He has a strong view about why Israel ranks so high in national happiness.

"The first element is a sense of purpose, which runs really deep," Herzog told us. "Definitely in the Jewish sector, but also among Arabs and among the Druze, there is a strong sense of identity and moving forward.

"The second element is a strong sense of family, which keeps the inner structure of society standing on a solid foundation. Many families are diversified across ethnic and religious lines, and multigenerational. It's a small country, so families can gather every Friday night. Both Jewish and non-Jewish families are really strong," Herzog continued.

The third element is a strong sense of perspective that comes from "absorbing so many layers of pain and being able to move on." Purpose. Family. Resilience. According to Herzog, these are the elements that make Israeli society "very impressive."

Matti Friedman is a journalist who moved to Israel from Canada at age seventeen. He served in the IDF when Israel held part of southern Lebanon as a "security zone" to protect the towns on Israel's northern border. He wrote about the experience in a powerful book called *Pumpkinflowers*, and has since written other insightful books that open windows into Israeli society.

"People here know how to live," Friedman told us. "Your life isn't just your job. The country really forces you to understand that there are things bigger than yourself and bigger than your job. One of those things is going to be the army. But even outside the army, the country is telling you that there are things that are more important. Your family is more important. The country is important. For many, religion is important. There's a lot here that draws you out of your own very narrow need to have a profession and status for yourself."

Idan Tendler and his wife, Dana, moved to San Francisco with their one-year-old daughter. Tendler was an executive at Palo Alto Networks, a large cybersecurity company. Seven years later, they had three children. They asked themselves, *Should we return to Israel?* It wasn't an easy decision. "You know California," Tendler told us. "Amazing weather, a backyard, beautiful nature—we had a great quality of life." After some debate, they decided to return to Israel.

Two years later, after they had a chance to settle into their home near Netanya, Tendler asked himself, *Why is it better here?* It was puzzling. It certainly wasn't that life was easier.

Just one month after he returned to Israel, Tendler was in a Zoom meeting with his U.S. team. Suddenly, he heard the piercing wail of air-raid sirens. He thought to himself, *How could this be? We're near Netanya* (a city well north of Tel Aviv, while the rocket fire was coming from Israel's southern border with Gaza). "I told my American colleagues that I had to run. I saw my kids standing at attention. They thought it was the siren for Memorial Day."

Tendler yelled at them, "What are you doing, we need to get in the shelter!" The kids said, "What is a shelter, Daddy?" Tendler asked himself, *What are we doing? This is crazy. One month ago, we were in California!*

So why was it better in Israel? "It's such a beautiful place for kids," Tendler said. "I think the essence is that Israel has a sense of meaning. We feel it, and I think the kids feel it—not just because of us. Because it's all around us."

The day before we spoke to Tendler, he and his family had been at a Holocaust memorial ceremony, where Dana's grandfather lit a memorial torch. He was a survivor who had fought in Israel's War of Independence.

"The kids feel they are part of history," Tendler said. "And I feel that you have a better quality of life if you feel that there is meaning, if you feel part of a bigger story. And you can contribute to that story. In California there's a better quality of life. But there was a lack of meaning."

Why are Israelis happier? Why is there less despair? Perhaps we have found the answer. For all its day-to-day coarseness, divisions, and struggles, Israeli society provides more of what humans really need.

At a time when people in many countries suffer from a shriveling sense of connection, belonging, and belief in the future, Israelis seem to have found a way to cultivate these treasures. A way to be modern *and* traditional. To be religious *and* secular. To embrace rapid technological change *and* build tight intergenerational families. To be ambitious individualists, achieve prosperity, *and* cradle a culture that persistently imprints that it's not just about you. That it is about service to the larger circles around you—the *hevre*, the country, and the world. That is the genius of Israel.

ACKNOWLEDGMENTS

Years after the publication of *Start-Up Nation*, we contemplated a sequel. We will write a sequel at some point, but this is not that book. As you now know, *The Genius of Israel* focuses on an aspect of Israel that is not just critical to understanding Israel's dynamism, but perhaps its greatest innovation: the extraordinary resilience of Israeli society.

We believe that no two societies are the same, just as no two people are the same. And that societies, like people, have their own stories, strengths, and weaknesses. The paradox of describing a society is that most outsiders and insiders are blind to it. Outsiders may not be familiar enough; insiders can be too close to see it. We are grateful to those who had some distance and also enough proximity to be our teachers, navigators, editors, and thought partners.

This book would not have been possible without Jonathan Karp, who put his confidence in us a second time. We were thrilled when Jon included *Start-Up Nation* in the roster of the twelve books that his imprint, Twelve, published every year. When Jon landed at the helm of Simon & Schuster, we had the chance to again benefit from his mentorship. He has also become a good friend along the way.

Ben Loehnen—the cofounder of Simon & Schuster's imprint Avid Reader—was our lead editor (and taskmaster). Ben bore the brunt of our frequent consultations. We are grateful for the speed, precision, and incisiveness of Ben's comments and, of course, his cajoling and directness.

While we wrote much of this book during our spare time during the pandemic lockdowns, it still took longer than promised, let's just say. Jon's and Ben's patience, as we blew through deadlines, was Herculean.

Jennifer Joel, our agent, was a quintessential professional, of course, on all business matters related to this book. But Jenn was also a sounding board and problem-solver extraordinaire whenever we got stuck (which happened a lot!).

Max August and Lia Wiener were more than our lead researchers, they also became part of our *hevre*. We benefited from Max's original research on Israel's innovation sector while he was a student at Harvard University and later his hands-on experience launching the Israeli office of the U.S. private equity firm General Atlantic. Max was crunching data right up to the publisher's deadline. Lia, Israeli-born with perfect English and Hebrew, served in the IDF's 8200 unit, and is a recent graduate of Stanford University's Graduate School of Business. She brought with her a wealth of knowledge, energy, contacts, and mission-orientation. She even set deadlines for us. Thanks, Max and Lia, it was a joy to work with both of you.

At various stages, Abigail Lyss, Avigail Rasol, Kayla Cohen, Jordan Esrig and Dore Feith were part of our crack research team. We thank you for all your hard work and indulgence as we disappeared and reappeared in a panic, always slotting us into your busy lives.

Leah Lerner was a researcher at different phases but especially at the critical one finalizing the manuscript—we may not have turned it in without her help.

Carolyn Kelly at Simon & Schuster ran a tight ship on the production process, especially on our truncated closing timeline—no small feat. David Kass and the publicity team at Simon & Schuster thoughtfully and creatively helped us make sure this book reached its audience.

We benefited from the suggestions of the many people who read our manuscript—some multiple drafts—and provided unvarnished feedback: Esther Abromowitz, Rebeca Becker, Tal Becker, Ilan Benatar, Daniel Bonner, Jon Chambers, Harry Zieve Cohen, Jared Cohen, Annette Furst, Mark Gerson, Jennie Goldstein, Yossi Klein Halevi, Jack Hidary, Judy Heiblum, David Hess, Terry Kassel, Jonathan Lewinsohn, John McConnell, Josh Opperer, Rachel Opperer, John Podhoretz, Dan Polisar, Matt Rees, Nati Ron, Adam Rubenstein, Matthew Scully, Meir Soloveichik, Daniel Taub, Josh Ufberg, Andrew Vogel, Sebastian Thurn, and Dana Hyde z"l. Dana's life ended tragically as we were submitting our manuscript. Her insights into Israel's story were invaluable.

Paul Golob read through the manuscript at different stages and made important suggestions on the book's structure.

To all our readers, we know this was a heavy lift and thank you for your time and speedy feedback.

Tom Nides, Ron Dermer, and Gil Messing—in addition to sharing their insights—helped us secure a number of important interviews.

Our own thinking on the promise of artificial intelligence is still evolving, but we are grateful for tutorials by Eric Schmidt, Reid Hoffman, Amnon Shashua, Sebastian Thrun, Jack Hidary, and Michal Braverman-Blumenstyk, who all helped inform the "No Place Like Home" chapter.

This book relied upon the research and work of many organizations, especially Start-Up Nation Central, cofounded by American philanthropists Paul Singer and Terry Kassel (and Dan). It is well known that Paul runs one of the world's most successful investment funds, but he also has become an informal teacher to Israeli business leaders and economic policy thinkers on the challenges facing Israel's economy. When Terry read the manuscript of our last book, she came up with the idea to launch an organization in Tel Aviv; Start-Up Nation Central is one of her many philanthropic projects thriving in Israel today. Paul and Terry are true friends of Israel. We encourage those interested in learning more about Israel's innovation sector to visit the organization's Tel Aviv headquarters and use the Start-Up Nation Finder (online).

Saul spent many hours working on this book ensconced in a library on the idyllic campus of Jerusalem's Van Leer Institute. Thank you to librarians Bayla Pasikov and Pinchas Maurer for hunting down endless studies and books.

Our wives, Campbell Brown (Dan) and Wendy Singer (Saul) were almost as married to this book as we were. We told you it would get done, just not when. There is probably not an idea contained herein that was not bounced off you. Thank you for being our reality check, and for believing that, some day, this book would see the light of day.

We will also never forget all the banter with Campbell and Wendy, and our children—Noa, Tamar, Yarden, Eli, and Asher—as we developed new themes for the book or discovered some fresh data. Lots of *gibush* over this project.

Finally, this book is dedicated to Dan's mother Helen Senor and Saul's parents, Max z"l and Suzanne Singer z"l.

Helen was born in Kosice, then part of Czechoslovakia, and today Slovakia. When the Nazis gathered the Jews in 1944, she went on the run and in hiding as a young child. Forty years later, in 1984, she lost her husband (Dan's father), and was a widow with children to raise. And thirty years after that, in 2014, she began a new and more hopeful chapter when she moved to Israel. Interspersed throughout these periods—1944, 1984 and 2014—she also lived in more places than we can count. Through it all, Helen's story is a model of resilience.

Both of Saul's parents were writers. Max wrote policy papers and op-eds on global strategy, Israel, and the Jewish world. Suzanne was the managing editor of the *Biblical Archaeology Review* and *Moment* magazine. Max and Suzanne brought their four boys for four years to Israel. All four sons decided to move back to Israel.

On September 15, 1987, his twenty-fifth birthday, IDF Lieutenant Alex Singer fell in battle during an operation in Lebanon to intercept terrorists bound for the Israeli border. Today, Alex's brothers Saul, Daniel, and Benjy live in Israel with their families. Many of the ideas in this book were polished by Max and Suzanne's endless curiosity and wisdom at their Shabbat table. We are happy that even if they didn't live to see this book, they lived and loved the Genius of Israel.

LIST OF INTERVIEWS

Over the years of researching and writing this book, we conducted numerous formal interviews and also benefited from many more informal discussions. We are grateful to all those listed (and those who requested not to be listed) for illuminating conversations on the issues we have written about in *The Genius of Israel*:

Mansour Abbas—Member of Knesset, Head of United Arab List

Esther Abramowitz

Yonatan Adiri—Founder and CEO, Healthy.io

Rotem Alaluf—CEO, Wand

Shira Anderson—Public Policy (Privacy) at Meta

Marc Andreessen—General Partner, Andreessen Horowitz

Amit Aronson—Culinary journalist

Amotz Asa-El—Columnist, *Jerusalem Post*

Mor Assia—Founding Partner, iAngels

Shlomo Avineri—Political Science Professor, Hebrew University

Ziv Aviram—Co-chairman, OrCam

Ran Balicer—Chief Innovation Officer, Clalit

Yair Bar-Haim—Psychology Professor, Tel Aviv University

Amnon Bar-Lev—Co-founder and CEO, Alike

Yona Bartal—Executive Director, Peres Circle

Yariv Bash—CEO, Flytrex

Rebecca Becker—VP, Alpha Tau Medical

Tal Becker—Senior Fellow, Shalom Hartman Institute

Eli Beer—Founder and President, United Hatzalah

LIST OF INTERVIEWS

Alexandra Benjamin

Tal Ben-Shahar—Founder, Happiness Studies Academy

Eshchar Ben-Shitrit—CEO, Redefine Meat

Dror Berman—Founding Partner, Innovation Endeavors

Rafi Beyar—Former Director General, Rambam Health Care

Jack (Tato) Bigio—Co-founder and Co-CEO, UBQ Materials

Elad Blumenthal—Founder and CEO, OneDay

Scott Bonham—Investor

Samuel Boumendil—Base Commander, Havat Hashomer

Meir Brand—Vice President, Google

Michal Braverman-Blumenstyk—Corporate VP at Microsoft,

Danny Brom—Director, METIV Psychotrauma Center

Arthur Brooks—Professor, Harvard Kennedy School

Mark Chess—Managing Partner, FinTLV Ventures

Eli Cohen—Founder and CEO, Ayala Water & Ecology

Eli Cohen—CEO, Mekorot

Glenn Cohen—CEO, Go Beyond

Guy Sgan Cohen—CAO, SolarEdge Technologies

Kfir Damari—Co-founder, SpaceIL

Fiona Darmon—Founder and Managing Partner, Sunvest Capital Partners

Sergio DellaPergola—Professor, Hebrew University

Ron Dermer—Minister of Strategic Affairs, State of Israel

Zaki Djemal—Founder and Managing Partner, fresh.fund

Shlomo Dovrat—Co-founder and General Partner, Viola Ventures

Ami Dror—Founder and CEO, BriBooks

Robin Dunbar—Professor, Oxford University

Nicholas Eberstadt—Wendt Chair, American Enterprise Institute

Michael Eisenberg—Equal Partner, Aleph

Shimon Elkabetz, CEO, Tomorrow.io

Erez Eshel—Co-founder, Ein Prat

Benedict Evans—Investor

LIST OF INTERVIEWS

Anat Fanti—PhD Candidate, Bar-Ilan University

Tvika Fayirizen—Former commander of Education Corps, IDF

Bruce Feiler—Author

Alan Feld—Founder and Managing Partner, Vintage Investment Partners

Maya Feldon—Company commander, IDF

Roni Flamer—Co-founder and CEO, Or Movement

Matti Friedman—Author

Moshe Friedman—Founder and CEO, Kamatech

Mark Gerson—Chairman, United Hatzalah

Michal Geva—Co-founder and Managing Partner, Triventures

Dedi Gilad—Co-founder and CEO, TytoCare

Brig. Gen. (Res.) Danny Gold—Head, Defense Research and Development Directorate

Daniel Goldman—Founding Partner, Goldrock Capital

Nir Goldstein—CEO, Good Food Institute Israel

Shafi Goldwasser—Co-founder and Chief Scientist, Duality

Micah Goodman—Author

Danny Gordis—Distinguished Fellow, Shalem College

Ron Gura—Co-founder and CEO, Empathy

Hossam Haick—Dean and Professor, Technion Institute of Technology

Jonathan Haidt—Professor, NYU Stern School of Business

Ofir Haivri—Vice President, Herzl Institute

Yossi Klein Halevi—Senior Fellow, Hartman Institute

Danny Hamiel—Director, School of Psychology, Reichman University

Avi Hasson—CEO, Start-Up Nation Central

Captain Udi Heller—Founder, Titkadmu unit, IDF

Isaac Herzog—President, State of Israel

David Horovitz—Editor in Chief, *Times of Israel*

Arnon Houri-Yafin—Founder and CEO, Zzapp Malaria

Eran Igelnik—Researcher, Start-Up Nation Policy Institute

David Ingber—Founding Rabbi, Romemu

LIST OF INTERVIEWS

Avi Issacharoff—Co-creator, *Fauda*

Luis Alberto Veronesi Joao—VP, Anheuser-Busch InBev

Sebastian Junger—Author

Eugene Kandel—Co-chair, Start-Up Nation Policy Institute

Leon Kass—Dean of Faculty, Shalem College

Tamar Katriel—Professor, University of Haifa

Asher Katz—Director, Me'ever Youth Movement

Yaakov Katz—Former Editor in Chief, *Jerusalem Post*

Tal Keinan—CEO, Sky Harbour Group

Kevin Kelly—Founding Executive Editor, *Wired* Magazine

Aviv Kohavi—Former IDF Chief of Staff

Manoj Kumar—Founder and CEO, Naandi Foundation

David Kushner—Author

Kai-Fu Lee—Chairman and CEO, Sinovation Ventures

Ariel Leventhal—CEO, UGLabs

Yuval Levin—Author, American Enterprise Institute

Sarah Levy-Schreier—Co-founder and CEO, Stealth

Fredrik Liljedah—Senior Manager, Karma

Erel Margalit—Founder and Executive Chairman, Jerusalem Venture Partners

Will Marshall—CEO, Planet Labs

Yossi Mattias—Vice President, Google

Arita Mattsoff—AVP, Mitrelli Group

Joe McCormack—Founder and CEO, SQDL

Jon Medved—CEO, OurCrowd

Raviv Melamed—Founder and CEO, Vayyar Imaging

Hadas Minka (Mamda)—Head of Behavioral Sciences, IDF

Alexis Mitelpunkt—Director of Pediatric Rehabilitation, Tel Aviv Medical Center

Jesse Moore—CEO and Co-founder, M-KOPA

Erez Naaman—Co-founder and CTO, Scopio Labs

LIST OF INTERVIEWS

Yaakov Nahmias—Founder and President Believer Meats

Benjamin Netanyahu—Prime Minister, State of Israel

Roni Numa—ret. Major General, IDF

Dele Olodeje—convenor, Africa in the World

Barbara Okun—Associate Professor, Hebrew University

Yoram Oron—Chairman, Red Dot Capital Partners

Raphael Ouzan—Founder and CEO, A.Team

Tamir Pardo—Former Director of Mossad

Shay Perchik—Senior Data Scientist, Ultima Genomics

Chemi Peres—Co-founder and Managing Partner, Pitango

Aya Peterburg—Managing Partner, S Capital

Anshel Pfeffer—Columnist, , *Ha'aretz*

Yehoshua Pfeffer—Rabbi, Tikvah Fund

Eran Pollack—CEO, N-Drip

Yossi Pollak—Co-founder, Sight Diagnostics

Jonathan Price—Professor, , Tel Aviv University

Maayan Rachmilevitz—Post-army traveler

Kira Radinsky—CEO and CTO, Diagnostic Robotics

Assaf Rappaport—CEO and Co-founder, Wiz

Eli Rata—VP, OurCrowd

Lior Raz—Co-creator, *Fauda*

Ben Roberts—Chief Technology and Innovation Officer, Liquid Intelligent
   Technologies

Nathaniel Rosen—Investor, Blackstone

Shmuel Rosner—Senior Fellow, Jewish People Policy Institute

Juliana Rotich—Head of Fintech Solutions, Safaricom PLC

Yaron Samid—Founder and CEO, TechAviv

Michael Sandel—Law professor, Harvard University

Laurie Santos—Professor, Yale University

Eric Schmidt—Former CEO and Chairman, Google

Eran Segal—Professor, Weizmann Institute of Science

LIST OF INTERVIEWS

Gadi Segal—Head of Education, Sheba Medical Center

Lihi Segal—Founder, DayTwo

Dan Shacham—Software Engineer, Nextdoor

Maya Shadmi—Former company commander, Havat Hashomer

Varda Shalev—Managing Partner, Team8

Amnon Shashua—CEO & Co-founder, Mobileye

Inbar Shashua—Co-CEO, The Social Solidarity Foundation

Yossi Shavit—Researcher, Taub Center

Nadav Shimoni—Founder, 81 HealthTech Network

Ophir Shoham—General Partner, Axon VC

Eden Shochat—Equal Partner, Aleph

Seth Siegel—Author

Avi Simon—Co-founder and CTO, Re-train.ai

Lenore Skenazy—President, Let Grow

Sammy Smooha—Sociology Professor, University of Haifa

Uzi Sofer—Founder and CEO, Alpha Tau Medical

Meir Soloveichik—Rabbi, Congregation Shearith Israel

Danna Stern—Founder, YES Studios

Yaniv Stern—Co-founder and Managing Partner, Red Dot Capital Partners

Yedidia Stern—President, Jewish People Policy Institute

Fred Swaniker—Founder and Chief Curator, The Room

Raz Yitzhaki Tamir—Co-founder and CEO, NSLcomm

Daniel Taub—Former Israeli Ambassador to the UK

Harel Tayeb—CEO, eTeacher Group

Idan Tendler—Founder and Chairman, Place-IL

Noa Tishby—Actor and author

Didier Toubia—Co-founder and CEO, Aleph Farms

Kathrine Tschemerinsky—Culture Editor, Weekendavisen, Denmark

Yoav Tzelnick—Former Head of Cyber Academy, 8200 Unit

Tal Vardi—Co-founder, Roim Rachok

Yael Vizel—Co-founder, Zeekit

LIST OF INTERVIEWS

Luis Voloch—Former CTO, Immunai

Alex Weinreb—Research Director, Taub Center

Tzahi Weisfeld—VP, Intel Ignite

Limor Weissbart—Co-CEO, Ein Prat

Yonatan Winetraub—Co-founder, SpaceIL

Avreimi Wingut—Managing Director, Kamatech

Aviv Wolff—Co-founder and CEO, Remilk

Harry Yuklea—President, Quantum Innovations Ltd.

Nadav Zafrir—Co-founder and Managing Partner, Team8

Daniel Zajfman—Former President, Weizmann Institute

Gil Zalsman—Psychiatry Professor, Tel Aviv University

Yahal Zilka—Managing Partner, 10D

Eyal Zimlichman—Chief Innovation Officer, Sheba Medical Center

Maty Zwaig—COO/CFO, Schusterman Family Philanthropies Israel

NOTES

Introduction: The Israeli Paradox

5   *its GDP per capita*: "GDP per Capita (Current US$)," World Bank, https://data.worldbank.org/indicator/NY.GDP.PCAP.CD?most_recent _value_desc=true.

6   *Income inequality and the cost of living*: Bar Peleg, "Income Inequality in Israel Widens in 2021, Despite a Drop Last Year," *Haaretz*, December 30, 2021, https://www.haaretz.com/israel-news/2021-12-30/ty -article/.premium/income-inequality-widened-in-2021-despiteeconomic rebound/0000017f-e302-df7c-a5ff-e37a1e1e0000.

6   *An average apartment costs*: "Israel: How Many Salaries Does an Apartment Cost?," *Yeshiva World*, June 14, 2013, https://www.theyeshiva world.com/news/headlines-breaking-stories/172858/israel-how-many -salaries-does-an-apartment-cost.html.

6   *"Why Are the Israelis So Damn Happy?"*: Tiffanie Wen, "Why Are the Israelis So Damn Happy?," *Daily Beast*, July 11, 2017, https://www .thedailybeast.com/why-are-the-israelis-so-damn-happy.

7   World Happiness Report: Sustainable Development Solutions Network and Gallup World Poll, "World Happiness Report 2023," March 20, 2023, https://worldhappiness.report/ed/2023/executive -summary/.

7   *Some countries, like the United Arab Emirates*: Robert Anderson, "Happiness in the GCC," *Gulf Business*, March 19, 2017, https://gulfbusiness .com/happiness-inthe-gcc/.

7   *The tiny country of Bhutan*: Adam Taylor, "The UAE Created a Minister of Happiness, but What Does That Even Mean?," *Washington Post*, February 10, 2016, https://www.washingtonpost.com/news/worldviews /wp/2016/02/10/the-uae-created-a-minister-of-happiness-but-what-does -that-even-mean/.

7   *The pollsters employed*: "Understanding How Gallup Uses the Cantril Scale," Gallup, https://news.gallup.com/poll/122453/understanding -gallup-uses-cantril-scale.aspx.

9   *Of all the wealthy countries polled*: Bruce Stokes, "Public Divided on

Prospects for the Next Generation," Pew Research Center, June 5, 2017, https://www.pewresearch.org/global/2017/06/05/2-public-divided-on -prospects-for-the-next-generation/.

10 *According to Waze*: "Tel Aviv Ranked 5th Worst in World for Traffic Congestion," *Haaretz*, November 4, 2019, https://www.haaretz.com/israel -news/business/2019-11-04/ty-article/.premium/tel-aviv-ranked-5th-worst -in-world-for-traffic congestion/0000017f-dc3c-df62-a9ff-dcffee460000.

10 *life expectancy in Israel*: "Life Expectancy and Healthy Life Expectancy, Data by Country," World Health Organization, https://apps.who.int /gho/data/node.main. 688.

10 *Israeli men have the fourth highest*: Ibid.

11 *Obesity levels*: Rossella Tercatin, "Health Report: Over Half of the Israeli Population Is Overweight," *Jerusalem Post*, February 3, 2021, https:// www.jpost.com/health-science/over-half-of-the-israeli-population-is -overweight-report-finds-657579.

11 *diabetes rates*: Ervin Stern et al., "Prevalence of Diabetes in Israel: Epide-miologic Survey," *Diabetes* 37, no. 3 (1988): 297–302, https://doi .org/10.2337/diab.37.3.297.

12 *In Japan, there are more people*: "Japan Population," *PopulationU*, https:// www.populationu.com/japan-population#:~:text=As%20per%20the%20 provincial%20June,are%2085%20years%20and%20over.

12 *More adult diapers*: Sam Jones and Ben McLannahan, "Hedge Funds Say Shorting Japan Will Work," *Financial Times*, November 29, 2012.

12 *"Japan is standing"*: George Wright, "Japan PM says country on the brink over falling birth rate," *BBC News*, January 23, 2023, https://www.bbc .com/news/world-asia-64373950.

13 *gap between Israel and Europe*: This chart is based on data from the United Nations World Population Prospects (2022). 1950 to 2021 show historical estimates. From 2022 the UN projections (medium variant) are shown.

13 *"sustained decline"*: Damien Cave et al., "Long Slide Looms for World Population," *New York Times*, May 22, 2021, https://www.nytimes .com/2021/05/22/world/global-population-shrinking.html.

13 *"replacement rate"*: In developed countries with low infant and child mor-tality rates the replacement rate is a fertility rate of 2.1. In countries with higher infant and child mortality, the replacement rate can be higher.

13 *fertility rate*: "Fertility rate" and "birth rate" are often used interchangeably, but they are not the same. Birth rate is the total number of births per year

per one thousand individuals in a population. Fertility rate is the number of live births in a year per one thousand women of reproductive age in a population.

14 *"deaths of despair"*: Anne Case and Angus Deaton, "Rising Morbidity and Mortality in Midlife Among White Non-Hispanic Americans in the 21st Century," *Proceedings of the National Academy of Sciences* 112, no. 49 (November 2, 2015): 15078–83, https://www.pnas.org/doi/10.1073/pnas.1518393112.

14 *the* Economist *reported*: "Deaths of Despair, Once an American Phenomenon, Now Haunt Britain," *The Economist*, May 4, 2019, https://www.economist.com/britain/2019/05/14/deaths-of-despair-once-an-american-phenomenon-now-haunt-britain.

15 *the Global Burden of Disease (GBD) study*: "Global Burden of Disease (GBD)," Institute for Health Metrics and Evaluation, https://www.healthdata.org/gbd.

15 *opioid abuse*: According to this report, opioid use in Israel is now very high, though thus far it does not have a notable mortality impact. The report also makes important recommendations for addressing the dangers of overuse of opioids in Israel. Nadav Davidovitch et al., "Are We Nearing an Opioid Epidemic in Israel?," Taub Center, March 2023, https://www.taubcenter.org.il/en/research/opioid-epidemic/.

16 *"CDC Report on Teen Mental Health"*: Lisa Jarvis, "CDC Report on Teen Mental Health Is a Red Alert," *Washington Post*, February 16, 2023, https://www.washingtonpost.com/business/cdc-report-on-teen-mental-health-is-a-red-alert/2023/02/16/8decdcbe-ae24-11ed-b0ba-9f4244c6e5da_story.html.

16 *"'overwhelming wave of violence and trauma'"*: Erika Edwards, "CDC Says Teen Girls Are Caught in an Extreme Wave of Sadness and Violence," NBC News, February 13, 2023, https://www.nbcnews.com/health/health-news/teen-mental-health-cdc-girls-sadness-violence-rcna69964.

16 *"alarming levels of violence"*: Megan Schiller, "CDC: Teen Girls Experiencing Record-High Levels of Violence, Sadness and Suicide Risk," CBS News, February 13, 2023, https://www.cbsnews.com/pittsburgh/news/cdc-teen-girls-experiencing-violence-sadness-and-suicide-risk/.

16 *"High school should be a time for trailblazing"*: "U.S. Teen Girls Experiencing Increased Sadness and Violence," Centers for Disease Control and Prevention, February 13, 2023, https://www.cdc.gov

/nchhstp/newsroom/2023/increased-sadness-and-violence-press-release .html#:~:text=%E2%80%9CHigh%20school%20should%20be%20 a,Director%20for%20Program%20and%20Science.

16 *American Academy of Pediatrics*: "AAP-AACAP-CHA Declaration of a National Emergency in Child and Adolescent Mental Health," American Academy of Pediatrics, October 19, 2021, https://www.aap.org/en/advo cacy/child-and-adolescent-healthy-mental-development/aap-aacap-cha-dec laration-of-a-national-emergency-in-child-and-adolescent-mental-health/.

16 *one Long Island hospital*: Azeen Ghorayshi and Roni Caryn Rabin, "Teen Girls Report Record Levels of Sadness, C.D.C. Finds," *New York Times*, February 13, 2023, https://www.nytimes.com/2023/02/13/health/teen -girls-sadness-suicide-violence.html.

16 *Israel's teen suicide rates*: "Teenage Suicides (15–19 years old)," OECD Family Database, October 17, 2017, https://www.oecd.org/els/family/CO_4_4 _Teenage-Suicide.pdf.

16 *social media and smartphones*: Elia Abi-Jaoude et al., "Smartphones, Social Media Use and Youth Mental Health," *Canadian Medical Association Journal* 192, no. 6 (February 2020): E136–E141, https://doi.org/10.15 03%2Fcmaj.190434.

16 *Derek Thompson chronicled*: Derek Thompson, "Why American Teens Are So Sad," *The Atlantic*, April 11, 2022, https://www.theatlantic.com/newslet ters/archive/2022/04/american-teens-sadness-depression-anxiety/629524/.

17 *CEO Jon Clifton*: "Unhappiness is soaring around the world, laments Jon Clifton," *The Economist*, June 17, 2022, https://www.economist.com /by-invitation/2022/06/17/unhappiness-is-soaring-around-the-world -laments-jon-clifton.

17 *loneliness, for example, dropped*: Loneliness is measured with standard questionnaires, such as the twenty-item UCLA Loneliness Scale.

18 *study comparing social connectedness*: Claude Fischer and Yossi Shavit, "National Differences in Network Density: Israel and the United States," *Social Networks*, Volume 17, Issue 2, 1995, https://doi.org/10.1016 /0378-8733(94)00251-5.

Chapter 1: Uber to the Moon

Much of this chapter relies on authors' interviews of Yariv Bash, Kfir Damari, Yonatan Winetraub, Will Marshall, Miri Adelson, and an article by Armin Rosen in *Tablet*: "Inside Israel's Crash-Landing on the Moon," May 22, 2019, https://www.tabletmag.com/sections/arts-letters/articles /israel-spaceil-moon.

20 *Kennedy asked*: David Harland and Richard Orloff, *Apollo: The Definitive Sourcebook* (Berlin: Springer, 2016), 12.

20 *In a secret memo*: Lyndon B. Johnson, "Evaluation of Space Program," NASA History, April 28, 1961, https://history.nasa.gov/Apollomon/apollo2.pdf.

21 *Membership in communal organizations soared*: Robert Putnam, *Bowling Alone: The Collapse and Revival of American Community* (New York: Simon & Schuster, 2000).

22 *$20 million*: Mike Wall, "Ex-Prize: Google's $20 Million Moon Race Ends with No Winner," Space.com, January 23, 2018, https://www .space.com/39467-google-lunar-xprize-moon-race-ends.html.

23 *The prize deadline:* Shawn Rodgers, "SpaceIL's Kfir Damari Looks to the Stars and Beyond," *Jewish Journal*, October 30, 2019, https://jewishjournal.com /community/306423/spaceils-kfir-damari-looks-to-the-stars-and-beyond/.

24 *Danny Grossman told* Tablet: Armin Rosen, "The Jews Make It to the Moon," *Tablet*, April 15, 2019, https://www.tabletmag.com/sections /israel-middle-east/articles/the-jews-make-it-to-the-moon.

25 *"That's why Israel is the only country"*: Ibid.

28 *"It's the first thing"*: *Rookie Moonshot: Budget Mission to the Moon*, directed by Tom Brisley (Arrow Media, 2019).

28 *three days, three hours, and forty-nine minutes*: Valerie Stimac, "How Long Does it Take to Get to the Moon?" How Stuff Works, March 31, 2021, https://science.howstuffworks.com/how-long-to-moon.htm.

29 *from kindergarten through twelfth grade*: Melanie Lidman, "Beresheet May Have Crashed, but for a Moment We Raised Our Eyes to the Heavens," *Times of Israel*, April 12, 2019, https://www.timesofisrael.com/beresheet -may-have-crashed-but-for-a-moment-we-raised-our-eyes-to-the-heavens/.

30 *the planned mission schedule*: Kenneth Chang, "Israel Wants to Land on the Moon. First Its Spacecraft Needs to Stick the Orbit," *New York Times*, April 3, 2019, https://www.nytimes.com/2019/04/03/science/israel -beresheet-moon.html.

30 *correct speed*: Melanie Lidman, "With Beresheet, Israel Becomes 7th Country to Achieve Lunar Orbit," *Times of Israel*, April 5, 2019, https:// www.timesofisrael.com/with-beresheet-israel-becomes-7th-country-to -achieve-lunar-orbit/.

31 *a soft landing on the lunar surface*: "Beresheet Spacecraft Reaches Moon but Landing Unsuccessful," Ynet, April 11, 2019, https://www.ynetnews.com/articles/0,7340,L-5493174,00.html.

31 *pajama party*: Abigail Klein Leichman, "Beresheet Reaches Moon, Crashes on Arrival," *Israel21c*, April 12, 2019, https://www.israel21c.org/beresheet-reaches-moon-crashes-on-arrival/.

31 *Benjamin Netanyahu sat*: "PM Netanyahu Attends Beresheet Lunar Landing Watch," Mission of Israel to the EU and NATO, April 11, 2019, https://embassies.gov.il/eu/NewsAndEvents/Pages/PM-Netanyahu-attends-Beresheet-lunar-landing-watch-event-.aspx.

31 *the rate of descent*: Stephen Clark, "Israel's Beresheet Lander Breaks into Lunar Orbit," Spaceflight Now, April 4, 2019, https://spaceflightnow.com/2019/04/04/israels-beresheet-lander-brakes-into-lunar-orbit/#:~:text=The%20Beresheet%20spacecraft%20ignited%20its,the%20mission%20to%20an%20end.

32 *Volkswagen headquarters*: The story of Yariv Bash speaking about his grandfather at Volkswagen headquarters is from Danny Spector, "Third Generation Spaceship," *Yedioth Ahronoth*, July 16, 2013.

33 *Speaking about the visit:* Ibid.

36 *Am Yisrael Chai*: The idea to inscribe the sign on the craft with the words "Am Yisrael Chai" originated with philanthropists Miri and Sheldon Adelson, who were strong supporters of the SpaceIL project.

37 *At the bottom were the logos*: Georgina Torbet, "Israel's Lunar Lander Just Snapped a Selfie on Its Way to the Moon," Digitaltrends, March 5, 2019, https://www.digitaltrends.com/cool-tech/beresheet-israeli-craft-posts-postsselfie/#:~:text=Curiosity%20and%20InSight%20aren't,above%20the%20Earth%20this%20week.

37 *"each Hebrew letter as small as a microbe"*: Rosen, "Inside Israel's Crash-Landing on the Moon."

37 *"ask what you can do for your country"*: "John Fitzgerald Kennedy, Inaugural Address (20 January 1961)," Voices of Democracy, https://voicesofdemocracy.umd.edu/kennedy-inaugural-address-speech-text/.

37 *"With all due respect"*: Rebecca Klar, "Markey Riffs on JFK Quote in New Ad Touting Progressive Bona Fides," *The Hill*, August 12, 2020, https://thehill.com/homenews/campaign/511929-markey-riffs-on-jfk-quote-in-new-ad-touting-progressive-bona-fides/.

39 *only SpaceIL*: Rosen, "Inside Israel's Crash-Landing on the Moon."

40 *the first-ever $1 million "Moonshot Award"*: "XPrize Foundation Awards
$1 Million 'Moonshot Award' to SpaceIL," XPRIZE Foundation,
April 11, 2019, https://www.xprize.org/articles/xprize-awards-1m-moon
shot-award-to-spaceil.

42 *Growing food on the moon*: "Growing Plants in Space," NASA, July 12,
2021, https://www.nasa.gov/content/growing-plants-in-space.

Chapter 2: Where's the Class?

Sections in this chapter rely on authors' interviews with Sebastian
Thrun, Avi Simon, Tal Vardi, Tamir Pardo, Liora Sali, Tamar Katriel,
Daniel Gordis, David Kushner (as well as his article "The Israeli Army's
Roim Rachok Program Is Bigger Than the Military"), and a number of
currently serving and alumni of the IDF's Roim Rachok program who
requested that their names not be published.

44 *one in ten of those enrolling*: The completion rate of MOOCs varies widely
depending on the platform, course, and cost. See this report published by
Coursera: https://about.coursera.org/press/wp-content/uploads/2020/10
/Coursera_DriversOfQuality_Book_MCR-1126-V4-lr.pdf.

47 *"conquered by individuals"*: Daniel Gordis, *Becoming a Jewish Parent* (New
York: Harmony Books, 1999).

48 *8200 EISP*: Data are from the 8200 EISP website, https://www.eisp.org.il.

49 *"Expect a great deal"*: "B.-P.'s Outlook," US Scouting Service Project,
http://www.usscouts.org/history/BPoutlook1.asp.

49 *"Association with Adults"*: "The Boy Scouts of America's Mission, Vision,
Aims, and Methods," Boy Scouts of America, https://troopleader.scout
ing.org/scoutings-aims-and-methods/.

50 *Hashomer describes*: "The Movement," Hashomer Hatzair, https://www
.hashomerhatzair.ca/the-movement.html.

50 *On March 7, 1929*: "A Bit of History," Bnei Akiva, https://bneiakiva.org
.il/historya/.

51 *Mizrahi eventually embraced Bnei Akiva*: "Bnei Akiva," Wikipedia,
https://en.wikipedia.org/wiki/Bnei_Akiva.

52 *The force from the 101st*: Yoav Zeyton, "The secret card against Hezbollah:
this is how the paratroopers will fight deep in Southern Lebanon," Ynet,
March 2, 2018, https://www.ynet.co.il/articles/0,7340,L-5079313,00
.html.

52 *The last time Israel*: Kali Robinson, "What Is Hezbollah?," Council on Foreign Relations, May 25, 2022, https://www.cfr.org/backgrounder /what-hezbollah.

53 *northern Lebanon*: Hezbollah is based in southern Lebanon along the Israeli border, but it possesses long-range missiles and could or does operate from northern Lebanon as well.

55 *From 1949 through 1950*: "On This Day, 1950: Final 'Operation Magic Carpet' Airlift Arrives in Israel," *Jerusalem Post*, September 25, 2017, https://www.jpost.com/israel-news/on-this-day-1950-last-flight-of-opera tion-magic-carpet-arrives-in-israel-505897.

57 *Boaz Keinan*: A pseudonym for this individual, who requested to remain anonymous.

61 *The mission of the IDF*: Tom Segev, *A State at Any Cost: The Life of David Ben-Gurion* (New York: Farrar, Straus and Giroux, 2019); Carrie Rubenstein, "This Israeli Innovation May Be the Answer to the U.S. Social Justice Crisis," *Forbes*, September 7, 2020, https://www.forbes.com/sites /carrierubinstein/2020/09/07/this-israeli-innovation-may-be-the-answer -to-the-us-social-justice-crisis/?sh=4e18a11cf0fb.

62 *As Noam, a young adult with autism*: A pseudonym for this individual, who requested to remain anonymous.

64 *"This project opens the doors"*: Anna Ahronheim, "IDF Aims to Recruit 500 Soldiers with Autism by End of 2022," *Jerusalem Post*, November 8, 2021, https://www.jpost.com/israel-news/idf-aims-to-recruit-500-sol diers-with-autism-by-the-end-of-2022-684354.

65 *A. J. Drexel Autism Institute*: "A. J. Drexel Autism Institute," Drexel University, https://drexel.edu/autisminstitute/.

65 *Morgan McCardell*: "Spy agency utilizes autistic analysts' unique skills," *CBS News*, April 21, 2022, https://www.cbsnews.com/news/spy-agency -utilizes-unique-skills-of-autistic-analysts/.

65 *eight hundred adults with autism*: Michael Bernick, "The State of Autism Unemployment in 2021," *Forbes*, January 12, 2021, https://www.forbes .com/sites/michaelbernick/2021/01/12/the-state-of-autism-employment -in-2021/?sh=fd81ae559a48.

Chapter 3: Perpetual Boom

Sections of this chapter rely on authors' interviews with Dr. Nicholas Eberstadt and Yossi Klein Halevi.

67   *British-American committee*: "Morrison-Grady Plan," Wikipedia, https://en.wikipedia.org/wiki/Morrison%E2%80%93Grady_Plan.

68   *"in the Negev"*: "Jewish National Fund Chairman of the Board—Emeritus Ronald S. Lauder Continues to Build on Ben Gurion's Dream of Making the Negev the Future," Jewish National Fund USA, https://www.jnf.org/menu-3/news-media/jnf-wire/jnf-wire-stories/jewish-national-fund-Lauder-build.

68   *eleven barren spots*: "11 points in the Negev," Wikipedia, https://en.wikipedia.org/wiki/11_points_in_the_Negev.

69   *According to what is perhaps*: "The Lancet: World Population Likely to Shrink after Mid-Century, Forecasting Major Shifts in Global Population and Economic Power," Institute for Health Metrics and Evaluation, July 14, 2020, https://www.healthdata.org/news-release/lancet-world-population-likely-shrink-after-mid-century-forecasting-major-shifts-global.

71   *The 1990s turned out to be*: Naoki Abe, "Japan's Shrinking Economy," Brookings, February 12, 2010, https://www.brookings.edu/opinions/japans-shrinking-economy/.

71   *2014 study by economists*: James Liang, Hui Wang, and Edward P. Lazear, "Demographics and Entrepreneurship," National Bureau of Economic Research, September 2014, http://www.nber.org/papers/w20506.

72   *Megan McArdle*: Megan McArdle, "Europe's Real Crisis," *The Atlantic*, April 2012, https://www.theatlantic.com/magazine/archive/2012/04/europes-real-crisis/308915/.

73   *In 2018, just thirteen countries*: "2018 World Population Data Sheet," Population Reference Bureau, https://www.prb.org/wp-content/uploads/2018/08/2018_World-Population-data-sheet.pdf.

73   *By 2040, there will be*: "S. Korea's 65-and-Up Population to Double by 2040 as Working-Age Demographic Plummets," *Hankyoreh*, April 15, 2022, https://english.hani.co.kr/arti/english_edition/e_national/1039139.html.

75   *Darya Maoz*: Miri Michaeli, "How Can You Run a Household with Ten Children?," Channel 13, https://13tv.co.il/item/parenthood/articles/ntr-1248456/.

76   *The "birth quake"*: Diane J. Macunovich, *Birth Quake: The Baby Boom and Its Aftershocks* (Chicago: University of Chicago Press, 2002).

78   *In every other country*: Matthias Doepke et al., "The New Economics of Fertility," International Monetary Fund, September 2022, https://www.imf .org/en/Publications/fandd/issues/Series/Analytical-Series/new-economics -of-fertility-doepke-hannusch-kindermann-tertilt#:~:text=It%20suggests%20 that%20as%20parents,across%20countries%20and%20over%20time.

Chapter 4: The Kids Are Alright

Sections of this chapter rely on authors' interviews with Yossi Klein Halevi, Micah Goodman, Lenore Skenazy, Danny Hamiel, Sarah Levy Schreier, and Daniel Gordis.

80   *"Is that a child?"*: "Conan Visits Waze HQ in Tel Aviv," Youtube video, uploaded by Team Coco, September 24, 2017, https://www.youtube .com/watch?v=CoRKrejQBjk.

83   *In Israel, fifteen weeks*: Mothers who worked for 10 of the 14 months (or 15 of 22) prior to the birth receive 15 weeks of paid leave, whereas mothers who worked for 6 of the 14 months before the birth receive 8 weeks of paid leave. "Bituach Leumi: Rights and Benefits," Chaim V'Chessed, March 21, 2023, https://chaimvchessed.com/information /bituach-leumi/bituach-leumi-rights-benefits/#:~:text=If%20you%20 worked%20for%2010,56%20days)%20of%20paid%20leave.

85   *Sharon Geva, a historian*: Roni Bar, "The Women Who Chose to Live Kids-Free in Procreation-Obsessed Israel," *Haaretz*, April 9, 2020, https://www.haaretz.com/israel-news/2020-04-09/ty-article-magazine /.premium/the-women-who-go-against-the-jewish-womans-mission -motherhood/0000017f-dbd2-df62-a9ff-dfd7addd0000.

86   *"It's really hard to be the one who doesn't want to be a mother"*: Jennifer Richler, "Saying No to Kids," *Tablet*, July 10, 2017, https://www.tablet mag.com/sections/community/articles/saying-no-to-kids.

87   *grandparental assistance*: Barbara Okun, "An investigation of the unex- pectedly high fertility of secular, native-born Jews in Israel," Popul Stud (Camb), July 2016, https://doi.org/10.1080/00324728.2016.1195913.

88   *She is the author*: Lenore Skenazy, *Free-Range Kids: How to Raise Safe, Self-Reliant Children (Without Going Nuts With Worry)*, (San Francisco: Jossey-Bass, 2010).

90 *"trustful parenting"*: Peter Gray, "Trustful Parenting: Its Downfall and Potential Renaissance," *Psychology Today*, July 16, 2009, https://www .psychologytoday.com/us/blog/freedom-learn/200907/trustful-parenting -its-downfall-and-potential-renaissance.

Chapter 5: Thanksgiving Every Week

93 *"Bowling Alone"*: Robert Putnam, *Bowling Alone: The Collapse and Revival of the American Community* (New York: Simon & Schuster, 2000).

93 *"Virtually all forms of family togetherness"*: Ibid., ch. 1.

94 *"A palace in time"*: Abraham Joshua Heschel, *The Sabbath* (New York: Farrar, Straus and Giroux, 1959).

95 *"senior citizens [in the U.S.]"*: Leon Neyfakh, "What Age Segregation Does to America," *Boston Globe*, August 31, 2013, https://www.boston globe.com/ideas/2014/08/30/what-age-segregation-does-america/o56 8E8xoAQ7VG6F4grjLxH/story.html.

96 *One government has gone so far*: "Grant to Help Extended Families Live Close Together," Today Online, August 23, 2015, https://www.todayon line.com/singapore/more-help-families-buy-hdb-flats-close-one-another; "Closer Families, Stronger Ties: Enhanced Proximity Housing Grant to Help More Families Live Closer Together," Ministry of National Development, February 19, 2018, https://www.mnd.gov.sg/newsroom/press -releases/view/closer-families-stronger-ties-enhanced-proximity-housing -grant-to-help-more-families-live-closer-together.

98 *For his book on the happiest*: Eric Weiner, *The Geography of Bliss: One Grump's Search for the Happiest Places in the World* (New York: Hachette Book Group, 2006).

99 *Ishay Ribo*: Patrick Kingsley, "Religious Pop Star Singing 'God and Faith' Wins Over Secular Israel," April 15, 2023, https://www.nytimes.com /2023/04/15/world/middleeast/israel-music-ishay-ribo.html?smid=url -share.

101 *"Despair is suffering without meaning"*: Viktor Frankl, *The Unconscious God* (New York: Washington Square Press, 1985).

101 *In September 2017*: "Where Americans Find Meaning in Life," Pew Research Center, November 20, 2018, https://www.pewresearch.org /religion/2018/11/20/where-americans-find-meaning-in-life/.

102 *A 2012 report by the Civil Service College*: Joel Kotkin, "The Rise of Post-

Familialism: Humanity's Future?," New Geography, October 10, 2012, https://www.newgeography.com/content/003133-the-rise-post-familial ism-humanitys-future#:~:text=Increasingly%2C%20family%20 no%2longer%2serves,%2C%20often%2C%20marriage%20as%20well.

103 *"We're actually quite social"*: Eric Klinenberg, *Going Solo: The Extraordinary Rise and Surprising Appeal of Living Alone* (London: Penguin, 2013).

Chapter 6: Touching History

This chapter is based on a series of authors' interviews with Micah Goodman and General Tzvika Fayirizen (Ret.), Alon Davidi, and Roni Flamer.

109 *"At the ceremony"*: Similar oaths are made by soldiers in the militaries of other nations. The difference is that in most countries, very few serve in the military, and even in countries with mandatory service, there is little expectation of being sent into battle. The letter can be found in Alex Singer, *Alex: Building a Life: The Story of an American Who Fell Defending Israel* (New York: Gefen, 1996), full-text PDF avalable here: https://www.alexsingerproject.org/book.

114 *"Residents have grown accustomed"*: Ethan Bronner, "A Town Under Fire Becomes a Symbol for Israel," *New York Times*, April 5, 2008, https://www.nytimes.com/2008/04/05/world/middleeast/05sderot.html.

116 *"The virtuous city will fragment"*: Justin Davidson, "The 15-Minute City: Can New York Be More Like Paris?," *New York*, July 17, 2020, https://nymag.com/intelligencer/2020/07/the-15-minute-city-can-new-york-be-more-like-paris.html.

Chapter 7: People of the Story

This chapter relies extensively on authors' interviews with Liel Leibovitz, Avi Issacharoff, Lior Raz, and Danna Stern, as well as the essay by Liel Leibovitz, "Why Israeli TV Is So Good," *Sapir Journal*, Winter 2023.

121 *Omar Said Salah Abu Sirhan*: Jackson Diehl, "Arab Worker Kills 3 Jews in Jerusalem," *Washington Post*, October 22, 1990, https://www.washing tonpost.com/archive/politics/1990/10/22/arab-worker-kills-3-jews-in -jerusalem/9c18f6d7-0c9d-4146-833f-1d6ee292325f/.

121 *Israeli government negotiated a prisoner exchange*: Ben Quinn et al., "Gilad Shalit Freed in Exchange for Palestinian Prisoners," *The Guardian*, Octo-

ber 18, 2011, https://www.theguardian.com/world/2011/oct/18/gilad
-shalit-palestine-prisoners-freed.

122 *"That's what's different about Israeli television"*: Joy Press, "Why Israeli TV
Is Irresistible to American Producers," *Vanity Fair*, October 2019, https://
www.vanityfair.com/hollywood/2019/08/why-israeli-tv-is-irresistible-to
-american-producers.

123 *"My father was a wandering Aramean"*: Deuteronomy 26:5–8.

123 *"Each person must see themselves as if they personally left Egypt"*: Pesachim
116b.

123 *"Stories give the group"*: Jonathan Sacks, "A Nation of Storytellers," *Covenant and Conversation*, https://www.rabbisacks.org/covenant-conversa
tion/ki-tavo/a-nation-of-storytellers/.

123 *Andrew Marr, a prominent BBC journalist*: Andrew Marr, *The Observer*,
May 14, 2000.

124 *"Israelis are probably the world's most neurotic TV audience"*: Gabe Friedman, "New Israeli HBO Series 'Valley of Tears' Reopens Wounds of the
Yom Kippur War," *Times of Israel*, November 14, 2020, https://www
.timesofisrael.com/new-israeli-hbo-series-valley-of-tears-reopens-wounds
-of-the-yom-kippur-war/.

125 *the* New York Times *published a ranking*: Mike Hale, "The 30 Best
International TV Shows of the Decade," *New York Times*, December 12,
2019, https://www.nytimes.com/2019/12/20/arts/television/best-inter
national-tv-shows.html.

125 *According to the* New York Times, *Israel has become*: Stephen Heyman,
"Israeli Television's Surprising Global Reach," *New York Times*, November 6, 2014, https://www.nytimes.com/2014/11/06/arts/international
/israeli-televisions-surprising-global-reach.html.

125 *decade beginning in 2010*: "Israeli Film & Television Industry 2018: Facts
and Figures at a Glance," Israeli Film Fund, http://intl.film
fund.org.il/CMS_uploads/EnglishSite/facts&figures2018.pdf.

126 *120 independent production companies*: Ibid.

126 *Gidi Raff, the creator and showrunner of* Hatufim: Ruth Margalit, "The
Israeli Inspiration for 'Homeland,'" *New Yorker*, September 26, 2012,
https://www.newyorker.com/culture/culture-desk/the-israeli-inspiration
-for-homeland.

126 *Hagai Levi is the creator of* BeTipul *(*In Treatment*)*: "Hagai Levi," Wikipedia, https://en.wikipedia.org/wiki/Hagai_Levi.

127 *One psychology journal described* BeTipul: Itay Harlap, *Television Drama in Israel: Identities in Post-TV Culture* (London: Bloomsbury, 2017).

127 *"when psychoanalysis was portrayed in TV or film"*: Shayna Weiss, "*Frum* with Benefits: Israel's Television Globalization, and *Srugim*'s American Appeal," *Jewish Film and New Media: An International Journal* 4, no. 1 (Spring 2016), https://doi.org/10.13110/jewifilmnewmedi.4.1.0068.

127 *"We have such small budgets"*: Joy Press, "Why Israeli TV Is Irresistible to American Producers," *Vanity Fair*, October 2019, https://www.vanityfair.com/hollywood/2019/08/why-israeli-tv-is-irresistible-to-american-producers.

127 *According to Keren Margalit*: Ed Power, "How Israel Became a Global Power in Television," *Sydney Morning Herald*, June 3, 2020, https://www.smh.com.au/culture/tv-and-radio/how-israel-became-a-global-power-in-television-20200602-p54yn0.html.

128 *Samuel "Shmulik" Maoz*: Rachel Cooke, "Samuel Maoz: My Life at War and My Hopes for Peace," *The Guardian*, May 2, 2010, https://www.theguardian.com/film/2010/may/02/israel-lebanon-samuel-maoz-tanks.

128 *"an astonishing piece of cinema"*: Roderick Morris, "War and Drugs in the Cross Hairs," *New York Times*, September 10, 2009, https://www.nytimes.com/2009/09/11/arts/11iht-venfest11.html.

128 *"intensely personal grasp of the subject-matter"*: Roger Clarke, "Film Review: *Lebanon*," British Film Institute, http://old.bfi.org.uk/sightandsound/review/5473.

128 *It also received a twenty-minute standing ovation*: Cooke, "Samuel Maoz: My Life at War and My Hopes for Peace."

129 *Applications from Israeli tech companies to a foundation that places workers with autism in jobs*: Scott Roxborough, "The World Is Watching Israeli Series," Deutsche Welle, March 25, 2019, https://www.dw.com/en/why-the-world-is-watching-israeli-tv-series/a-48049546.

130 *the most popular courses*: Seph Fontane Pennock, "Positive Psychology 1504: Harvard's Groundbreaking Course," Positive Psychology, June 16, 2015, https://positivepsychology.com/harvards-1504-positive-psychology-course.

132 *"I Have No Other Country"*: Gali Atari, "Ein Li Eretz Acheret (I Have No Other Country)," YouTube video, https://www.youtube.com/watch?v=l84xo1pb-Uo.

Chapter 8: Vaccination Nation

Much of this chapter is based on interviews with Ran Balicer, Benjamin Netanyahu, Yonatan Adiri, and Ron Dermer.

135 *The "Spanish flu" pandemic*: "1918 Pandemic (H1N1 Virus)," Centers for Disease Control and Prevention, https://www.cdc.gov/flu/pandemic -resources/1918-pandemic-h1n1.html.

135 *Life expectancy in the United States*: Andrew Noymer and Michel Garenne, "The 1918 Influenza Epidemic's Effects on Sex Differentials in Mortality in the United States," *Population and Development Review* 26, no. 3 (September 2000): 565–81, https://doi.org/10.1111%2Fj.1728 -4457.2000.00565.x.

135 *The clear answer was*: "Oseltamivir," Wikipedia, https://en.wikipedia.org /wiki/Oseltamivir.

136 *Indeed, just a year later*: "SARS," Wikipedia, https://en.wikipedia.org /wiki/SARS.

136 *Crunching the numbers*: Ran D. Balicer et al., "Cost-Benefit of Stockpil- ing Drugs for Influenza Pandemic," *Emerging Infectious Diseases* 11, no. 8 (August 2005), https://doi.org/10.3201%2Feid1108.041156.

139 *"Twice a year, five hundred million birds"*: Dennis Zinn, "The Hula Valley, Israel's Bird Paradise," *Israel21c*, March 8, 2016, https://www.israel21c .org/the-hula-valley-israels-bird-paradise/.

140 *Bourla had grown up*: Albert Bourla, "My Family's Story: Why We Re- member," LinkedIn, January 29, 2021, https://www.linkedin.com/pulse /my-familys-story-why-we-remember-albert-bourla/.

143 *The average time to develop*: Will Brothers, "A Timeline of COVID-19 Vaccine Development," BioSpace, December 3, 2020, https://www .biospace.com/article/a-timeline-of-covid-19-vaccine-development/.

143 *"Not good enough"*: Nathan Vardi, "The Race Is On: Why Pfizer May Be the Best Bet to Deliver a Vaccine by the Fall," *Forbes*, May 20, 2020, https:// www.forbes.com/sites/nathanvardi/2020/05/20/the-man-betting-1-billion -that-pfizer-can-deliver-a-vaccine-by-this-fall/?sh=26d47bea382e.

147 *Gideon Levy, a columnist*: Gideon Levy, "A Good Word for Netanyahu, for a Change," *Haaretz*, December 27, 2020, https://www.haaretz.com /israel-news/2020-12-27/ty-article-opinion/.premium/israel-covid-19 -vaccination-good-word-for-netanyahu-for-a-change/0000017f-e346 -d38f-a57f-e756f57f0000.

148 *As Netanyahu put it*: "82% Vaccinated in Israel; Race on Between Vaccination & Mutation: Netanyahu," *Business Standard*, January 27, 2021, https://www.business-standard.com/article/international/82-vaccinated-in-israel-race-on-between-vaccination-mutation-netanyahu-121012701556_1.html.

150 *obscure band of data crunchers*: The main data scientists who worked with Ran Balicer on the predictive model for COVID-19 were Dan Riesel and Shay Perchik. Perchik told the authors in an interview: "In February 2020, Dan [Riesel] and I had a meeting over a cup of coffee. There were no cases in Israel yet, but we knew the virus was coming." Taking a model they already had from flu season and tweaking it with data from China, Riesel and Perchik were able to predict which areas of the country were at highest risk, how the disease might spread, and the likely caseload of each hospital. Riesel and Perchik had met when they were officers in the IDF's Computer Science Academy. Perchik worked in programming and information security and later earned a master's degree in neuroscience. Riesel served as a data science team leader, and as a commander in programming courses designed to integrate Haredi soldiers into the military.

150 *An October 2020 study*: Manfred S. Green et al., "The Confounded Crude Case-Fatality Rates (CFR) for COVID-19 Hide More Than They Reveal—A Comparison of Age-Specific and Age-Adjusted CFRs Between Seven Countries," *PLOS One*, October 21, 2020, https://doi.org/10.1371/journal.pone.0241031.

152 *A 2019 survey*: Jarrett Lewis, "Patient Data Sharing: The Public's Opinion," Medium, October 7, 2019, https://medium.com/swlh/patient-data-sharing-the-publics-opinion-6c385d6d7eda.

152 *In a 2018 poll*: Leigh Dodds, "Who Do We Trust with Personal Data?," Open Data Institute, July 5, 2018, https://theodi.org/article/who-do-we-trust-with-personal-data-odi-commissioned-survey-reveals-most-and-least-trusted-sectors-across-europe/.

152 *HMOs are among*: "IDI's 2020 Democracy Index: Trust in HMOs is Higher Than All Other Public Institutions," The Israel Democracy Institute, January 11, 2021, https://en.idi.org.il/articles/33422#:~:text=Overall%2C%20HMOs%20ranked%20highest%20in,77%25%3B%20Arabs%2C%2083.5%25.

155 *As the* Telegraph *put it*: Abbie Cheeseman, "The World's Fastest Covid

Inoculation Drive: Israel Vaccinates Half a Million in Nine Days," *The Telegraph*, December 29, 2020, https://www.telegraph.co.uk/global -health/science-and-disease/worlds-fastest-covid-inoculation-drive-israel -vaccinates-five/.

156   *"It's really being treated"*: Ibid.

Chapter 9: No Place Like Home

This chapter is largely based on interviews with Amnon Shashua, Ziv Aviram, Inbar Shashua Bar-Nir, Nadav Zafrir, Michal Braverman-Blumenstyk, Noam Bardin, and Uri Levine.

160   *WannaCry*: "WannaCry Ransomware Attack," Wikipedia, https://en .wikipedia.org/wiki/WannaCry_ransomware_attack.

166   *"Wazers"*: "130 Million Reasons to say Thanks for Wazers," Waze, August 17, 2020, https://medium.com/waze/130-million-reasons-to-say -thanksto-wazers-bcc9f9521378.

167   *"WTF Is Waze"*: Rip Empson, "WTF Is Waze and Why Did Google Just Pay a Billion+ for It?," Techcrunch, June 12, 2013, https://techcrunch .com/2013/06/11/behind-the-maps-whats-in-a-waze-and-why-did-google -just-pay-a-billion-for-it/?guccounter=1&guce_referrer=aHR0cHM6Ly93 d3cuZ29vZ2xlLmNvbS8&guce_referrer_sig=AQAAANsF27svtVuQwr yY3MoeBzd0MnQmCHHnE0D0rqLAT75EcQmNCYKzjnStxFr5KhC 4CrTgInTUfd8BFHJI7wknFcYp2eru3T0k1afMbDk4Dq9u7sXM6Rn Q22AAxeV3jhAWdv1cetLtm7KMqxcYSrnkYayjYC8msg3_nuAWit -PmfYM.

167   *"the mob is the map"*: Vindu Goel, "Maps That Live and Breathe with Data," *New York Times*, June 10, 2013, https://www.nytimes.com/2013 /06/11/technology/mobile-companies-crave-maps-that-live-and-breathe .html.

174   *It was 1985*: Matthew Libby, "The Brain Across the Table: Garry Kasparov vs. Deep Blue, 1997," Medium, June 9, 2019, https://medium .com/@matthewlibby_75648/the-brain-across-the-table-garry-kasparov -vs-deep-blue-1997-7904f77cebf7.

176   *according to industry analysts, Mobileye was a global leader*: "Mobile Named Industry Leader by Two Industry Research Groups," Mobileye press release, March 2, 2023, https://www.mobileye.com/news/mobileye -named-av-leader-by-two-industry-research-groups/.

181   *easy to do business*: In 2020, Israel ranked thirty-fifth globally, below most
      European countries, in ease of doing business. "Doing Business 2020:
      Comparing Business Regulation in 190 Economies," World Bank Group,
      https://openknowledge.worldbank.org/bitstream/handle/10986/32436
      /9781464814402.pdf.

Chapter 10: The Wars of the Jews

183   *The national lockdown*: "New Virus Rules Keeping People Within 100
      Meters of Home Go into Effect," *Times of Israel*, March 25, 2020,
      https://www.timesofisrael.com/from-5-p-m-wednesday-no-walks
      -farther-than-100-m-from-home-synagogues-shut/#:~:text=The%20
      government%20on%20Wednesday%20announced,and%20the%20
      shuttering%20of%20synagogues.

189   *"The real tragedy"*: History and quote in this paragraph are from an in-
      terview with Jonathan Price, professor of classics and ancient history, Tel
      Aviv University.

191   *On June 20, 1948*: Joanna M. Saidel, "Fire in the Hole: Blasting the
      Altalena," *Times of Israel*, June 20, 2013, https://www.timesofisrael.com
      /fire-in-the-hole-blasting-the-altalena/.

191   *Claiming that Begin*: David M. Castlewitz, "The Altalena Affair," History
      Net, February 26, 2020, https://www.historynet.com/the-altalena-affair/.

191   *In 1952, when the state*: Ofer Aderet, "September 10, 1952: Israel Splits
      over Reparations with West Germany," *Haaretz*, June 16, 2013, https://
      www.haaretz.com/jewish/2013-06-16/ty-article/september-10-1952-is
      rael-splits-over-reparations-agreement-with-west-germany/0000017f
      -f7ae-d47e-a37f-ffbe3c4a0000.

192   *This war was the first*: Shawn Cochran, *War Termination as a Civil-
      Military Bargain* (Berlin: Springer, 2016).

192   *"War had always united Israelis"*: Yossi Klein Halevi, "Netanyahu's
      Betrayal of Democracy Is a Betrayal of Israel," *The Atlantic*, January 12,
      2023, https://www.theatlantic.com/ideas/archive/2023/01/benjamin
      -netanyahu-coalition-israel-democracy/672693/.

192   *350,000 people*: William E. Farrell, "Israelis, at Huge Rally in Tel Aviv,
      Demand Begin and Sharon Resign," *New York Times*, September 26,
      1982, https://www.nytimes.com/1982/09/26/world/israelis-at-huge
      -rally-in-tel-aviv-demand-begin-and-sharon-resign.html.

192　*A few months later*: Yael Gruenpeter, "Revisiting Israeli Peace Activist Emil Grunzweig's Murder, 33 Years Later," *Haaretz*, February 16, 2016, https://www.haaretz.com/israel-news/2016-02-16/ty-article /.premium/revisiting-peace-activist-emil-grunzweigs-murder/0000017f -e484-d804-ad7f-f5fe02d70000.

192　*The Oslo Accords, named after*: Grace Wermenbol, "The Oslo Accords 25 Years On," Middle East Institute, October 3, 2018, https://www.mei .edu/publications/oslo-accords-25-years.

193　*the agreement was ultimately signed*: "The Oslo Accords and the Arab-Israeli Peace Process," Office of the Historian, https://history.state.gov /milestones/1993-2000/oslo.

193　*On November 4, 1995*: Jonathan Freedland, "The Assassination of Yitzhak Rabin: 'He Never Knew It Was One of His People Who Shot Him in the Back,'" *The Guardian*, October 31, 2020, https://www .theguardian.com/world/2020/oct/31/assassination-yitzhak-rabin-never -knew-his-people-shot-him-in-back.

193　*According to* din rodef: "Pursuing the 'Rodef,'" *Forward*, July 16, 2004, https://forward.com/news/5026/pursuing-the-e2-80-98rodef-e2-80-99/.

193　*The widowed Leah Rabin*: Dan Perry, "Rabin's Widow: Would Rather Shake Arafat's Hand Than Netanyahu's," AP News, November 15, 1995, https://apnews.com/article/0e0f1a27ed412d11a252b60f295c6096.

194　*Sharon, who during his whole career*: Tzvi Joffre, "On This Day in 2005: Israel Completes Disengagement from the Gaza Strip," *Jerusalem Post*, September 13, 2021, https://www.jpost.com/israel-news/on-this-day-in -2005-israel-completes-disengagement-from-the-gaza-strip-679288.

198　*Two hundred reservist pilots*: Some opponents of the overhaul opposed using refusal to serve as a form of protest. Former IDF chief of staff Gadi Eisenkot, who was serving as an MK in the opposition, responded to the pilots' letter: "As a citizen and member of the Knesset who opposes the legal reform, I urge you to refrain from boycotting the reserves. I understand your great pain . . . but without the IDF there is no State of Israel. We must keep it out of this important and just struggle." Lilach Shoval et al., "As Pilots' Protest Intensifies, Former IAF Chiefs Appeal to PM to End Judicial Crisis," *Israel Hayom*, March 5, 2023, https://www.israel hayom.com/2023/03/05/iaf-reservists-shorten-duty-in-protest-against -judicial-reform/.

Chapter 11: The Other Israel

Much of this chapter is based on interviews with Chemi Peres.

201 *The true issue*: Yehoshua Pfeffer, "No Longer a Minority: Behind the Veil of Israel's Public Arrest," Tzarich Iyun, March 2023, https://iyun.org.il /en/sedersheni/no-longer-a-minority/.

202 *"rejects outright"*: "Haredim and Zionism," Wikipedia, https://en .wikipedia.org/wiki/Haredim_and_Zionism. There is a wide range of stances among Haredim toward Israel as a nation state, all the way from opposing Israel's existence to ultranationalism.

203 *Shoresh Institution*: "Graph Gallery," Shoresh Institution for Socioeconomic Research, https://shoresh.institute/graphs.html.

204 *Other economists and demographers*: Ofir Haivry, "Israel's Demographic Miracle," *Mosaic*, May 7, 2018, https://mosaicmagazine.com/essay/israel -zionism/2018/05/israels-demographic-miracle/; Sarah Ridner, "What Others Can Learn from Israel About Having Children," *Mosaic*, May 14, 2018, https://mosaicmagazine.com/response/israel-zionism/2018/05 /what-others-can-learn-from-israel-about-having-children/.

204 *15 percent of Haredim leaving*: Alex Weinreb and Nachum Blass, "Trends in Religiosity Among the Jewish Population in Israel," Taub Center, May 2018, https://www.taubcenter.org.il/wp-content/uploads/2020/12 /trendsinreligiosity-1.pdf.

210 *Shira Carmel writes*: Shira Carmel, "The Kollel-Man Masculinity Crisis," August 2022, https://iyun.org.il/en/sedersheni/the-kollel-masculinity -crisis/.

212 *not drafted*: Israeli Arabs are not drafted, but the Druze community is drafted and proudly serve in the military and the police. Zeidan Atashi, "Druze in Israel and the Question of Compulsory Military Service," Jewish Virtual Library, https://www.jewishvirtuallibrary.org/druze-in-israel -and-the-question-of-compulsory-military-service.

213 *only religious subjects*: Haredi women do learn secular subjects in preparation for joining the workforce. The labor force participation of Haredi women has risen sharply and is now similar to non-Haredi Jewish women. Gilad Malach and Lee Cahaner, "80% of Ultra-Orthodox Women Participate in the Workforce—2022 Statistical Report on Ultra-Orthodox Society in Israel," Israel Democracy Institute, January 2, 2023, https://en.idi.org.il/articles/47009.

214 *"We have lost control"*: Ruth Margalit, "The Arab-Israeli Power Broker in the Knesset," *The New Yorker*, October 25, 2021, https://www.newyorker.com/magazine/2021/11/01/the-arab-israeli-power-broker-in-the-knesset.

214 *2020 poll*: Israel Democracy Institute, https://en.idi.org.il/tags-en/1465.

215 *"Ninety percent of Jews and Arabs"*: "Dr. Nasreen Haddad Haj-Yahya," Israel Democracy Institute, https://en.idi.org.il/experts/1444.

216 *"Israel was born as a Jewish state"*: Aaron Boxerman, "Arabs Should Move Past Contesting Israel's Jewish Identity, Ra'am Chief Abbas Says," *Times of Israel*, December 21, 2021, https://www.timesofisrael.com/arabs-should-move-past-contesting-israels-jewish-identity-raam-chief-abbas-says/.

216 *"The message of change"*: Michael Milshtein, "This Is the Most Radical Experiment Israeli-Arab Society Has Undergone," *Haaretz*, December 17, 2021, https://www.haaretz.com/israel-news/2021-12-17/ty-article-magazine/.highlight/this-is-the-most-radical-experiment-israeli-arab-society-has-undergone/0000017f-ef8e-d8a1-a5ff-ff8e47fc0000.

Chapter 12: Second Chances

233 *640,000 men and women*: Authors' email exchange with the IDF Spokesperson's Office.

233 *9.7 million*: "Israel's Population Nears 10 Million, a 12-Fold Increase Since State's 1948 Founding," *Times of Israel*, April 24, 2023, https://www.timesofisrael.com/israels-population-nears-10-million-a-12-fold-increase-since-states-1948-founding/.

236 *air traffic is diverted*: Agence France-Presse, "Flight Bans Police Escorts as Half a Million South Koreans Sit Annual 'Suneung' College Exam," *Young Post*, November 18, 2022, https://www.scmp.com/yp/discover/news/asia/article/3199964/flight-bans-police-escorts-half-million-south-koreans-sit-annual-suneung-college-exam.

239 *one hundred* mechinot: This includes both full- and half-year *mechinot*.

239 *"I am here"*: Nina Beth Cardin, "The Deepest Meanings of Hineini," 929, April 19, 2022, https://www.929.org.il/lang/en/page/53/post/40815.

241 *the "odyssey" years*: David Brooks, "The Odyssey Years," *New York Times*, October 9, 2007, https://www.nytimes.com/2007/10/09/opinion/09brooks.html.

Chapter 13: The Genius of Israel

245 *Sacks asked*: Rabbi Jonathan Sacks, "Individual and Collective Responsibility," *Covenant & Conversation*, https://www.rabbisacks.org/covenant-conversation/noach/individual-and-collective-responsibility/.

245 *"There have been, in the course"*: Ibid.

245 *No system of justice*: Paul Johnson, *A History of the Jews* (New York: Harper Perennial, 1988).

246 *individualism-collectivism spectrum*: Here you can see the United States, Israel, and South Korea compared on individualism and five other parameters. Note that Israel scores 13 in Power Distance (a measure of how hierarchical a society is), compared to 60 for the U.S., and 80 for South Korea. Israel had the second-lowest Power Distance score of all seventy countries that Hofstede studied—not surprising in a place where saluting military officers is rare and soldiers call their officers by their first names. "Country Comparison Tool," Hofstede Insights, https://www.hofstede-insights.com/country-comparison-tool?countries=israel%2Csouth+korea%2Cunited+states.

249 *"having no friends"*: Robin Dunbar, *Friends: Understanding the Power of Our Most Important Relationships* (London: Little, Brown, 2021).

249 *In 1938, Arlie Bock*: Joshua Shenk, "What Makes Us Happy?," *The Atlantic*, June 2009, https://www.theatlantic.com/magazine/archive/2009/06/what-makes-us-happy/307439/.

251 *"The clearest message"*: "Robert Waldinger: What Makes a Good Life? Lessons from the Longest Study on Happiness," YouTube video, uploaded by TED, January 25, 2016, https://www.youtube.com/watch?v=8KkKuTCFvzI.

252 *these trends have made it harder*: Robert D. Putnam and Shaylyn Romney Garrett, *The Upswing: How America Came Together a Century Ago and How We Can Do It Again* (New York: Simon & Schuster, 2020).

252 *trend toward greater individualism*: Huang Zihang et al., "Increasing Individualism and Decreasing Collectivism? Cultural and Psychological Change Around the Globe," *Advances in Psychological Science* 26, no. 11 (2018): 2068–80, January 2018, https://journal.psych.ac.cn/xlkxjz/EN/10.3724/SP.J.1042.2018.02068.

253 *Amos Oz*: "Amos Oz Still Dreams of Life on the Kibbutz," *Tablet*, September 13, 2013, https://www.tabletmag.com/podcasts/vox-tablet/amos-oz-interview.

INDEX

Page numbers beginning with 271 refer to notes.

INDEX

INDEX

ABOUT THE AUTHORS

DAN SENOR is coauthor of the bestseller *Start-Up Nation: The Story of Israel's Economic Miracle*. He was a senior advisor to Paul Ryan's 2012 campaign for vice president and foreign policy advisor to Mitt Romney's presidential campaigns. A former Defense Department official, Senor has been based in Baghdad and at U.S. Central Command in Qatar, and was a U.S. Senate aide in the 1990s. He has written for the *Financial Times*, the *Wall Street Journal*, the *New York Times*, *USA TODAY*, and the *Washington Post*. He is the host of the popular *Call Me Back* podcast. Today, he is a media communications and public policy executive at a global investment firm.

SAUL SINGER is coauthor of the bestselling book *Start-Up Nation: The Story of Israel's Economic Miracle*. He is a former editor and columnist at the *Jerusalem Post* and has written for the *Wall Street Journal*, the *Washington Post*, and other publications. Singer has given keynote speeches at innovation conferences around the world including in Beijing, Sydney, Singapore, London, Madrid, Amsterdam, Oslo, Nairobi, and São Paulo. Before moving to Israel in 1994, he served for ten years as an advisor to U.S. members of Congress. He lives in Jerusalem with his wife and three children.